Contents

About your AQA GCSE Sociology exam

Units

The AQA GCSE specification in Sociology has two Units. If you are doing the Short Course, you will study Unit 1 and sit one written exam. If you are doing the Full Course, you will study both Unit 1 and Unit 2 and sit two written exams.

Unit 1 the Short Course	+ Unit 2 equals the Full Course
Studying Society	Crime and Deviance
Education	Mass Media
Families	Power
	Social Inequality

The exam papers

- There are two exam papers, Paper 1 and Paper 2. Paper 1 tests *Unit 1* and Paper 2 tests *Unit 2*.

- If you are doing the *Short Course*, you will complete *Paper 1*. This is worth 100 per cent of the total marks you can get in the Short Course.

- If you are doing the *Full Course*, you will complete *Paper 1* and *Paper 2*. Each paper is worth 50 per cent of the total marks you can get in the Full Course.

See the chart opposite: **GCSE Sociology at a glance**.

The skills you are assessed on

When the examiners mark your answers, they are looking for particular skills. These are called **assessment objectives**. This book covers all the assessment objectives (AOs) for Unit 1 and Unit 2.

In Paper 1 and Paper 2, you will be assessed on your:

- **Knowledge and understanding (AO1)**

  You must show that you know and understand the social structures (such as families and the education system), social processes (such as socialization and social control) and social issues (such as fear of crime and poverty) that you have studied during your course.

- **Application of knowledge and understanding (AO2)**

  You also need to show that you can apply or relate your knowledge and understanding of the sociological concepts, terms and explanations to the set exam questions.

- **Interpretation, analysis and evaluation (AO3)**

  This means you must show that you can make sense of any written and statistical information presented to you. This might involve picking out relevant information from a written source, such as a description of a study, or an extract from a newspaper. It might also involve picking out relevant information from a graph or table of statistics.

  You also need to show that you can assess and criticize sociological ideas, concepts, views and explanations.

Collins Revision

GCSE
Sociology
AQA

Revision guide

Pauline Wilson

Contents

GCSE Sociology at a glance

Sociology (Short Course)

Unit 1:   **Studying Society**
          Education
          Families

Paper 1   90 marks
1.5 hours   100 per cent of the total marks

Section A: Studying Society

Section B: Education

Section C: Families

Answer all questions in all three sections of the paper.

Each section consists of one question that is subdivided into different parts.

In **Section B** and **Section C**, the final part of the question gives two options: you only have to answer one of these.

Sociology (Full Course)

Unit 1:   **Studying Society**
          Education
          Families

Unit 2:   **Crime and Deviance**
          Mass Media
          Power
          Social Inequality

Paper 1   90 marks
1.5 hours   50 per cent of the total marks

Section A: Studying Society

Section B: Education

Section C: Families

Answer all questions in all three sections of the paper.

Paper 2   90 marks
1.5 hours   50 per cent of the total marks

Section A: Crime and Deviance

Section B: Mass Media

Section C: Power

Section D: Social Inequality

Choose three sections from the four options and answer all questions in each of the three chosen sections.

Each section of Paper 1 consists of one question that is subdivided into different parts.

In **Section B** and **Section C**, the final part of the question gives two options: you only have to answer one of these.

Each section of Paper 2 consists of one question that is subdivided into different parts. In each section, the final part of the question gives you two options and you only have to answer one of these.

Key points

- Section A of Paper 1 will focus on **Unit 1, Studying Society**.

- This section of the exam paper is compulsory.

- It is marked out of 30 and accounts for 33 per cent (one third) of your total mark for Paper 1.

- You should spend no more than 30 minutes on this question. This includes the time spent on studying the Items, reading the questions and planning your answers.

Paper 1 consists of three sections. Only Section A (Studying Society) is given here.

Remember to read the instructions and the Items carefully before answering the questions.

Use a ruler to help you read tables of statistics.

About the Studying Society exam question

Here is an example of the sort of exam question that could be asked on Studying Society. The question is divided into parts (a) to (e) and for each part, the assessment objectives (AOs) (see page 4) have been identified for you. This will help you to recognize which skills each part is testing. The comments are there to provide you with guidance on how to go about answering exam questions on Studying Society.

In the exam, the 'Items' could contain sources such as written extracts, charts, graphs or photographs. In the question below, Item A shows official statistics on GCSE results and is a secondary source of quantitative data. Item B describes a research study related to the sociology of education. Item C gives an insight into the sociological approach.

SECTION A: STUDYING SOCIETY

Answer **all** questions from this section.

Total for this question: 30 marks

1 Study **Items A, B and C** and then answer parts (a) to (e).

ITEM A			
Percentage of students achieving five or more GCSE grades A*–C by sex and ethnic origin – 2006			
SEX		**ETHNIC ORIGIN**	
Male	54%	White	58%
Female	63%	Black	50%
		Asian	64%
		Other ethnic group	56%

Source: Department for Children, Schools and Families (© Crown Copyright, 2008)

ITEM B
Diane Reay and her colleagues studied how male and female students from different social class and ethnic backgrounds went about choosing which university to attend. The researchers carried out research in six schools and colleges. During the study, they gave a questionnaire to over 500 students in Year 12, Year 13 and in Further Education colleges. They also interviewed 120 students in depth.

It's worth skim reading all of the questions before you begin answering them. Underline the command words such as 'identify', 'outline', 'describe' and 'explain'. Note that each question in (e) contains two command words.

ITEM C

The term 'sex' refers to whether a person is considered male or female. It refers to biological differences between males and females such as their roles in human reproduction. Sociologists tend to use the term 'gender' rather than 'sex'. The term 'gender' describes the different social practices and expectations that are linked to masculinity and femininity. Gender is seen as based on socialization rather than on biology.

This question is asking you to pick out the relevant information from Item A.

(a) From **Item A**, what percentage of female students achieved five or more GCSE A*–C grades? AO3 *(1 mark)*

You can answer questions worth one mark briefly in a few words, a short sentence or by giving the relevant figures.

(b) (i) Identify a research method referred to in **Item B**. AO3 *(1 mark)*

(ii) Outline **one** advantage and **one** disadvantage of using this research method. AO1 *(2 marks)*

Aim to answer questions worth two marks in one or two sentences.

The command word in this question is 'outline'. So it is asking you to give a brief description of one advantage and one disadvantage.

(c) (i) Study **Item C**. Describe how the sociological idea of 'gender' differs from the biological idea of 'sex'. AO1 AO2 *(4 marks)*

(ii) Explain what sociologists mean by the term 'socialization'. AO1 *(4 marks)*

Aim to answer questions worth four marks in a paragraph (around 4–7 lines).

(d) Explain **one** way in which the findings from sociological research studies could help educational authorities in Britain to develop policies that tackle discrimination in schools, colleges or universities. AO1 AO2 *(4 marks)*

The command word here is 'explain'. This question is testing your knowledge and understanding of a key sociological process. You should define the term clearly and give examples to support your definition.

(e) As a sociologist, you have been asked to investigate attitudes towards citizenship education among students in a large comprehensive school.

(i) Identify and explain **one** possible ethical issue that you might need to address while you are carrying out your research. AO1 AO2 AO3 *(4 marks)*

(ii) Identify **one** secondary source of information that you would use in your study **and** explain why you would use this source. AO1 AO2 AO3 *(4 marks)*

This question is asking you to state briefly which primary research method you would use to investigate this topic and then to set out the reasons why you would use this method rather than another primary method.

(iii) Identify **one** primary method of research that you would use in your study **and** explain why this method would be better than another primary method for collecting the data that you need. AO1 AO2 AO3 *(6 marks)*

Task

Answer questions (a) and (b)(i).

The sociological approach

Key points

- In Section A of Paper 1, you may be asked to **distinguish between the sociological approach and that of psychology, biology or journalism**.

- In practice, this is likely to mean that you should be able to:
  - explain what sociology is and what sociologists study
  - identify differences between sociology and psychology, biology and journalism.

Examiner's tip

When you are revising Studying Society (and all other sections), it is a good idea to begin by writing a revision checklist of the relevant topics, key terms and concepts. Once you have revised an item on your checklist you can tick it off.

Defining sociology

When writing about what sociology is, you should include the following important points:

- Sociology explores the **social factors** that shape human behaviour and the way that society influences our daily lives.

- Sociology is often defined as the **study of society**. A 'society' can be defined as a group of people who share a culture or a way of life.

What sociologists study

In studying society, sociologists ask questions about its social structures and social processes and they explore the social issues facing people in society. The table below gives some examples of this. Copy out this table and add your own examples to it.

Social structures	Social processes	Social issues
The different groups and institutions that make up society.	The means by which something takes place in society.	Issues and problems that affect individuals, groups and communities in their daily lives.
Families.	Primary socialization. Gender socialization.	The quality of parenting. Teenage parenthood.
The education system.	Secondary socialization. Labelling. The development of subcultures.	Educational underachievement.
The legal system.	Formal and informal social control.	Knife crime. Teenage crime. Fear of crime.
The social stratification system.	Discrimination.	Poverty. The causes and effects of inequality.

Sociology and other approaches

Sociologists, psychologists and biologists all study people and human behaviour (i.e. what people do). They base their explanations on evidence from their research.

When you write about the differences between these subjects in your answers, be sure to contrast them rather than just describing each subject separately.

Contrasting sociology and psychology

- Psychologists focus on individual behaviour. They study topics like mental illness.

- Sociologists study the social influences on human life. They focus on group (rather than individual) behaviour.

Contrasting sociology and biology

- Biologists look for biological causes or characteristics when studying human behaviour.
- Sociologists view behaviour as social or cultural rather than biological.

Contrasting sociology and journalism

- Sociologists and news journalists sometimes research into similar social issues. However, journalists' research is less thorough and reporting may be biased or one-sided.
- Sociologists must select and use evidence in a balanced way or their research may be criticized by other sociologists.

Here is how one student answered question (c)(i) on page 7:

'Study Item C. Describe how the sociological idea of 'gender' differs from the biological idea of 'sex'.' *(4 marks)*

> The command word in this question is 'describe'. The question is assessing AO1 and AO2 and is marked out of four.

Gender refers to being masculine or feminine (e.g. blue jeans and Spiderman for boys but pink dresses and Barbie dolls for girls). Sex refers to biological differences between males and females (e.g. men can grow facial hair and women can bear children).

3/4

Good point

It's a good idea to use relevant examples to illustrate a point. However, the answer could focus more fully on the nature/nurture debate or biological/cultural differences.

Task

Match the term in the first column with the correct meaning in the second column.

Term	Meaning
1 Sociology	a) The way of life of a society or group including its values, norms, beliefs and language.
2 Society	b) The process through which we learn the culture and values of the society we are born into.
3 Social structures	c) The study of human social life, groups and societies.
4 Social processes	d) Issues and problems that affect individuals, groups and communities in their daily lives such as fear of crime, inequality and poverty.
5 Social issues	
6 Culture	e) The way society is structured or divided into hierarchical strata or layers with the most privileged group at the top and the least privileged at the bottom.
7 Socialization	
8 Social stratification	f) Processes such as socialization, social control and social change.
	g) A group of people who share a culture.
	h) The groups and institutions that make up society such as families, the education system and the social stratification system.

Examiner's tip

It is helpful to have a clear idea in your mind of how each subject is defined before considering the differences between them. For example:

- **Psychology**
  The science of mind and behaviour.
- **Biology**
  The study of living organisms, such as animals and plants.
- **Journalism**
  Writing or reporting for newspapers, news broadcasts or the internet.

Key concepts

culture	social issues	social structures
gender	social policies	socialization
norms	social problems	society
poverty	social processes	values
social control	social stratification	

The research process in sociology

Key points

- In Section A of Paper 1, you may be asked about the **research process in sociology**.

- In practice, this is likely to mean that you should be able to describe how sociologists carry out their research.

Carrying out sociological research

Sociologists carry out research to collect information in an organized way. This information gives them the evidence they need to explain the social world. The process of research involves several key stages.

Stage in the research process	Brief explanation
Developing research aims and hypotheses	Research aims set out what the researcher intends to investigate and they provide the study's focus. A hypothesis is a hunch or an informed guess and is written as a statement that can be tested. It will either be supported by the evidence or proved wrong.
Carrying out a pilot study	A pilot study is a small-scale trial run carried out before the main research.
Selecting a sample	Rather than study the whole population, a researcher often selects a sample. This is done by using a sampling technique such as stratified random sampling or snowball sampling.
Collecting the data	Sociologists collect data using primary research methods such as questionnaires or observation. They may also use secondary sources such as official statistics or mass media reports. Data may be either quantitative or qualitative.
Analysing the data	Data analysis involves interpreting or making sense of the information and presenting the main findings or results.
Evaluating the study's aims, methods, findings and conclusions	Sociologists write articles about their research in journals and present papers at conferences. These articles and papers are reviewed and evaluated by other sociologists. This is known as peer review.

Examiner's tip

Make sure that you understand what the command words are asking you to do:

- **identify** – state a point briefly
- **explain one reason why** – develop this point by discussing the reason in more depth.

Here is how one student answered the question:

'Identify and explain one reason why sociologists use a pilot study in questionnaire-based research'. *(4 marks)* AO1, AO2

Good points

- The student has focused on the set question. The answer identifies one appropriate reason and then goes on to explain this reason.

- The answer shows a sound knowledge and understanding of why pilot studies are used in questionnaire-based research.

> One reason is because a pilot study often shows up mistakes or problems. For example, by piloting a questionnaire, a sociologist can check whether the wording of questions is clear to the respondents. The sociologist can also check that the questionnaire doesn't take too long to complete. If it takes up too much time or some questions are unclear, the sociologists can change the questionnaire before sending out lots of copies.

4/4

Sampling techniques

Researchers select their samples by using sampling techniques. With **probability** (or random) **sampling**, each member of the sampling frame has a known chance of being selected. If the sample is selected randomly, it is likely to be representative of the population. Examples of probability sampling include simple random sampling, systematic sampling and stratified random sampling.

Non-probability sampling is used when a sampling frame is not available. The sample is not selected randomly so it is unlikely to be representative of the population. Snowball, quota and purposive sampling are examples of non-probability sampling.

Task 1

Match the term in the first column with the correct meaning in the second column.

Term	Meaning
1 Population	a) A subgroup of the population that is selected for study.
2 Sample	b) General statements and conclusions that apply not only to the sample studied but also to the broader population.
3 Sampling frame	c) The particular group being studied, for example students in Higher Education or families.
4 Representative sample	d) A list of members of the population, such as a school register.
5 Generalizations	e) A sample that has the same characteristics as the population but is a smaller version of it.

Task 2

Match each sampling technique in the first column with its correct description in the second column.

Sampling technique	Description
1 Simple random sampling	a) Researchers divide the population into strata (subgroups) according to characteristics such as age, gender and ethnicity. They then randomly draw a sample from each subgroup in proportion to the numbers in the population.
2 Systematic sampling	b) Each member of the population has an equal chance of being selected.
3 Stratified random sampling	c) Through contact with one member of a population (e.g. one member of a youth culture), the researcher is introduced to, or identifies others in the same population.
4 Snowball sampling	d) Researchers take every 'nth' item from the sampling frame, for example every 20th name from a school register.

Key concepts

generalizations
hypothesis
peer review
population
primary research methods
qualitative data
quantitative data
representative
sample
secondary sources

Examiner's tip

Remember to check how many marks are available for each question and to divide your time according to the marks.

Quantitative methods

Key points

- In Section A of Paper 1, you may be asked about **social surveys, questionnaires, structured interviews and longitudinal studies, their uses, value and limitations**.

- In practice, this is likely to mean that you should be able to:
  - describe what a social survey, questionnaire, structured interview and longitudinal study involve
  - explain how they are used, their strengths and weaknesses.

A social survey is an example of a primary research method that is usually used to collect **quantitative data**. In other words, a survey produces statistical information that counts or measures something. The results are presented as graphs or tables of statistics with the sociologist's comments and analysis. If follow-up surveys are carried out several times over a number of years, in a **longitudinal study**, it is possible to identify social changes over time.

Social surveys

Social surveys are used to collect information from large numbers of people. They may be based on questionnaires or on structured interviews. A questionnaire consists of a list of pre-set questions. These questions are **standardized** so all respondents answer identical questions in the same order. When you are revising social surveys, it is helpful to distinguish between postal questionnaires, hand-delivered questionnaires and structured interviews:

- Self-completion **postal questionnaires** are sent to respondents by post or email. Each respondent completes a copy of the questionnaire and returns it to the researcher.

- With **hand-delivered questionnaires**, the researcher hands the self-completion questionnaire to the respondent and returns to collect the completed questionnaire.

- In **structured** (or formal) **interviews**, a trained interviewer asks the set questions and records the respondents' answers. Structured interviews are conducted either face-to-face or by telephone.

Survey questions may be 'open-ended' or 'closed'. Here is how one student answered the question: '**Outline one advantage and one disadvantage of using closed questions**'. *(2 marks)*

> The command word here is 'outline' – that is, state briefly.

Good points

- The student has focused on the set question by outlining or briefly stating one advantage and one disadvantage.

- The answer shows a very good knowledge and understanding of the relevant material (AO1).

One advantage is that the <u>answers are already provided</u> so respondents can answer closed questions quite quickly, e.g. by just ticking boxes. One disadvantage is that respondents must choose pre-set answers and cannot expand on their responses.

> The question is assessing AO1.

2/2

Task 1

Outline one advantage and one disadvantage of using open-ended questions.

Structured interviews

The table below summarizes the advantages and disadvantages of structured interviews.

Advantages of structured interviews	Disadvantages of structured interviews
• The trained interviewer can explain what the questions mean.	• The use of pre-set questions assumes that the sociologist has the skills to decide, before the interview takes place, what questions need to be asked, how to ask them and in what order.
• With standardized questions, all respondents answer the same questions. Sociologists can compare respondents' answers. Any differences are seen as reflecting real differences in their attitudes or opinions.	• Interviewees have few opportunities to raise new issues.
• Sociologists can identify connections between different factors (e.g. interviewees' attitudes to marriage and their gender).	• The interview effect – in a formal interview setting, interviewees may give answers that are socially acceptable or that show them in a positive light. If interview bias occurs, the results will not be valid.
• Structured interviews can be replicated or repeated to check the reliability of the findings. If the results are consistent the second time round, they are seen as reliable.	• The interviewer effect – the interviewer's personal or social characteristics (such as their age or class) may influence the interviewees' responses. If interviewer bias occurs, the results will be invalid.
• Sociologists can generalize from reliable results taken from a representative sample.	

Task 2

The following points cover the advantages and disadvantages of postal questionnaires. For each point, note down whether it describes an advantage or a disadvantage.

1 The questions are not explained face-to-face so some may be misunderstood or skipped.

2 Postal questionnaires are one of the cheapest and quickest ways of getting information from lots of people.

3 The questionnaire might not be completed by the person it was sent to.

4 As the researcher is not present, respondents may be more willing to answer personal or sensitive questions.

5 Postal questionnaires are not appropriate for some populations (e.g. homeless people).

6 With standardized questions, respondents' answers to a particular question can be compared. When they give different answers, this is seen as showing real differences in their attitudes or opinions.

7 Standardized postal questionnaires can be replicated to check whether the results are reliable. If the results are consistent the second time round, they are seen as reliable.

8 The response rate is usually low. Those who respond may not be representative or typical of the population being studied. If so, the researcher cannot generalize from the sample to the population.

Examiner's tips

• Remember to refer to your textbook or lesson notes if you are not clear about the meaning of any terms listed under Key concepts.

• When you are revising, try using tables like this to help you summarize the key points or the advantages and disadvantages.

Key concepts

interview effect
interviewer effect
longitudinal studies
reliability
replication
validity

Qualitative methods

Key points

- In Section A of Paper 1, you may be asked about **unstructured interviews, their uses, value and limitations.** You may also be asked about **participant observation (PO)**.

- In practice, this is likely to mean that you should be able to:
  - describe what an unstructured interview involves
  - explain the strengths and weaknesses of unstructured interviews
  - describe what PO involves
  - explain the strengths and weaknesses of PO.

Unstructured interviews and participant observation are examples of primary research methods that are used to collect **qualitative data**. In other words, they produce information in the form of words, quotations from interviewees and detailed descriptions.

Unstructured interviews

An unstructured (or informal) interview is like a guided conversation. Rather than asking pre-set questions from a standardized interview schedule, the interviewer is guided by a short list of prompts that they have prepared in advance. Group interviews are usually unstructured and they are like small group discussions.

The advantages and limitations of unstructured interviews are summarized in the table below. Try this method of organizing your work for other topics that you want to focus on during your revision.

Advantages of unstructured interviews	Limitations of unstructured interviews
• The trained interviewer can rephrase questions and clear up any misunderstandings.	• Compared with other methods, unstructured interviews are often time consuming and expensive for the amount of data that is collected.
• Rather than sticking to pre-set questions, interviewers can probe and ask follow-up questions. This allows them to explore complex issues.	• The interviewer must have the skills needed to keep the conversation going and encourage interviewees to 'open up'.
• Interviewees can develop their answers and explain their views in detail.	• The interview effect: if interview bias occurs the results will not be valid.
• Unstructured interviews give an in-depth and rich account of the topic being studied.	• The interviewer effect: if interviewer bias occurs the results will be invalid.
• They provide a more valid or authentic picture of the topic.	• Unstructured interviews are not standardized so they are difficult to replicate in order to check whether the findings are reliable.
	• Compared with social surveys, fewer unstructured interviews can be carried out so the sample size is smaller. This makes it difficult to generalize from the sample to the wider population.

Good point

The student has used an appropriate sociological term to identify the disadvantage. However, to achieve higher marks, 'interviewer bias' should be explained more fully, e.g. by pointing out that interviewer bias affects the validity of the data.

Here is how one student answered the question: '**Identify and explain** one disadvantage of using unstructured interviews to study truancy among secondary school pupils'. *(4 marks)*

> The command words here are 'identify' and 'explain'.

> Interviewer bias – when the interviewer is biased during the unstructured interview.

> The question is assessing AO1 and AO2.

2/4

Participant observation

In research based on participant observation (PO), the researcher joins a group and takes part in its daily activities in order to study it. The researcher watches and listens to the group and records what is observed over a period of time. PO may be carried out either overtly or covertly.

> Remember that some sociologists observe behaviour without joining in. They are non-participant observers.

Task 1

Read through the information below which discusses participant observation. Fill in each gap by selecting the correct answer from the following:

a) are not harmed	d) daily life	g) observer effect	j) unethical
b) consent	e) full member	h) overt	
c) covert	f) illegal activities	i) too many questions	

With participant observation (PO), the researcher studies a group by becoming a (1) _____ of the group and participating in its (2) _____ . In an (3) _____ PO study, the group's members are aware that the participant observer is doing research on them. However, this may lead to the (4) _____ – whereby group members change their behaviour because they know they are being studied.

In a (5) _____ PO study, the researcher does not tell the group that they are carrying out research. This avoids the observer effect but means that the researcher may avoid asking (6) _____ in case they 'blow their cover'.

Some supporters of covert PO argue that it may be the only way to study (7) _____ and that it is acceptable so long as participants (8) _____ as a result of taking part in the research. Others argue that covert PO is justified because it removes the observer effect.

However, critics argue that covert PO is (9) _____ or morally unacceptable. This is because participants are not informed that they are being studied so they do not get the chance to give, withhold or withdraw their (10) _____ .

Task 2

Draw up a table to summarize the advantages and disadvantages of participant observation. Try to include at least two advantages and two disadvantages.

Task 3

Drawing on relevant information from your class notes and your textbook, answer the following questions:

a) Identify two advantages and two disadvantages of non-participant observation.

b) Identify two advantages and two disadvantages of group interviews.

Examiner's tip

If a question asks you to identify and explain one disadvantage, you should identify the disadvantage briefly and then go on to explain it in more depth.

Secondary sources of data

Key points

- In Section A of Paper 1, you may be asked about **secondary sources of data**.

- In practice, this is likely to mean that you should be able to:
  - explain the difference between primary and secondary sources
  - give some examples of secondary sources
  - describe how secondary sources are used
  - describe the strengths and limitations of official statistics and qualitative secondary sources.

Good point

The student identifies several secondary sources. However, the explanation is not developed. The student could argue that they would use information about citizenship education from the prospectus to help them write better or more relevant questions when devising a questionnaire on students' attitudes.

Primary and secondary sources

- **Primary data** are collected first hand by the researcher using methods such as structured interviews or participant observation.

- **Secondary data**, such as official statistics or mass media reports, are collected and put together by other people, or organizations such as government agencies, so they already exist.

Opinion polls can be a useful source of secondary data. They are a type of survey and use fixed-choice questions to find out people's voting intentions or their opinions on topical issues. Organizations such as Gallup and GfK NOP are often commissioned to carry out surveys of voting intentions and political attitudes. In the months before a general election in the UK, you may notice that opinion poll findings on political issues are regularly published in newspapers.

Quantitative and qualitative secondary data

- **Quantitative secondary data** are presented as statistical information that counts or measures something. Examples include the results of opinion polls and official statistics such as numbers and rates of marriage and divorce.

- **Qualitative secondary data** are presented in visual or verbal form, for instance as words. Examples include newspaper and magazine articles, TV documentaries, diaries, letters, notes, memos, emails, photographs, school inspection reports, college prospectuses, internet websites, novels and autobiographies.

Question (e)(ii) on page 7 focuses on the use of secondary sources in sociological research. Have another look at this question. It assesses AO1, AO2 and AO3. In other words, it tests your ability to apply your knowledge and understanding of secondary sources to the set question. In answering question (e)(ii), you should explain how the information from your chosen secondary source meets the needs of the particular study.

Here is how one student answered this question.

> Statistics on GCSE exam results, and the school website, are examples of secondary sources. However, for this investigation, I would use the school's prospectus to find information about citizenship education there.

2/4

> The first sentence identifies possible secondary sources but the question asks for just one secondary source. The student does not use this information to address the set question.

Task 1

Read through the examples of different sources of data on the left hand side. Draw a line from each one to connect it to the correct type on the right hand side.

a) Observation

b) Written documents such as biographies, novels, letters and diaries

c) Mass media sources such as magazine articles and TV documentaries

Sources of quantitative primary data

d) Questionnaires

Sources of qualitative primary data

e) Official statistics such as birth, death and unemployment rates

f) Structured (or formal) interviews

Sources of quantitative secondary data

g) Statistics on GCSE exam results published by a government department

Sources of qualitative secondary data

h) Unstructured (or informal) interviews

Examiner's tip

Remember to address only the question that is asked. Don't waste time by including material that is not linked to the question.

Task 2

Read through statements 1 to 7 below and fill the gaps in these statements by selecting the correct answer from the following:

a) definitions	c) few sources	e) statements of fact	g) validity
b) cheap	d) primary	f) trends	

Advantages of official statistics

1 Official statistics are relatively _____ , easy to access and cover many aspects of social life.

2 In some cases, they are one of the _____ of data available on a topic.

3 Official statistics allow sociologists to examine _____ (that is, increases or decreases over time) related to issues such as divorce, teenage pregnancy, crime and poverty.

4 They can be used with _____ sources of data to get a fuller picture of a topic. For example, in research on ethnicity and educational achievement, official statistics on GCSE exam results could be used alongside classroom observation and unstructured interviews with teachers.

Limitations of official statistics

5 Official statistics are put together by officials so sociologists have little say on the _____ used.

6 Sociologists cannot check the _____ of official statistics, i.e. whether they give a valid or true picture of what they claim to be measuring. For example, official statistics may not give a true measurement of classroom violence.

7 Official statistics are 'socially constructed' – they are the outcome of decisions and choices made by the people involved in their construction. For example, statistics on domestic violence are published as _____ . However, they are the outcome of decisions made by people such as victims and police officers. The victims, for instance, must decide whether or not to report violent incidents to the police. As a result, domestic violence is likely to be under-reported to the police.

Planning a research project

Key points

- In Section A of Paper 1, you may be asked to **discuss how you would investigate a given topic and to justify your choice of methods**.

- In practice, this is likely to mean that you should be able to:

  - show that you can plan a simple research project

  - identify a primary research method that you would use to investigate the given topic and explain why you would use this method rather than another primary research method

  - identify a secondary source that you would use and explain why you would use this source

  - explain an ethical issue that might arise during the course of doing your research.

Key concepts

ethical issues
informed consent

Ethical issues in research

Research ethics focus on conducting research that is morally acceptable. When planning and carrying out research, sociologists are expected to follow ethical guidelines. When writing about the ethical issues that could arise during the research process you could include:

- **Informed consent** – before agreeing to take part in research, participants should be told clearly what the study is about and why it is being done. They should also be told what taking part will involve, e.g. that their words will be quoted in books. Individuals have the right not to consent and to withdraw their consent at any time.

- **Anonymity** – participants should not be identified by name or in other ways in books or articles about the research.

- **Confidentiality** – personal information about the participants should be kept private.

Exam questions on planning a research project

Part (e) of the sample question on Studying Society (see pages 6–7 and pages 16–17) focuses on planning a research project. Each of the subquestions assesses AO1, AO2 and AO3. This question is worth 14 marks altogether – almost half of the total marks for Section A, the Studying Society question – so it is important that you understand how to address questions like this.

Here is how one student answered question (e)(i) on page 7. *(4 marks)*

> One ethical issue that I might need to address while I am doing my research on students' attitudes to citizenship education in a large comprehensive school is how to go about getting informed consent from everyone at the school. I would have to get informed consent as part of the ethical research process.

2/4

Remember that you don't need informed consent from 'everyone at the school' – only from the people who participate in the research.

Good point

The answer identifies an appropriate ethical issue. However, it does not explain 'informed consent'.

Here is how another student answered question (e)(ii). *(4 marks)*

> One secondary source would be studies of students' attitudes towards citizenship education carried out by other researchers (e.g. the Citizenship Education Longitudinal Study).

This is a good example to use.

Continued >

I could compare my findings to those of other studies, highlight any similarities and differences between them and try to explain the differences.

4/4

Here is how the student answered question (e)(iii). *(6 marks)*

I would use self-completion questionnaires – the students could complete them quickly during lessons so the response rate would be high.

Questionnaires would be better than unstructured interviews with students when studying attitudes. By giving questionnaires to a large sample, I would get lots of statistical information about the students' views. Informal interviews usually involve small samples and take more time.

Also, questionnaires are standardized so I could repeat the questionnaire to check the reliability of the findings. If the results are reliable and from a representative sample then I can generalize from them to the wider population of students. However, informal interviews are not standardized so they are hard to replicate to check whether the findings are reliable. The sample is usually small and not representative. So it would be difficult to generalize from the findings of informal interviews.

6/6

> There is a clear focus on doing research in a school setting.

> The student applies relevant terms such as 'response rate', 'sample' and 'population'.

> The student discusses key issues such as standardization, replication, reliability and generalizations.

Good points

- The student addresses both parts of the question.

- This is a good example of how studies by other researchers can be used as a secondary source.

Good points

- This is an excellent response. The student shows a very sound understanding of how and why questionnaires could be used in this particular investigation.

- The answer compares questionnaires and informal interviews in terms of sample size, time factors, ease of replication, reliability and generalizations.

Task

Write an answer to the following question. Try to spend no more than 12 minutes on this as this is roughly how long you will have for this kind of question in the exam.

Imagine that you are a sociologist investigating male and female attitudes to divorce.

(i) Identify and explain **one** ethical issue that you might need to address while you are carrying out your research. *(4 marks)*

(ii) Identify **one** secondary source of information that you would use in your study **and** explain why you would use this source. *(4 marks)*

(iii) Identify **one** primary method of research that you would use in your study **and** explain why this method would be better than another primary method for collecting the data that you need. *(6 marks)*

Examiner's tip

The first student answer on page 18 tends to repeat the wording of the question. Don't copy out the wording of the question as this wastes valuable time.

Paper 1 Section B: Education

Key points

- Section B of Paper 1 will focus on **Unit 1, Education.**

- This section of the exam paper is compulsory.

- It is marked out of 30 and accounts for 33 per cent (one third) of your total mark for Paper 1.

- You should spend no more than 30 minutes on this question.

Paper 1 consists of three sections. Only Section B (Education) is given here.

It's essential to manage your time carefully during the exam. Although you have 30 minutes to answer a question worth 30 marks, this does not work out at one minute per mark. Remember that you have to spend time studying the Items, reading the questions, planning your answers, writing them and re-reading them at the end.

About the Education exam question

Here is an example of the sort of exam question that could be asked on Education. The question is divided into parts (a) to (g) and for each part, the assessment objectives (AOs) have been identified to help you recognize which skills are being tested.

Item D discusses home education and the lack of reliable statistical evidence on the number of children being educated at home. Item E looks at some of the links between educational achievement and home background.

SECTION B: EDUCATION

Answer **all** questions from this section.

Total for this question: 30 marks

2   Study **Items D and E** and then answer parts (a) to (g).

ITEM D

Education at home

Home education, whereby parents or carers provide education for their children at home rather than sending them to school, is an alternative form of educational provision. In 2006, there was no reliable information on the number of children who were educated at home in the UK. However, some estimates from home education groups suggest that thousands of families in the UK educate their children at home and that the number of home-educated children is on the increase.

ITEM E

Educational success and family background

Research evidence suggests that children's attitudes towards learning begin to develop from an early age. These attitudes influence their educational achievements. There are significant differences between children from different social groups in their attitudes towards school and their experiences of school. Children from less-advantaged backgrounds are more likely to feel that they lack control over their learning. They are also less likely to feel confident about school.

Note that questions (e) and (f) both ask you to do two things – to describe and also to explain.

Remember to use the marks as a guide to how long you should spend on each answer. Aim to spend around three minutes on questions worth four marks, four minutes on questions worth five marks and around 10 minutes on questions worth 12 marks.

Aim to answer questions worth five marks in a paragraph (around 5–8 lines).

Part (g) is an extended-answer or mini-essay question worth 12 marks. Aim to answer this question in three or more paragraphs.

The command words here are 'Discuss how far sociologists would agree...', so they are asking you to:

- put forward the different views and explanations in a debate
- discuss, compare or evaluate these different views and explanations
- come to a clear conclusion based on your discussion.

It's a really good idea to practise answering questions under timed conditions. This will give you valuable experience of writing your answers in the appropriate times. It will also give you an opportunity to check whether there are any gaps in your knowledge.

(a) From **Item D**, identify **one** alternative form of educational provision. AO3 *(1 mark)*

(b) From **Item E**, which children are more likely to feel that they lack control over their learning? AO3 *(1 mark)*

(c) Identify **two** reasons why some parents may want their children to be educated at home rather than at school. AO1 *(2 marks)*

(d) Explain what sociologists mean by 'social cohesion'. AO1 *(4 marks)*

(e) Describe **one** way in which British governments have increased the use of testing in primary schools over the past 25 years **and** explain the criticisms of this policy. AO1 AO2 *(5 marks)*

(f) Describe **one** type of school that pupils aged 11–16 might attend **and** explain the advantages of this type of school. AO1 AO2 *(5 marks)*

(g) **EITHER**

   (i) Discuss how far sociologists would agree that teachers' expectations are the most significant influence on children's educational achievements. AO1 AO2 AO3 *(12 marks)*

   OR

   (ii) Discuss how far sociologists would agree that serving the needs of the economy is the most important function of the education system in Britain today. AO1 AO2 AO3 *(12 marks)*

As you work through this revision chapter on Education, you will have the opportunity to read examples of how students have answered questions (d) to (g). These sample student answers have all been given a mark and there is also a written comment about each one. It is important to study all of this information carefully because it will give you further guidance on how to tackle exam questions on Education.

Task 1

Answer questions (a) and (b).

Task 2

Once you have worked through this chapter on Education, you should answer questions (d), (e) and (f) and then compare your own responses to the sample student answers provided.

The role of education

Key points

- In Section B of Paper 1, you may be asked to **describe and explain the different functions that education is expected to fulfil today**.

- In practice, this is likely to mean that you should be able to:
  - explain what education is for
  - discuss the different functions of education such as secondary socialization and serving the needs of the economy.

Key concepts

capitalism
function
functionalist approach
hidden curriculum
hierarchy
Marxist approach
meritocracy
official curriculum
social class
social cohesion
social inequalities
social mobility

Formal and informal education

Education involves building up knowledge and learning new skills. It can take place formally or informally.

- **Formal education** takes place in educational institutions such as schools and universities where people learn knowledge and skills across a wide range of subjects.

- **Informal education** takes place when people develop knowledge and skills by observing what is happening around them in everyday life.

The purposes of formal education

Sociologists disagree about what **formal education** is for. The functionalist approach focuses on the **positive functions** that the education system performs in society. When revising this approach to education, it can be helpful to set out the functions in a spider diagram like the one below.

As part of your revision, try using a spider diagram to summarize your notes on other topics.

1 Serving the needs of the economy

6 Social control

The functionalist approach to the functions of the education system in society

2 Selection

5 Secondary socialization

3 Facilitating social mobility

4 Encouraging 'Britishness' and social cohesion

In contrast, the **Marxist approach** is critical of the role of the education system in capitalist society. This approach sees the education system as benefiting privileged groups and reinforcing **social inequalities** over time.

Question (d) on page 21 is testing your knowledge and understanding (AO1) of an important sociological concept. One way of answering questions like this is to define the term clearly and give examples to support your definition. To get full marks on such questions, you need to provide a clear (rather than a basic or limited) explanation of the term.

Here is how one student answered question (d) on page 21.

Here is how one student answered question (d) on page 21.

The question assesses AO1 and is marked out of four.

Social cohesion is like the glue that bonds everybody in a society together and unites them all. Without social cohesion, society would have more divisions and conflicts. Social cohesion, socialization and social control are three important functions of education.

3/4

Although the last sentence is factually accurate, this question is not directly asking about the different functions of education. So the reference to social control and socialization in this context is not strictly relevant. As the question does not ask about other functions of education, it's best to focus more directly on 'social cohesion'.

Good points

- The student shows some understanding of the concept of 'social cohesion'.

- The answer recognizes that social cohesion is a function of the education system. However, it could go on to explain how education is expected to contribute to, or build, social cohesion.

Task 1

This table summarizes the role of the education system according to the functionalist approach. Match each function in the first column with the correct explanation.

The functions of the education system	Explanation
1 Serving the needs of the economy 2 Selection 3 Facilitating social mobility 4 Encouraging 'Britishness' and social cohesion 5 Secondary socialization 6 Social control	a) The education system is expected to enable individuals to move up (or down) the social ladder. Able students from disadvantaged backgrounds have opportunities to achieve qualifications that allow them to move up the layers of the social class system. b) While at school, pupils learn the culture (way of life), norms and values of their society. c) Through their formal education (e.g. citizenship classes), pupils identify with British culture and see themselves as British citizens. Schools help to reinforce the 'glue' or the social bonds that unite different people in society. d) Education has an economic role in teaching the knowledge and skills that future workers will need in a competitive global economy. e) Schools teach pupils to conform and to accept rules (e.g. punctuality) and adult authority. f) The education system works like a sieve, grading people and allocating them to jobs based on their individual merit, abilities and exam results.

Task 2

This table summarizes the Marxist approach. Match the role of the education system in the first column with the correct explanation in the second column.

The role of the education system in a capitalist society	Explanation
1 Serving the interests of the ruling class 2 Reproducing the class system 3 Breeding competition 4 Secondary socialization	a) Through sports and exams at school, students are encouraged to accept values such as competition. If most people value competition, this helps to maintain the capitalist system because it is based on competition. b) By passing on ideas and beliefs that benefit the ruling class (for example, that capitalist society is fair and meritocratic), the education system serves ruling class interests. c) The education system socializes working-class children to accept their lower position in capitalist society. For example, they learn to accept hierarchy at school and to obey rules. d) Education appears to reward pupils fairly based on their individual abilities. However, it actually favours pupils from more advantaged backgrounds. Over time, education recreates (or reproduces) the advantages that some social class groups have over others.

The structure of the education system

Key points

- In Section B of Paper 1, you may be asked to **describe and explain the structure of the education system and discuss debates about education**. You may also be asked to **explain why educational reforms have been made and to criticize these reforms**.

- In practice, this is likely to mean that you should be able to:
  - explain the structure of the education system
  - discuss the advantages and disadvantages of special schools, faith schools, home education and testing
  - discuss how effective particular reforms (such as the introduction of league tables and OFSTED Inspections) have been in raising standards.

The education system is structured into five different **stages**. The table below summarizes these stages. When you are revising, try to summarize your notes in this way to make them more manageable.

1	Pre-school or early years education	State nursery schools and nursery classes in primary schools offer free, part-time provision for children aged 3–4.
2	Primary education	Most state primary schools cater for girls and boys aged 5–11.
3	Secondary education	Most state secondary schools cater for students aged 11–16 but some have a sixth form. In some areas, middle schools take pupils from 8–12, 9–13 or 10–13 years old. Secondary schools include academies, comprehensives, grammar, specialist, faith and private schools.
4	Further education (FE)	FE mainly caters for students aged 16 and over who have completed compulsory education. Further education (e.g. A-level and vocational qualifications) is provided by Sixth Form and FE Colleges.
5	Higher education (HE)	The HE sector includes universities that provide higher level academic and vocational courses (e.g. degree level study). However, much HE is now also provided in colleges.

Debates about the structure of education

Debates about how education is organized focus on issues such as the merits of:

- different **types of school** such as faith schools, private schools, special schools and selective schools
- **testing** in primary schools
- alternative forms of **educational provision** such as home education
- **special** schools and **mainstream** schools.

Part (f) of the Education question (see page 21) relates to different types of secondary school. Read this question carefully and underline the command words. You will see that it assesses AO1 and AO2 and is marked out of five. Two marks are available for an appropriate description. An additional three marks are available for a clear explanation of the advantages of the type of school that you have described. Here is how one student answered this question.

Examiner's tip

Remember to read the question carefully and to answer the question that is set. If a question asks for advantages, you should give more than one.

Good point

The student both describes and explains an advantage of a comprehensive school. However, the answer is quite short for five marks and it only gives one advantage.

One type of school is a state comprehensive school. The advantage of this is that it accepts pupils of all abilities. Grammar schools select on the basis of ability and exclude . many pupils.

The question asks for advantages rather than for one advantage.

3/5

Education as a political issue

The different political parties each have ideas on how education should be organized. Once in **government**, a party has the power to introduce new educational **policies and reforms**. Most recent governments have aimed to improve educational standards and have introduced reforms to **raise standards**. However, critics often question how far government policies have actually achieved their aims. For example, the Education Reform Act 1988 introduced **SATs tests** for 7-, 11- and 14-year-olds as a way of measuring pupils' performance against national targets. Critics argued, however, that there was too much formal testing in schools. Testing at 7, 11 and 14 has now been abolished in Wales and the government has decided to end testing at 14 in England.

Read through part (e) of the Education question on page 21, which focuses on testing in primary schools. This question is marked out of five. Two marks are available for an appropriate description. An additional three marks are available for a clear explanation of the criticisms of testing. Here is how one student answered this question.

> One way is through SATs tests. When these were first introduced, all primary school pupils aged 7 and 11 did national tests in English, maths and science. A pupil's performance could be measured against national targets.
> These tests were criticized because too much time was spent preparing for them and education was now being driven by testing. Many pupils found the tests stressful and some parents kept their children off school on test days.

5/5

This question assesses AO1 and AO2.

The answer gives an appropriate description.

The explanation is clear.

Good points

- The student gives a clear description of SATs tests.
- The answer explains several relevant criticisms of the use of SATs tests in primary schools.

Key concepts

marketisation of education
selective education

Task 1

Some parents and carers want their children to attend a faith school such as a Church of England or Muslim school. Others want their children to attend community schools that admit pupils regardless of their religious beliefs. Copy out and complete the table below by identifying two reasons why some people support faith schools and give two criticisms of faith schools.

Reasons why some parents and carers want their children to attend faith schools	Criticisms of faith schools
1	1
2	2

Task 2

Copy out and complete the table below by identifying two reasons why some people support private education and give two criticisms of private education.

Reasons why some people support private education	Criticisms of private education
1	1
2	2

Differential educational achievement

Key points

- In Section B of Paper 1, you may be asked to **describe and explain variations in educational achievement in terms of social class, ethnicity and gender**.

- You may also be asked to **identify the different influences on educational achievement**.

- In practice, this is likely to mean that you should be able to:
  - define the term 'differential educational achievement'
  - outline the patterns of educational achievement by social class, ethnicity and gender
  - discuss the different influences on a child's educational achievement linked to home factors, school factors and government policies.

Key concepts

institutional racism
labelling
minority ethnic group
school ethos
self-fulfilling prophecy
streaming

The term '**differential educational achievement**' refers to the variations in educational attainment (e.g. in Key Stage test results and in exam results at GCSE and A-level) between students according to their social class background, gender and ethnicity.

The patterns of educational achievement

When revising differential educational achievement, it is important to be clear in your own mind what the **general patterns** or variations in achievement are. You should be aware that:

- In general, students from **middle-class backgrounds** tend to achieve better results in public examinations than those from **working-class backgrounds**.

- Generally, students from **some minority ethnic groups** (such as Chinese, Indian and Irish heritage students) tend to perform better than others (such as African Caribbean, Pakistani and Bangladeshi heritage students) within education.

- During the 1970s and 1980s, **subject choice was gendered** with girls tending to specialize in some secondary-school subjects and boys in others. In the sciences, for example, girls tended to choose biology while boys tended to choose physics. This could be seen at 'O' level, when more boys sat exams in subjects such as physics and mathematics while more girls sat exams in biology and English Language.

> At 16, many students sat 'O' level exams before 'O' levels were replaced by GCSEs.

- Traditionally, boys got better results at A-level than girls. However, towards the end of the 1980s, this **gender gap in achievement** began to narrow. By the early 2000s, girls were doing better than boys at GCSE and at A-level. They were also tending to perform better in key stage tests. In 2008, for example, girls performed better than boys in English and science tests at Key Stage 2.

- Not all students who are working-class, male, or from a minority ethnic background **underachieve**. For example, boys from schools in very affluent areas generally perform better than boys and girls from schools in very deprived areas; middle-class boys tend to achieve better results than working-class girls.

Influences on educational achievement

When you are revising the different influences on educational achievement, it can be helpful to set out the various factors as key points in a table. The table on the next page shows one way of doing this. It summarizes the **home-based** and **school-based factors** as well as the impact of **government policies** and reforms.

Influences on educational achievement

Home factors
Children's experiences in the home and neighbourhood

Parental values and expectations
- Parents in professional occupations often have **high expectations** of their children and expect them to do well at school. They are more likely than other parents to **monitor** their children's school performance.

Parents' educational backgrounds
- If parents have high-level educational qualifications (for example, a degree), they are more able to **help with homework** and to **monitor** progress.

Economic circumstances
- Students from relatively well-off backgrounds are more likely to have access to **facilities (such as a PC, books and a quiet space)** to help them study at home.
- Students from some minority ethnic backgrounds are far more likely than white British students to attend the most **deprived** schools.

Cultural background
- Research suggests that British Chinese parents **value education** and that in Chinese culture, children respect older people. So British Chinese pupils develop high educational ambitions and get positive self-esteem from being 'good pupils'.

School factors
Children's experiences at school

School-based resources
- School factors include how **well-resourced** the school is. Fee-charging private schools, for example, often have better resources and facilities than most state schools.

The school curriculum
- The school **curriculum** can be seen as biased towards white European cultures. Critics argue that African Caribbean cultures, histories and experiences should be included more in the curriculum.

Teacher expectations and labelling
- Some teachers may have lower **expectations** of students from working-class or minority ethnic backgrounds. This may affect how much **attention** such teachers give to these students during lessons. If particular students are not expected to succeed, they may become demotivated.
- Negative **labelling** of working-class or black students (e.g. as 'unlikely to do well') can lead to a **self-fulfilling prophecy**. In this case, students perform as badly or as well as their teachers expect them to.

Pupil cultures and school ethos
- Some pupils may experience **peer pressure** to conform to the norms of an 'urban' or 'street' culture that does not value education.
- 'Laddish' cultures may emphasize that it's 'uncool' to work hard. This informal peer culture may encourage **anti-learning attitudes** and affect the progress of particular boys (and girls) in some schools.
- Among schools in middle-class neighbourhoods, boys may not see education as 'uncool'. They may achieve **status** among their peers by displaying academic abilities.
- **School ethos** refers to the character or culture of a school. Some schools (e.g. selective schools) have an academic ethos that promotes exam success and progression to university.

Institutional racism
- This occurs when an organization fails to provide an appropriate service to people because of their ethnic origin, culture or colour. Institutional racism is an **unintended consequence** of the way institutions such as schools are **organized**. For example, the relatively high rate of exclusion of students from African Caribbean backgrounds has been linked to institutional racism.

Government policies
The impact of government policies and reforms

The specialist schools programme
- Research suggests that some government policies such as the **specialist schools programme** have helped to tackle low achievement and raise standards in schools.

Schools' admissions policies
- Some policies can work against students from disadvantaged backgrounds. For example, if a school's admissions policy gives it scope to **select** its intake, this can work against students from disadvantaged backgrounds.

Marketisation, competition and league tables
- The emphasis on parental choice and competition between schools to **raise standards** may have made life more difficult for some urban schools that have an intake of working-class or minority ethnic students.
- National **league tables** were introduced to help raise standards in schools. However, they can have negative effects for low achievers from disadvantaged backgrounds if schools focus their resources on the better performers rather than on those who are not entered for GCSE exams.

EMAs
- **Education Maintenance Allowances** (EMAs) were introduced so that students from low-income backgrounds could get financial help if they **stayed on** within education and training after GCSEs.

Equal opportunities policies and legislation
- Equal opportunities policies and anti-discrimination legislation (for example, the Sex Discrimination Act and the Race Relations Act) made it **illegal** for schools to **discriminate** on the basis of gender or ethnicity.

Teachers' expectations and educational achievement

Part (g)(i) of the question on Education (see page 21) focuses on teachers' expectations and children's educational achievement. Read this question carefully and underline the command words. This is an example of an extended-answer question that is marked out of 12 and assesses AO1, AO2 and AO3. Here is how one student answered this question.

The student starts well with an example of how educational achievement can be measured.

Sociologists have identified several significant influences on children's educational achievements (such as their exam results). Teachers' expectations are one key influence. In this answer, I have to discuss the different influences and say whether teachers' expectations are the most important of all.

The student confirms what they have to do in this answer.

The student makes good use of sociological concepts.

Some teachers have lower expectations of working-class pupils than middle-class pupils. Other teachers may underestimate the abilities of some minority ethnic pupils compared to white pupils or the abilities of girls compared to boys (e.g. in Physics). This labelling can lead to a self-fulfilling prophecy and so pupils' achievements are as good or bad as their teachers expect.

The student discusses alternative influences.

Parents' values and attitudes are also important. It is argued that parents in professional jobs have higher expectations for their children than working-class parents. So they are more likely to check up on their child's progress. Their values fit in with the values of the education system.

This reference to Kellett and Dar is accurate and up to date. However, don't worry if you forget the names of the researchers who carried out a particular study. You can make the point without referring to the researchers by name and still earn full marks. For example, you could replace 'Kellett and Dar found …' with 'Research has found …'.

Material factors are another home-based factor influencing children's educational achievements. Kellett and Dar found that many disadvantaged primary school pupils do homework in noisy conditions while more well-off pupils do homework in their own bedrooms at home.

This is a good point.

Government policies can also affect children's educational achievements. For example, the EMA has encouraged more students from low income backgrounds to stay on at 16 and get A Level qualifications.

A clear conclusion that addresses the 'how far' aspect of the question.

To conclude this answer, sociologists would agree that teacher expectations are one of the significant influences on children's achievements. However, the different school and home-based influences can overlap and are hard to disentangle.

The answer is well-structured. It begins with a clear introduction that shows an understanding of the issues. The answer discusses teachers' expectations before moving on to examine other relevant factors that influence achievement. It also refers to government policies. The answer comes to a clear conclusion.

12/12

Good points
- The student examines achievement in relation to class, gender and ethnicity.
- The answer looks at both school-based and home-based factors. It also refers to government policies.
- It directly addresses the set question.

Task 1

When explaining the improvements in girls' educational achievements since the 1980s, several factors have been identified. These include equal opportunities policies and anti-discrimination legislation. Copy out and complete the following table by providing an explanation of how each of the four factors has helped to improve the educational achievements of girls.

Factor	Explanation
1 Equal opportunities policies in education	
2 Anti-discrimination laws	
3 The impact of feminism	
4 The National Curriculum	

Task 2

Match the term in the first column with the correct meaning in the second column.

Term	Meaning
1 Streaming	a) This refers to the culture and character of a particular school. For example, selective schools (such as grammar schools and many private schools) have an academic culture that stresses the importance of exam success and progression from school to university.
2 Selective education	b) A form of teaching in which students are grouped according to their general ability and then taught in this group for all of their subjects.
3 School ethos	c) A way of recruiting pupils to a school, based on a form of selection. For example, pupils may be selected on the basis of their results in an entrance exam, or on the basis of their parents' or guardians' ability and willingness to pay annual school fees.

Task 3

Drawing on the information provided here, as well as relevant information from your textbook or class notes, answer the following questions:

a) Identify and explain one way in which peer groups may influence pupils' educational achievements. *(4 marks)*

b) Explain what sociologists mean by 'institutional racism'. *(4 marks)*

Examiner's tips

- Remember to check the lists of Key concepts and refer to your textbook or lesson notes if you are unsure what any of them mean.

- The student's answer on page 28 is relatively long. Bear in mind that it is possible to write a shorter answer and still earn full marks as long as the answer demonstrates the relevant skills. When an examiner marks your answers, he/she will be looking for evidence of skills such as knowledge and understanding (A01), application (A02) and evaluation (A03).

- Remember that one potential problem with writing very long answers to extended-answer questions is that you risk running out of time.

Answering extended-answer questions

An extended answer is like a **mini-essay** and it is important that you have a clear idea of how to respond to this particular style of question.

Part (g) of the question on Education gives you a choice between two extended-answer questions (see page 21 and page 28). The part (g) question is worth 12 marks. This represents 40 per cent of the total mark for Section B of Paper 1 so you need to make sure that you understand what is expected of you.

Your answer should have a **clear and logical structure** with an introduction, a main body and a conclusion. You should aim to write three or more paragraphs and spend no more than 10 minutes writing your answer.

You have already looked at an example of a student's answer to part (g)(i) of the question on Education so we will now look at part (g)(ii).

> Remember that you will also have to spend time on things like reading the Items and checking through your work.

Focusing on the set question

Let's look at question (g)(ii) more closely and begin to unpack it.

> **Discuss how far sociologists would agree that serving the needs of the economy is the most important function of the education system in Britain today.**
>
> *(12 marks)*

This question relates to the different functions of the education system and it refers to the economic function in particular. The command words are 'Discuss how far sociologists would agree ...'.

In your response, you need to discuss the different functions of the education system today, including serving the needs of the economy, secondary socialization, social control and encouraging social cohesion.

You also need to assess to what extent sociologists would agree that serving the needs of the economy is the most important of these functions. So you should try to assess the arguments and evidence and reach a conclusion on this (AO3).

Your answer should aim to say:

> *'There are several important functions of the education system today but this answer will discuss whether serving the needs of the economy is the most important of these.'*

The question gives you a **time frame** (today) so you need to stay focused on up-to-date issues.

> If a question refers to a particular time frame, you must ensure that you respond to this time frame in your answers.

Planning your answer

It's worth spending time in the exam planning your answer. This will help you to organize your ideas and present them more clearly and logically. Spend no more than a couple of minutes on this. Just jot down the main points that you intend to cover. Make sure that you refer back to your plan as you write your answer.

Getting started

Start your extended answer with an **introduction** in which you briefly define or explain the meaning of any sociological **terms or concepts** in the question. For example, you could explain that the term 'function' refers here to a role carried out by the education system in society and that it is linked to the functionalist approach. This shows that you know and understand (AO1) the sociological terms, concepts and approaches.

You could begin the **main body** of your answer by arguing that the most important function of the education system today is to serve the needs of the economy. For example, you could argue that the education system meets the needs of a competitive global economy by providing a well-educated and highly skilled workforce.

> See pages 22–3 for a summary of the different functions of the education system according to the functionalist approach.

Once you have put forward an argument to **support** the view, you could then put forward an argument **against** this view. For example, you could argue against this view by discussing other important functions of the education system today such as **social control**, **secondary socialization** and **social cohesion**.

You could also put forward an alternative view by referring briefly to the **Marxist approach** to the role of the education system in a capitalist society. In this way, you are building up an argument in response to the set question and you are criticizing or evaluating information. This shows that you can analyse an issue and evaluate the different viewpoints on this issue (AO3).

> Task 2 on page 23 provides some information about the Marxist approach to education.

Answering the set question

When writing your mini-essay, it is important that you respond directly to the question that is asked. Try to link each point or section of your answer directly to the set question so that it is clear why you have included it. By doing this, you will show that you can **apply** your knowledge and understanding (AO2) to the question.

Concluding your answer

Finish your answer by summing up and reaching a **clear conclusion** that responds directly to the 'how far' aspect of the question. You need to conclude on whether serving the needs of the economy is the most important function of the education system today. Your conclusion should follow on from your discussion. You might conclude that most sociologists **agree** with the view expressed in the question or that many sociologists **disagree** with this view. By summing up and addressing 'how far', you will show that you can analyse and evaluate (AO3).

> Bear in mind that sociologists from the different approaches (such as the functionalist and Marxist approaches) tend to disagree rather than agree on the key issues.

Task

Write a mini-essay to answer question (g)(ii) on page 21. Try to spend no more than 10 minutes on this question as this is more or less how long you will have to write a 12-mark answer in the exam.

Examiner's tips

- The quality of your written communication will be assessed in your extended answer. Try to make sure that your handwriting is readable and that your spelling, punctuation and grammar are accurate.

- Always leave time at the end of the exam to read through your answers and make any necessary changes or corrections.

Paper 1 Section C: Families

Key points

About the Families exam question

Here is an example of the sort of exam question that could be asked on Families. The question is divided into parts (a) to (g). For each part, the assessment objectives (AOs) (see page 4) have been identified for you. This will help you to recognize which skills each part is testing. The comments are there to give you some guidance on how to go about answering exam questions on Families.

In the exam, the 'Items' could contain material such as written extracts from books or newspapers, charts, bar graphs, tables of statistics or photographs. In the question below, Item F presents a set of official statistics on divorce and Item G outlines findings from the *British Social Attitudes Survey* about who does the housework.

SECTION C: FAMILIES

Answer **all** questions from this section.

Total for this question: 30 marks

3   Study **Items F and G** and then answer parts (a) to (g).

ITEM F

Number of divorces: by length of marriage. 1996 and 2006
United Kingdom

Length of marriage	1996	2006
Under 5 years	37 016	25 005
5–9 years	48 670	37 116
10–19 years	51 538	48 891
20 years and over	34 487	37 116

Source: adapted from *Social Trends* 39, (2009) Office for National Statistics. (© Crown Copyright)

ITEM G

The *British Social Attitudes Survey* found that in 1994, 77 per cent of men with partners and 84 per cent of women with partners said that laundry was always or usually done by the women. In 2006, 71 per cent of men with partners and 80 per cent of women with partners said that laundry was always or usually done by the women. Crompton and Lyonette argue that, while attitudes to gender roles have changed a lot since the late 1980s, men's participation in household tasks has not changed much.

The assessment objectives (AOs) are shown here to help you to recognize which skills are being tested. However, the AOs will not appear alongside the questions on the AQA examination papers.

(a) From **Item F**, how many divorces in the UK in 2006 were granted to couples who had been married for 5–9 years? AO3   *(1 mark)*

(b) From **Item G**, what percentage of men with partners in 2006 said that laundry was always or usually done by the women? AO3   *(1 mark)*

(c) Identify **two** reasons for the increase in the number of one-person households in Britain over the last 30 years. AO1   *(2 marks)*

(d) Explain what sociologists mean by an 'ageing population'. AO1   *(4 marks)*

It's important to get lots of practice at writing answers under timed conditions. Aim to spend around three minutes writing answers to 4-mark questions, four minutes writing answers to 5-mark questions and around 10 minutes writing answers to 12-mark questions.

(e) Describe **one** way in which the infant mortality rate has changed in Britain over the last 100 years **and** explain the reasons for this change. AO1 AO2   *(5 marks)*

(f) Describe **one** way in which an individual's family or household situation might change over the course of their life **and** explain why this change may have occurred. AO1 AO2   *(5 marks)*

Part (g) is an extended-answer or mini-essay question worth 12 marks. Aim to answer this question in three or more paragraphs.

(g) **EITHER**

(i) Discuss how far sociologists would agree that changing attitudes are the most important reason for the general increase in divorce in Britain since 1945. AO1 AO2 AO3   *(12 marks)*

OR

You can draw on relevant information from the Items when answering extended-answer questions. For example, you could use relevant information from Item G when answering (g)(ii). However, you should avoid copying from the Items.

(ii) Discuss how far sociologists would agree that the roles of men and women in families have changed significantly since the 1960s. AO1 AO2 AO3   *(12 marks)*

Four of these part-questions (c, e, g(i) and g(ii)) specify a timescale. It's important to respond to these timescales in your answers. Bear in mind that some timescales (e.g. 'since 1945') are precise whilst others (e.g. 'since the 1960s') are less exact.

As you work through this revision chapter on Families, you will have the opportunity to read examples of how students have answered questions (c), (e), (g)(i) and some other questions. These sample student answers have all been given a mark and there is also a written comment about each one. It is important to study all of this information carefully because it will give you further guidance on how to answer exam questions on Families.

The command words here are 'Discuss how far sociologists would agree...'.

It's a good idea to start your answer by explaining the view stated in the question and then put forward contrasting or different views. Finish your answer by coming to a conclusion based on your discussion and remember to address the 'how far' aspect of the question. In your answer to (g)(i), for instance, you would need to discuss the different reasons before coming to a conclusion about whether the most important of these reasons is changing attitudes.

Task 1

Answer questions (a) and (b).

Task 2

Once you have worked through this chapter on Families, you should answer questions (c), (e) and (g)(i) and then compare your own responses to the sample student answers provided.

Defining a 'family' and a 'household'

Key points

- In Section C of Paper 1, you may be asked to **define a 'family' and to explain the different types of family found in Britain today**.

- In practice, this is likely to mean that you should be able to:
  - explain what the terms 'family' and 'household' mean
  - explain the different family types such as nuclear and extended families.

Key concepts

beanpole family
civil partnership
cohabitation
cultural diversity
extended family
family
family diversity
gay or lesbian family
household
lone-parent family
migration
nuclear family
reconstituted family

Examiner's tip

It's important to recognize that people have been migrating to Britain for centuries and that Britain is a culturally diverse society.

Defining a 'family'

The term **'family'** can be defined as a couple who are married, civil partners or cohabiting, with or without dependent children, or a lone parent with their child or children. Some sociologists prefer to use the term **'families'** rather than 'the family' because it recognizes the **diversity** or the variety of family types living in Britain today. When you are revising these different family types, it can be useful to set them out in a diagram.

1 Nuclear families

2 Extended families

3 Lone-parent families

Different family types in Britain today

4 Gay or lesbian families

5 Reconstituted (blended or step) families

Families differ in several respects. For example, they vary according to whether they are headed by a couple or a lone parent. If they are headed by a couple, they can differ according to whether the partners are married, in a civil partnership or cohabiting. They also differ in terms of whether the couple is heterosexual or gay.

Defining a household

Most people in the UK live in **households**. A household can be defined as either one person living alone or a group of people who share a house or flat. Some, but not all, households are family households.

A family household could contain:	A non-family household could contain:
- one family or - one family plus people who are not family members such as a live-in housekeeper or - two or more families.	- one person living alone (e.g. in a flat) or - two or more unrelated people (e.g. a group of students) living in a shared house and sharing a daily meal or facilities such as a living room.

Around one per cent of the UK population live in residential establishments such as care homes, nursing homes or prisons.

Data from the 2001 Census highlights variations in households by **ethnicity**. For instance:

- **household size varies**; households of Bangladeshi and Pakistani heritage, on average, contained more people than other households

- ten per cent of households of Bangladeshi and Pakistani heritage, three per cent of households of black Caribbean heritage and two per cent of white British households contained a **multigenerational extended family**.

Question (c) on page 33 is an example of a question that tests your knowledge and understanding of one-person households. Read this question carefully. The command word here is 'identify', so the question is asking you to state briefly two reasons for the increase. Here is how one student answered this question.

One reason for the increase in one-person households is the changing age structure of the population. People are generally living longer now and this has resulted in more elderly, one-person households. These households often contain older women who have outlived their husbands.

Another reason is the increase in households containing widows.

1/2

> This question tests AO1 and is marked out of two. You will get one mark for each of the two appropriate reasons that you identify.

> The question asks you to identify two reasons but it doesn't ask you to explain these reasons. So the third sentence could be cut from the answer without losing the mark.

> In the first part of the answer, the student identifies one reason. However, this is quite long given that it can earn only one mark out of two.

Good points

- The student clearly identifies one appropriate reason. However, the second reason is very similar to the first one. As a result, it does not earn the second mark.

- The student could have identified the increase in solo living among younger people as the second reason.

Examiner's tip

Some questions ask you to identify 'two reasons' or 'two ways'. In your answers, try to make sure that you give two separate reasons or two different ways in order to earn the two marks.

Life course diversity

One way of looking at **diversity** is to examine the different family and non-family households that a particular individual experiences over their **life course** (during the course of their lifetime). For example, a baby could be born into a lone-parent family and later become part of a reconstituted family. As a young adult, they could live with friends in a shared house before living on their own in a single-person (i.e. non-family) household. After this, they could live with their partner before having children and forming a nuclear family and so on.

Task

This table defines the main terms related to households and family types. Each definition contains a highlighted word or phrase and you have to decide whether the highlighted text is correct. If it is incorrect, you should replace it with a correct word or phrase. The first one has been done to help you get started.

Term	Definition
1 Non-family household	a household containing either one person living alone or a group of related people such as students who live together and share facilities (e.g. a living room) or one meal every day. *Incorrect. Correct = unrelated.*
2 Family household	a household containing a family group such as a nuclear or a lone-parent family.
3 Nuclear family	a two-generation family containing married or cohabiting parents and their child or children who live apart.
4 Extended family	a group of relatives extending beyond the nuclear family. In the classic extended family, three generations live together or nearby. In the modified extended family, members live apart geographically but have regular contact and provide support.
5 Gay or lesbian family	a family in which a heterosexual couple (civil partners or cohabiting) live together with their child or children.
6 Reconstituted family	a blended family in which one or both partners have a child or children from a previous relationship living with them.
7 Lone-parent family	a family in which two parents live with their child or children.
8 Beanpole family	a multigenerational family in which each generation has one or very few members.

Different sociological approaches to families

Key points

- In Section C of Paper 1, you may be asked to **describe and explain the different sociological approaches to the family**.

- In practice, this is likely to mean that you should be able to:

  - describe and explain the functionalist, New Right, feminist and Marxist approaches to the role of the family in society.

Examiner's tip

When answering extended-answer questions, you should put forward alternative explanations of the issue under discussion. One way of tackling this is to think about how the different sociological approaches might address the issue. For example, when answering question (g)(ii) on Families (see pages 32–3), you could discuss the feminist approach. You will find a discussion of changing gender relationships in families on pages 38–9.

There are several different sociological approaches to the study of families and family life. Some of these, such as the **functionalist approach**, emphasize the **positive** aspects of the nuclear family and the key role it plays in society. Others, such as the **feminist approach**, are **critical** of the family and its role in society.

The functionalist approach

During the 1940s and 1950s, the functionalist approach viewed the nuclear family in positive terms as a necessary and important part of society. This approach argued that the nuclear family performed **essential functions** for individuals and for society including:

- **reproduction** – the nuclear family produces the next generation of society's members

- **primary socialization** – the nuclear family is the agency of socialization through which young children learn the basic behaviour patterns, language and skills needed in later life

- **emotional support** – the nuclear family provides for its members' emotional well-being

- **economic support** – the nuclear family provides its members with financial support.

The New Right approach

The New Right approach of the 1980s and 1990s is a more recent reworking of the functionalist approach. Both approaches see the nuclear family as the family type that works best in meeting the needs both of society and of children. The New Right approach suggests that women should have the **caring role** within nuclear families while their husbands should have the **breadwinner role**. It views some changes in family structures (such as increases in one-parent families and births outside marriage) as damaging to society. For example, children in fatherless families are seen as being more prone to crime than other children.

> The New Right approach to crime and deviance is outlined on page 50.

The Marxist approach

The Marxist approach is critical of the nuclear family and the role it plays in maintaining the capitalist system. According to this approach, the nuclear family:

- **supports the capitalist** system by supplying future generations of workers

- **socializes working-class children** to accept their lower position in an unequal society

- **recreates inequalities** between the social classes over time. For example, members of the bourgeoisie (the upper class who own property and capital) can buy their children a privileged education and pass on their wealth to the next generation of the family.

The feminist approach

The feminist approach is also critical of the nuclear family and its role in society. Many feminist sociologists see society as based on **patriarchy**, or on male power and dominance over women. Living in nuclear families is seen as benefiting men more than women. In many families, for example, women have most responsibility for housework and childcare even if they work in full-time employment. Feminist sociologists also see primary socialization in families as a **gendered process**. In other words, it contributes to the creation of gender differences between girls and boys.

The following question tests your knowledge and understanding of a key sociological concept: **'Explain what sociologists mean by primary socialization.'** *(4 marks)*

The command word here is 'explain' and the question is asking you to define the term 'primary socialization'. Here is how one student answered this question.

> Primary socialization is the process of early learning in childhood. It usually takes place in families. During primary socialization, babies and infants learn the language, skills and behaviour they will need as they get older. So primary socialization prepares very young children to fit into society. **4/4**

This question tests AO1 and is marked out of four.

Here is an example of another question that tests your knowledge and understanding of the concept of socialization: **'Explain what sociologists mean by gender socialization.'** *(4 marks)*

This is how one student answered this question.

> Gender socialization describes people being socialized into their gender by agencies of socialization such as the family. **2/4**

This is another example of a question that tests AO1 and is marked out of four.

Task 1

1 Identify one similarity between the functionalist and the New Right approaches to the family.

2 Identify one similarity between the Marxist and the feminist approaches to the family.

3 Identify one difference between the functionalist and the Marxist views on families.

4 Identify one difference between the New Right and the feminist views on families.

Task 2

Write your own answer to the following question. Try to spend between three and four minutes on it – this is roughly how long you will have for this kind of question in the exam. In your answer, remember to address the 'gender' aspect of the question as well as the 'socialization' aspect.

Explain what sociologists mean by gender socialization. *(4 marks)*

Key concepts

agency of socialization
bourgeoisie
feminist approach
gender socialization
New Right approach
patriarchy
primary socialization
role

Good point

The student gives a clear explanation of the concept of 'primary socialization' that addresses 'primary' and 'socialization'.

Good point

The student uses the term 'agencies of socialization' and refers to the 'family' as an example. However, the answer does not define or explain clearly the concepts of 'gender' or 'socialization'. In order to earn full marks, the student would need to give a clear explanation that relates both to 'gender' and 'socialization'.

Role and authority relationships in families

Key points

- In Section C of Paper 1, you may be asked to **describe and explain role and authority relationships within families**. You may also be asked to **describe changes in these relationships and discuss the factors influencing these changes**.

- In practice, this is likely to mean that you should be able to:
  - describe and explain changes in gender roles, changing patterns of parenting and childcare and changes in relationships with members of the wider family.

Changing gender roles in families

Some sociologists argue that the **roles of men and women** in families have changed quite significantly since the 1960s. However, other approaches disagree with this view.

Gender roles and relationships in families have changed since the 1960s	Gender roles and relationships have not changed markedly since the 1960s
• Young and Willmott (1973) argued that the '**symmetrical family**' was now typical in Britain. Conjugal roles were more equal. • Young and Willmott (1973) also found that **decisions on spending money** (a measure of who has power in relationships) were shared more **equally**. • Pahl (1989) found that, compared with 30 years ago, more couples **shared decisions** on spending the household income. • Gatrell (2008) found that many **fathers** in dual-worker couples today play a **bigger role** in their children's lives compared with fathers in the past. • Reasons for these changes include: the rise of **feminism**; the availability of effective **contraception**; women's increased participation in **full-time paid employment**; and the increase in **home-based leisure activities**.	• **Feminist approaches** reject the idea of symmetry. In her study of housework, Oakley (1974) found little evidence of symmetry. Women in paid employment still had the responsibility for housework. • Crompton and Lyonette (2008) argue that men's involvement in household work has increased **less** than women's involvement in paid work. Also, the gap between men's and women's contribution to domestic work narrowed between the 1960s and 1980s because women spent **less time** on it rather than because men did more of it. • Crompton and Lyonette (2008) also argue that **attitudes** to gender roles have changed a lot but men's **participation** in household tasks has not changed much. Women still usually do the laundry and ironing. • Some feminist sociologists argue that family life is still **patriarchal**. Males benefit from living in families but females lose out.

Examiner's tip

You don't have to quote lots of sociological research with names and dates, but it is helpful to mention one or two as examples of a particular approach or view that you are describing. However, this is not a requirement, even to reach the top grades.

Good point

The student recognizes that joint roles are related to an equal division of labour. However, the answer is quite brief for four marks and the term 'conjugal roles' is not explained fully. To get full marks, the student would need to give a clear explanation that addresses both 'joint' and 'conjugal roles'.

Here is how one student answered the question: '**Explain what sociologists mean by 'joint conjugal roles'**. *(4 marks)* AO1

Where conjugal roles are described as joint, this means that all the household jobs (e.g. doing the shopping and the DIY) are shared out equally.

2/4

It's not clear from this explanation whether the household jobs are shared out equally between the adult partners or between all household members including any children.

Changing parent–child relationships

Many sociologists argue that **parent–child relationships** have changed over time.

- Relationships are less **authoritarian** – there is less emphasis on parental authority and discipline. There is more emphasis on children's rights and individual freedom. However, Pryor and Trindor (2004) note that middle-class families are more likely than working-class families to involve their children in decision making.

- Relationships are more **child-centred** – there is more focus on children's interests and needs. The average family size is smaller today than 100 years ago so children get more individual attention from parents. However, many young children are regularly separated from parents who work in full-time employment.

- Young people are now more **financially dependent** on their family and for a longer time compared with the past. As a result of the raising of the participation age, all teenagers will remain in education or training until the age of 17 from 2013 and 18 from 2015. This is likely to mean that many teenagers will be financially dependent for longer. However, Scott (2004) argues that some children may contribute by helping out in family businesses or with childcare and housework.

Task 1

Write an answer to the extended-answer question (g)(ii) on page 33. Try to spend no more than 10 minutes on this – this is roughly how long you will have for this kind of question in the exam.

Task 2

The information below discusses relationships with the wider family. Fill in each gap by selecting the correct answer from the following:

a) face-to-face contact	e) geographical mobility	i) telephone
b) adult children	f) wider family	j) grandchildren
c) financially	g) less important	
d) 1950s	h) mother	

Young and Willmott (1957) found that during the (1) _____ in East London, extended family ties were strong and 43 per cent of daughters had seen their (2) _____ during the last 24 hours. Some sociologists argue that family members see less of each other today due to increasing (3) _____ and women's involvement in full-time employment. Consequently, the wider family is becoming (4) _____ and family ties are weakening.

Other recent studies, however, have found regular (5) _____ between family members. Charles *et al* (2008) found that in Swansea, grandmothers regularly cared for their (6) _____ so that mothers could work. Furthermore, fathers often helped their (7) _____ with DIY and adult children cared for their parents. When family members lived some distance away they still maintained contact by (8) _____ or visits and provided support by helping out (9) _____ or by exchanging gifts. So while contact and support may be changing, the (10) _____ is not necessarily becoming less important.

Key concepts

conjugal roles
democratic relationships
division of domestic
    labour
dual-earner household
dual-worker families
feminism
gender roles
geographical mobility
joint conjugal roles
kinship relationships
male-breadwinner
    household
power
segregated conjugal
    roles
symmetrical family

Examiner's tip

Remember to try to get as much practice as possible at answering questions under timed conditions.

Changing patterns of fertility and life expectancy

Key points

- In Section C of Paper 1, you may be asked to **describe and explain changes in the patterns of fertility and expectations of life**. You may also be asked to **describe the significance of these changes for individuals, family structures and society**.

- In practice, this is likely to mean that you should be able to:
  - discuss changes in fertility
  - discuss changes in life expectancy and in the infant mortality rate
  - explain how these changes affect individuals, families and society.

You can link this to material on the welfare state and the NHS in the chapter on Power.

Changing patterns of fertility

The term **'fertility'** refers to the average number of children that women of childbearing age (usually defined as between 15 and 44) give birth to in a particular society. Women born in the UK are having **fewer children** than 30 years ago and they are having them at a later age. So there is a trend towards a **smaller family size**. These changes in patterns of fertility are linked to:

- **Changing attitudes to family size**. During the 19th century, many poorer parents relied on their children's income from paid work to survive. Having big families meant a larger income. Today, this financial incentive to have a large family no longer exists; in fact the opposite is true – children are expensive.

- **Later marriage**. In the 1970s, people generally married younger than is usual today. Nowadays, some women will marry later and delay having children until they are older.

- **Women's increased participation in education and paid employment**. This means that they now have more options open to them in addition to (or instead of) motherhood.

- **The availability of effective birth control methods**. Contraception gives women more control over their fertility (e.g. whether and when to have children).

Changing patterns of life expectancy

Life expectancy at birth is the average number of years a newborn baby is expected to live. In the UK, life expectancy has risen over the last century. In 2006 it was 77 years for men and 82 years for women and in the future it is expected to increase further.

Increased life expectancy is linked to:

- The **decrease in infant mortality rates** (the number of deaths of infants aged under one per 1000 live births per year) since the early 20th century.

- **Welfare state provisions**, including free healthcare through the National Health Service.

- Improvements in **public health and sanitation** during the 19th and early 20th centuries (e.g. clean water supplies and sewerage systems) so fewer people die from contagious or waterborne diseases.

- Improvements in **preventive measures** such as national screening programmes for breast cancer and vaccinations to prevent diseases like diphtheria and tetanus.

- **Advances in medicine and surgery** (e.g. open-heart surgery) during the 20th century.

- Healthier lifestyles and improvements in **diet and nutrition** over the last 30 years.

Part (e) of the sample question on Families (see page 33) focuses on infant mortality. Read this question carefully. The command words are 'describe' and 'explain' and it tests AO1 and AO2. The question is marked out of five. You will get two marks for a relevant description of one way in which the infant mortality rate has changed (AO1). You will get another three marks for explaining some of the reasons for this change (AO2).

Here is how one student answered this question.

The term 'infant mortality' refers to the number of babies who die before they reach the age of one. The infant mortality rate has fallen in Britain over the last one hundred years. In 1930, there were 60 infant deaths for every 1000 live births in England and Wales but by 2006, there were only five deaths per 1000 live births.

One reason for the improvement in the infant mortality rates is developments in the level of care provided to pregnant women and to babies through the NHS. Also, during the early 20th century, a midwifery service was developed so more babies were delivered by qualified nurses. Advances in medicine and surgery over the last 100 years mean that many more babies now survive serious illnesses and diseases.

5/5

> The student understands the term 'infant mortality' and how it is measured.

> The student draws on relevant statistics to illustrate the change in infant mortality rates.

Good point

The student gives a clear description of how the infant mortality rate has changed and explains some of the main reasons for this change.

Examiner's tip

You do not need to have a detailed knowledge of the different statistics. However, it's important to have a good idea of the trends, with the occasional statistic to illustrate.

The ageing population

As a result of declining fertility and longer life expectancy, the **age structure** of the UK population is changing. It now has a smaller proportion of children and young people and an increasing proportion of older people. In other words, it has an **ageing population**.

Longer life expectancy and an ageing population may lead to changes in families and households such as:

• an increase in one-person households

• an increase in 'beanpole' families.

Examiner's tip

When writing about 'retired people' or 'older people', bear in mind that they include:

• the 'young old', in their late 60s and early 70s

• the 'old old' who are in their 80s, 90s or older.

Task 1

The question below (question (d) from the Families question on page 33) tests your knowledge and understanding (AO1) of the term 'ageing population'. The command word is 'explain'. Write an answer to this question. Try to spend between three and four minutes on it.

Explain what sociologists mean by an 'ageing population'. *(4 marks)*

Key concepts

ageing population
demography
fertility
infant mortality rate
life expectancy
welfare state

Task 2

Drawing on information in your textbook and class notes, identify two social consequences of an ageing population.

Marriage, cohabitation and divorce

Key points

- In Section C of Paper 1, you may be asked to **describe and explain changes in the patterns of marriage and cohabitation**. You may also be asked to **explain changes in the pattern of divorce in Britain since 1945 and to be aware of the consequences of divorce for family members and family structures**.

- In practice, this is likely to mean that you should be able to:
  - discuss the reasons for the changing patterns of marriage and cohabitation
  - give reasons for the general increase in divorce since 1945 and understand how divorce can affect family structures (e.g. lone-parent and reconstituted families) and family members (e.g. children).

Changing patterns of marriage and cohabitation

The **marriage rate** in the UK has declined from 7.1 marriages per 1000 people in 1981, to 5.2 marriages per 1000 people in 2005. The proportion of people **cohabiting** (living with a partner outside marriage or civil partnership) has doubled over the last 20 years in Britain. This increase is linked to **changing social attitudes** towards sex outside marriage. Before the 1960s, it was seen as unacceptable for unmarried women to be sexually active.

During the 1960s and 1970s, the number of **births outside marriage** increased, and in 2006 over 40 per cent of babies were born outside marriage. However, many of these babies are born to cohabiting couples. The increase is related to changing social attitudes towards births outside marriage which, in general, are now less disapproved of. Other important changes linked to marriage and cohabitation include the introduction in 2005 of **civil partnerships** and the **increase** in the average age of first marriage.

Changing patterns of divorce

In general, the number of divorces per year has increased since the 1940s. In 1970, 63 000 divorces were granted in the UK. The number of divorces peaked at around 180 000 in 1993 but fell to 144 000 in 2007.

Several factors have been identified to explain the general increase in divorce since 1945.

- **Changing attitudes** mean that divorce is now more socially acceptable.

- **Legal changes** have made divorce easier, quicker and cheaper to obtain. The Divorce Reform Act (1969), for instance, introduced 'irretrievable breakdown of marriage' as the ground for divorce. In 1984, new legislation allowed couples to petition for divorce after one rather than three years of marriage.

- **Changes in the social position of women** have meant that a woman in an unhappy marriage is less tied to her husband through economic dependence.

- **The secularization process** has weakened the religious barrier to divorce.

- **The media's emphasis on mutual attraction and romance** in relationships may encourage couples to have high expectations of marriage. If these expectations do not match the reality of married life, this may result in an increase in divorce.

The consequences of divorce

Divorce has consequences for individuals and for society:

- Rising divorce rates have contributed to an **increase in some household and family types** (e.g. one-person households, lone-parent and reconstituted families).

Examiner's tip

Modern Britain is a culturally diverse society and is home to a rich mix of cultural, ethnic and religious groups. When you are writing about social attitudes, it's important to appreciate that attitudes to issues such as births outside marriage, abortion, cohabitation and divorce may vary quite significantly from group to group. Some religions, for example, do not approve of cohabitation, births outside marriage or divorce.

Examiner's tip

You don't need to have a detailed knowledge of the different divorce laws. However, it's important to know the approximate dates and what main legal changes were introduced.

- Living in a **reconstituted family** may cause problems for individual family members who have to adjust to different expectations of behaviour. On the other hand, more people may be available to provide attention and support.

- Some children **lose contact** with their father following their parents' divorce.

- **Conflict** between the former husband and wife may continue after they divorce because of disputes about parenting and property issues.

- Divorce can lead to a **loss of income** for the former partners. After divorce, lone-parent families with dependent children may face financial hardship.

- Divorced people, particularly men, may experience **loss of emotional support**.

Part (g)(i) of the sample question on Families (see page 33) is an extended-answer question. Read this question carefully. It assesses AO1, AO2 and AO3 and is marked out of 12. Here is how one student answered this question.

Changing attitudes are one important reason for the increase. Attitudes to divorce have changed and there is now less social stigma linked to divorce compared to 1945 (the end of World War 2).

Another important reason is legal changes, which introduced irretrievable breakdown of marriage as a ground for divorce. So it is now easier to get divorced than it was in 1945.

A third reason is secularization. Religion is less important in today's society and fewer people get married in religious ceremonies (e.g. in churches). So religion is less of a barrier to getting divorced.

To sum up, sociologists argue that the reasons for the general increase in divorce are changing attitudes, less social stigma, new legislation and secularization.

7/12

> The answer is beginning to resemble a list of reasons. Try to relate the material more directly to the question by assessing the importance of these different reasons.

> These reasons are all important. However, to pick up more marks, the student must address whether the most important reason is changing attitudes. If not, which is the most important reason?

Examiner's tip

Extended-answer questions test the quality of your written communication. In your own extended answers, try to ensure that your writing is readable and that your spelling, punctuation and grammar are accurate so that the meaning is clear.

Good points

- The student has identified several appropriate reasons for the general increase in divorce since 1945.

- They have also used sociological terms such as 'secularization'.

  However, the answer does not respond directly to the 'how far' aspect of the question. See page 33 which explains this aspect of the question.

Key concept

secularization

Task

The following list includes issues such as cohabitation and divorce. For each one, make a note of whether it has increased or decreased, in general, in Britain since the 1960s.

1 births outside marriage

2 cohabitation

3 divorce

4 the average age of first marriage

5 the birth rate

6 the marriage rate

7 the number of reconstituted families

8 the proportion of households containing lone parents with dependent children

9 the proportion of households containing one person

10 the proportion of households containing traditional nuclear families.

How to raise your Unit 1 exam paper grade

The information on pages 96–97 explains how the examiners calculate your grade if you are completing the GCSE Sociology Full Course. If you are doing the Full Course, you should read this additional information as well.

Key point

The advice and tips provided here are designed to help you to **maximize your mark in the Unit 1 exam paper**. They cover:

- the assessment objectives (AOs) and the skills that you need to demonstrate in the exam
- the command words that you need to respond to
- advice on the key 'dos and don'ts' to guide you when approaching your GCSE Sociology exam.

If you are doing the **GCSE Sociology Short Course**, you will study Unit 1 and sit the Paper 1 exam. When the examiner marks your Paper 1 exam script, they will add up your marks for the three questions and calculate your total mark out of 90. This is referred to as your raw mark. They will convert your raw mark into a uniform mark out of 100 and then convert your uniform mark into a grade. To achieve a good grade in the Short Course, you should focus on getting as high a mark as you can in the Paper 1 exam.

The assessment objectives

To achieve a good grade in the Paper 1 exam, you need to maximize your marks by demonstrating the **skills** that the examiners are looking for. These skills are:

- **Knowledge and understanding** (AO1)
- **Application of knowledge and understanding** (AO2)
- **Interpretation, analysis and evaluation** (AO3)

You need to demonstrate a sound knowledge and understanding of the relevant Unit 1 topics. So it is essential to revise the subject content thoroughly in order to maximize your AO1 marks.

To maximize your AO2 marks, you need to apply the appropriate concepts, terms and theories effectively.

To maximize your AO3 marks, you need to:
- interpret data from the Items accurately
- evaluate different sources and methods when answering the Studying Society questions about investigating a given topic
- evaluate different explanations and outline appropriate conclusions when answering extended-answer questions.

The command words on Paper 1

The exam questions are all carefully worded to test your sociological skills. The command words are a key part of each question. They make it clear exactly what you are required to do in order to answer a particular question. So to maximize your chances of getting high marks and a good grade it is important to ensure that you understand what the different command words are asking you to do.

Command words	Examples of questions from Paper 1	What you are required to do
Identify	From **Item A**, what percentage of female students achieved five or more GCSE A*–C grades? *(1 mark)*	• Pick out the relevant information from an Item.
	Identify two reasons for the increase in the number of one-person households in Britain over the last 30 years. *(2 marks)*	• Briefly state two different reasons.
Outline	**Outline one** advantage and **one** disadvantage of using informal interviews. *(2 marks)*	• Give a short description of an advantage and a disadvantage.
Explain	**Explain** what sociologists mean by a nuclear family. *(4 marks)*	• Define the term clearly and give examples to support your definition.
Describe … and explain why …	**Describe one** way in which an individual's family or household situation might change over the course of their life **and explain why** this change may have occurred. *(5 marks)*	• Give both a description and an explanation; briefly outline one way (**describe**) and then discuss the possible reasons why (**explain why**) this change may have taken place.

Command words	Examples of questions from Paper 1	What you are required to do
Identify ... and explain why ...	Identify **one** secondary source of information that you would use in your study **and explain why** you would use this source. *(4 marks)*	• State briefly (**identify**) and develop your answer by discussing the reasons why (**explain why**).
	Identify **one** primary method of research that you would use in your study **and explain why** this method would be better than another primary method for collecting the data that you need. *(6 marks)*	• State which primary method you would use in a given study (e.g. a study that investigates parents' attitudes towards faith schools, private education or testing in primary schools). • Discuss the reasons why this method is a better choice than an alternative method. • Remember to take into account the focus of the given study.
Discuss how far sociologists would agree ...	**Discuss how far sociologists would agree** that teachers' expectations are the most significant influence on children's educational achievements. *(12 marks)*	• Put forward relevant arguments in favour of the statement for discussion, drawing on sociological explanations, concepts and evidence. • Put forward arguments against the statement for discussion. • Come to a clear conclusion which directly addresses the issue of 'how far'.

Exam 'Dos and Don'ts'

Do	Don't
Think about how you will use your time in the exam to: • read the Items and the questions carefully • plan your extended answers • write your answers • check and, if necessary, improve your answers.	Rush straight into writing the answer to a question.
Make sure you have a 'big picture' of the unit in your head, as well as the detail.	Worry about memorizing lots of sociologists' names and dates.
Study the 'command' words in the questions and respond to them.	Worry about memorizing lots of detailed statistics.
Write answers of the right length for the marks available.	Write 'all you know' about the topic in the question.
Try to make links in your answer between the different parts of the specification, for example, between Crime and Deviance and Mass Media.	Copy out chunks from the Items.
Look at the Chief Examiners' reports on previous exams with your teacher. Even if the specification has changed, the advice on how to get a good grade still applies.	Think that you have to write the 'perfect answer' to get full marks; the examiner knows that you are working under exam conditions and allows for this.

Examiner's tips

• Remember to read the instructions on the first page of the exam paper.

• Some questions refer to a particular time frame such as 'during the last 30 years'. In this case, you must respond to this time frame.

• If an Item contains figures, remember to check what units the figures are presented in. For example, they may refer to percentages or to millions.

Key points

- Paper 2 is divided into **four** sections (one of which is Crime and Deviance). In the exam, you will choose **three** sections and then answer all questions from each of the three sections you choose. Make sure that you choose three sections that you have revised thoroughly.

- Section A of Paper 2 will focus on **Unit 2, Crime and Deviance**.

- It is marked out of 30.

- If you choose Crime and Deviance, it will account for 33 per cent (one third) of your total mark for Paper 2.

- You should spend no more than 30 minutes on each of your three chosen sections. This includes the time you spend writing your answers but it also includes the time you will need to spend studying the Items, reading the questions, planning your answers and checking them at the end. Remember that on Paper 2 you may also need to spend a little time choosing which three sections you are going to answer.

About the Crime and Deviance exam question

Here is an example of the sort of exam question that could be asked on Crime and Deviance. The question is divided into parts (a) to (g). For each part, the assessment objectives (AOs) have been identified for you. This will help you to recognize which skills each part is testing. The comments are there to give you some guidance on how to go about answering exam questions on Crime and Deviance.

In the question below, Item A draws on official statistics and looks at the likelihood of men and women being found guilty of, or cautioned for, serious offences. Item B presents statistics from the British Crime Survey (BCS). So these Items are both based on secondary sources of quantitative data.

Paper 2 consists of four sections. Only Section A (Crime and Deviance) is given here. The questions are similar to those you have looked at in the Education and Families chapters in that they are a mixture of short-answer and extended-answer questions.

SECTION A: CRIME AND DEVIANCE

Answer **all** questions from this section.

Total for this question: 30 marks

1 Study **Items A and B** and then answer parts (a) to (g).

ITEM A

Figures from the Ministry of Justice show that males are more likely than females to be found guilty of, or cautioned for, serious offences. In 2007, for example, 5.2 per cent of males and 1 per cent of females aged 20 were found guilty of, or cautioned for, serious offences in England and Wales. Similarly, 1.5 per cent of males and 0.4 per cent of females aged 40 were found guilty of, or cautioned for, serious offences.

ITEM B

Offences recorded by the British Crime Survey

England and Wales

Millions

2001–02	12.6		2006–07	11.3
2002–03	12.3		2007–08	10.2
2004–05	10.9		2008–09	10.7
2005–06	10.9			

The British Crime Survey is an example of a victim survey.

These figures are in millions so 12.6 is actually 12 600 000.

Source: adapted from the *British Crime Survey*, Home Office Research Development Statistics, 2009
© Crown Copyright

The marks for questions are shown in brackets. Remember to use these marks as a guide to how much time you spend on each question.

This question asks for two ways. Make sure that you spend more or less the same amount of time writing about each of these ways.

It's important to get lots of practice at writing your answers under timed conditions. This will help you not only to get your timings right but also to check your knowledge of particular topics. Aim to spend around three minutes writing your answers to 4-mark questions, four minutes writing your answers to 5-mark questions and around 10 minutes writing your answers to 12-mark questions.

Note that questions (e) and (f) both ask you to do two things. Make sure that you provide a description and an explanation.

The command words here are 'Discuss how far sociologists would agree...'.

In your answer, you should:
- start by explaining the view that is stated in the question before putting forward the contrasting views
- discuss, compare or evaluate the different views and alternative explanations
- come to a conclusion based on your discussion.

(a) From **Item A**, what percentage of females aged 20 were found guilty of, or cautioned for, serious offences in England and Wales in 2007? AO3 *(1 mark)*

(b) From **Item B**, how many offences were recorded in 2007–08? AO3 *(1 mark)*

(c) Identify **two** ways in which people are encouraged to conform to formal social rules. AO1 *(2 marks)*

(d) Explain what sociologists mean by the term 'agencies of informal social control'. AO1 *(4 marks)*

(e) Describe **one** way in which crime and deviant behaviour could have a negative impact on communities **and** explain why this impact is seen as a problem by some members of the public. AO1 AO2 *(5 marks)*

(f) Describe how a self-report study is carried out **and** explain why it provides a different account of the number of crimes committed compared to police statistics. AO1 AO2 *(5 marks)*

(g) **EITHER**

(i) Discuss how far sociologists would agree that deviant and criminal behaviour among young people is due to peer group pressure. AO1 AO2 AO3 *(12 marks)*

OR

(ii) Discuss how far sociologists would agree that females are less likely to commit criminal offences than males. AO1 AO2 AO3 *(12 marks)*

As you work through this revision chapter on Crime and Deviance, you will have the opportunity to read examples of how students have answered questions (c), (d), (e), (f), (g)(ii) and another extended-answer question. These sample student answers have all been given a mark and there is also a written comment about each one. It is important to study all of this information carefully because it will give you further guidance on how to answer exam questions on Crime and Deviance.

You can draw on relevant information from the Items when answering extended-answer questions. For example, you could use relevant information from Item A when answering (g)(ii). However, you should avoid copying from the Items.

Task 1

Answer questions (a) and (b).

Task 2

Once you have worked through this chapter on Crime and Deviance, you should answer questions (c), (d), (e), (f) and (g)(ii) and then compare your own responses to the sample student answers provided.

Definitions of crime and deviance

Key points

- In Section A of Paper 2, you may be asked to **distinguish between the concepts of crime and deviance**. You may also be asked to **describe the ways in which individuals are encouraged to conform to formal and informal social rules**.

- In practice, this is likely to mean that you should be able to:
  - define 'crime' and 'deviance' and explain the difference between them
  - explain the difference between formal and informal rules
  - describe how the processes of formal and informal social control work.

The student uses a relevant sociological term.

Examples are included which support the explanation.

It's acceptable to use historical and cross-cultural evidence in your answers. However, you must make it very clear why you are referring to this evidence.

Defining crime and deviance

- A **crime** is an illegal act that is punishable by law. Examples include robbery, fraud and shoplifting. If a person commits a crime and it is detected, they could be arrested, charged and prosecuted. If found guilty, they will receive a sentence such as a community order, fine or imprisonment.

- **Deviance** refers to behaviour that does not conform to a society's norms or social rules, for instance, talking loudly in a library or in a cinema. If a person behaves in a way that is seen as deviant and this is discovered, it could lead to negative sanctions such as being told off, ignored or ridiculed.

- Some, but not all, deviant acts are also illegal. **Legal deviance** is behaviour that is seen as 'abnormal' by most people in a society but it does not break the law. **Illegal deviance** involves criminal behaviour that is punishable by the state.

- Some illegal acts are not necessarily seen as deviant. For example, many people park their car on double yellow lines or use a handheld mobile phone whilst driving even though these activities are against the law.

Question (d) on page 47 tests your knowledge and understanding (AO1) of the term 'agencies of informal social control' and is marked out of four. Read this question carefully. Here is how one student answered this question.

> Whereas formal social control operates through laws and written rules, informal social control operates through unwritten rules. It is enforced by social pressure from people such as family members, friends, workmates or peer groups who might, e.g. praise someone or ignore them. These groups are known as agencies of informal social control because they control or constrain people's behaviour informally through social pressure.

4/4

Good point

On questions like this, the examiners will give four marks for a clear and detailed (rather than a basic or incomplete) explanation of a particular sociological concept. In this answer, the student earns full marks by giving a clear explanation of what sociologists mean by the term 'agencies of informal social control'. The answer addresses the 'agencies' as well as the 'informal social control' aspects of the question.

Deviance as socially defined

Many sociologists argue that while crime involves legally defined behaviour, deviance is **socially defined**. Whether or not an act is seen as deviant depends on how other people react to it – how they view and label the act. This means that deviance is judged according to the social setting or the context in which it takes place.

Historical evidence suggests that what is considered as deviant can change over time. For example, attitudes to smoking and to homosexuality have changed in Britain since the Second World War. **Cross-cultural evidence** suggests that what is seen as deviant can vary between cultures. For example, cultures differ in terms of how women dress and what is seen as appropriate within their group or society.

Historical and cross-cultural evidence also suggests that what is classed as **criminal behaviour** can change over time and vary between cultures. For example, it was illegal to drink alcohol in the US during the 1920s and alcohol consumption is illegal or restricted in some countries today.

Formal and informal social control

Formal social control is based on formal written rules that are set out in laws or in codes of conduct such as school rules. The **agencies** of formal social control are the bodies that make the formal written rules, enforce them or punish people who break them. The role of the Houses of Parliament, for example, is to make the laws that regulate our behaviour while the police enforce those laws. The courts deal with alleged offenders and sentence those found guilty of crimes. The role of prisons is to punish convicted offenders, to rehabilitate them by giving them the opportunity to turn away from crime in the future, and to deter others from committing crime.

Informal social control is based on unwritten or 'taken-for-granted' rules and is enforced through social pressure from groups such as families, friends or peers. Parents, for example, may use positive sanctions, such as going out for a pizza, in order to reward their children's good behaviour. They may use negative sanctions, such as stopping pocket money, in order to punish bad behaviour and encourage conformity in the future.

Question (c) on page 47 tests your knowledge and understanding (AO1) of the process of formal social control and is marked out of two. Read this question carefully. Here is how one student answered this question.

> One way is by having a police force to enforce the law, investigate crimes and arrest suspected offenders. Another way is by having prisons to punish convicted offenders and to rehabilitate them.

2/2

Task 1

Match the term in the first column with the correct meaning in the second column.

Term	Meaning
1 Formal social control	a) Control of people's behaviour that is based on social processes such as the approval or disapproval of others. It is enforced through social pressure from groups such as peer groups and families.
2 Informal social control	b) The various groups (such as peer groups) and organizations (such as the police force) in society that control or constrain people's behaviour and actions.
3 Agencies of social control	c) Control of people's behaviour that is based on written laws and rules. It is usually associated with the ways in which the state regulates and controls people's behaviour through, for example, the police force, the courts and prisons.

Task 2

Describe two ways in which individuals are encouraged to conform to informal social rules.

(2 marks)

Examiner's tips

• If questions are worth just one or two marks, try to keep your answers brief. Lengthy answers use up valuable time.

• If you do write a lengthy and detailed answer to a question worth just two marks, the examiners won't be able to award you more than the maximum two marks. So remember to check how many marks are available (they will be shown in brackets) and use the marks as a guide to how long your answers should be.

Good points

• The student identifies two appropriate ways and gets one mark for each of these.

• The answer is well balanced in that the student has written one sentence about each of the two ways.

Key concepts

agencies of social control
crime
deviance
formal social control
informal social control
negative sanctions
peer group
peer pressure
positive sanctions
social order

Different explanations of crime and deviance

- In Section A of Paper 2, you may be asked to **outline different sociological explanations of criminal and deviant behaviour**.

- In practice, this is likely to mean that you should be able to:
  - describe different explanations linked, for example, to inadequate socialization, sub-cultural theories, labelling theory and relative deprivation.

Examiner's tip

You can contrast sociological and biological explanations for crime and deviance when answering relevant Paper 1 questions on the sociological approach (see pages 8–9).

- Sociological explanations focus on social factors such as inadequate socialization or labelling.

- Biological explanations focus on biological causes of criminal activity. One explanation, for instance, looks at the genetic basis of crime and antisocial behaviour.

Explaining crime and deviance

There are several different sociological explanations for criminal and deviant behaviour. These explanations focus on **social factors** rather than biological or psychological causes. When answering questions on sociological explanations for crime and deviance, you should be aware of the following approaches.

Inadequate socialization within families	This is one explanation for some young people's involvement in crime and deviance. It highlights the negative influence of the **home environment** and the failure of some parents to socialize their children to accept society's norms and values. **New Right** approaches, for example, argue that children whose parents fail to take responsibility for socializing them correctly are more prone to crime.
Sub-cultural theories	Sub-cultural theories explain crime and deviance in terms of the values of a particular **subculture** and the influence of the **peer group**. Vandalism and 'joyriding', for example, are carried out in groups. Young males in particular learn such deviant behaviour by joining a peer group or gang in which this is already the 'done thing'. Albert Cohen argued that working-class boys joined delinquent subcultures to gain **status** within their peer group.
Relative deprivation	People feel **relatively deprived** when they see themselves as badly off relative to the living standards of the particular group that they compare themselves to. Experiencing feelings of relative deprivation may motivate criminal behaviour. For example, a bank clerk who wants a mansion with a pool like that owned by their regional manager may commit fraud to acquire the necessary funds because they could never afford it any other way.
Marxist explanations	This approach links crime to the **social inequalities** that are built into capitalism. In a capitalist society, not everyone can access wealth and status so some people commit crime to acquire the consumer goods and material possessions that others have and that the media promote. According to the Marxist approach, the legal system operates in favour of the rich. For example, rich people who commit expense account fraud or tax evasion are less likely to be convicted than working-class people who commit benefit fraud.
Labelling theory	Labelling theory explores how and why some people (e.g. working-class boys) become **labelled** as deviant or criminal. Cicourel argued that a delinquent is someone who has been labelled as such. Being labelled a deviant or criminal may result from the **reaction** of other people (such as the police) and may not be entirely due to an individual's actions or behaviour. Labelling someone as deviant may help to create a **self-fulfilling prophecy** by pushing someone further towards deviance.

> It's important to look for links between the different topics that you have studied. For the concept of socialization, you can make links to Families and Education.

> Remember to use the relevant concepts and ideas (such as peer groups, socialization and labelling) in your answers.

Key concepts

relative deprivation	stereotype
status	subculture
status frustration	wealth

Here is how one student answered the extended-answer question: **'Discuss how far sociologists would agree that crime and deviance among teenagers result from their membership of deviant subcultures'.** *(12 marks)* AO1, AO2, AO3

In a deviant subculture, the group members' behaviour does not conform to society's norms.

Sub-cultural theory links crime and deviance among some teenagers (and adults) to the values of their subculture. In the 1950s, Cohen argued that young males learned to become delinquents by joining gangs in which delinquency already existed. Cohen linked delinquency among working-class boys to status frustration at school. These boys gained status through their delinquent subculture rather than from doing well at school.

On the other hand, the Marxist approach links crime to the workings of capitalist society. Labelling theory also disagrees with the sub-cultural theory and argues that working-class boys may end up labelled as criminals because of the reactions and stereotypes of people such as probation officers, police officers or teachers. Middle-class teenagers who behave in the same way often avoid being labelled.

In conclusion, sub-cultural theorists would agree that teenage crime and deviance is linked to membership of deviant subcultures. Marxist approaches put more emphasis on capitalism and labelling theory puts more emphasis on labelling and stereotyping of teenagers. However, sociologists would all agree that teenage crime and deviance results from social factors rather than from biological or psychological factors.

12/12

This extended answer is carefully planned and very well structured. It follows a logical sequence by starting with an introduction, followed by a main body and finishing with a conclusion. The answer begins by defining the concept of deviant subculture. The second paragraph explains the view that teenage crime and deviance result from membership of deviant subcultures. The third paragraph argues against this view by discussing alternative sociological explanations for teenage crime and deviance. The final paragraph draws the answer to a close and directly addresses the 'how far' aspect of the question.

Don't worry if you can't remember the names of all the sociologists you have studied. You can discuss the relevant explanations (e.g. sub-cultural theory) without referring to the work of particular sociologists and still get full marks.

The Marxist approach is not discussed fully. However, the examiners are experienced teachers who appreciate that it is impossible to include everything when writing under timed conditions. They are not looking for perfection.

By writing 'on the other hand', the student signals that they are going to examine an alternative explanation.

Good points

- The student links the view in the question to sub-cultural theory and goes on to explain this approach before looking at other relevant sociological explanations. It would also be acceptable to include 'inadequate socialization' or 'the opportunity structure' as explanations of teenage crime and deviance.

- The answer effectively contrasts sub-cultural and labelling theories.

- Although this answer could be improved, it is the best that can reasonably be expected under exam conditions and so it gets full marks.

Task

Question (g)(i) on page 47 is an example of an extended-answer question that focuses on sociological explanations of crime and deviance.

Write an answer to this question. Try to spend around 10 minutes on it – this is roughly how long you will have for this kind of question in the exam.

Sources of statistical data on the extent of crime

Key points

- In Section A of Paper 2, you may be asked to **assess the usefulness of official crime statistics, self-report studies and victim surveys**.

- In practice, this is likely to mean that you should be able to:
  - describe how official crime statistics are put together and explain their advantages and disadvantages
  - describe how victim surveys and self-report studies are carried out and explain their advantages and disadvantages.

Key concepts

official statistics
self-report study
social construction
victim survey
white-collar crime

When writing about sources of statistical data on the extent of crime, you should be aware that the two **main measures of crime levels** in Britain are:

- official statistics of crimes recorded by the police
- surveys of the public such as victim surveys and self-report studies.

Official statistics of crimes recorded by the police

Official statistics of crimes recorded by the police are an important secondary source of quantitative data. However, although they appear to provide a factual measure of the extent of crime in any one year, they cannot be taken at face value. Police recorded crime statistics exclude the '**hidden figure**' of crime including **unreported and unrecorded crime**. In your answers, you could include the following reasons for this:

- Some crimes are **not witnessed or discovered** and so they cannot be reported to the police. For example, white-collar crimes such as fraud or misuse of expense accounts may not be discovered in the first place.
- Some crimes that are witnessed or discovered are **not reported to the police**.
  - **Less serious crimes** such as vandalism tend to be under-reported while most car theft is reported, probably for insurance purposes.
  - People tend not to report crimes that they see as **private**.
  - The victim might not report a crime such as sexual assault because they think that the **police** will handle it **insensitively**.
  - **Employers** might not report crimes that their employees commit. For example, if a company's directors discovered that one of their managers had stolen company funds, they might decide not to report this to the police in order to avoid negative publicity. Such **white-collar crime** is under-represented in police-recorded crime statistics.
- The police do not necessarily **record** all crime that is reported to them. They may see the crime as too trivial to record, doubt the complainant's report or have insufficient evidence that a crime has actually been committed.

Sociologists argue that statistics of police recorded crime are '**socially constructed**'. In other words, the statistics are the outcome of the decisions and choices made by the people, such as the witnesses, victims and police officers, who are involved in their construction.

Victim surveys

Victim surveys ask people about their **experiences of crime**. The *British Crime Survey*, for example, measures crime via surveys with large samples of households in England and Wales. It interviews people about whether they have been a victim of particular offences during the last year and, if so, whether they reported the crimes to the police.

> You could refer to victim surveys when answering exam questions on social surveys or on secondary sources in Section A of Paper 1, Studying Society.

Victim surveys indicate that many victims do not report crimes to the police. This **under-reporting** helps to explain why the police-recorded crime statistics are lower than the estimated statistics based on victim surveys.

Self-report studies

Self-report studies ask people to **reveal offences they have committed**. The *Offending, Crime and Justice Survey* (OCJS), for example, is a **longitudinal study** that measures the extent of self-reported offending, drug use and antisocial behaviour in England and Wales, particularly among 10–25 year olds. The 2004 OCJS interviewed around 5000 young people about their involvement in various offences during the previous year. Each interview lasted for around one hour. Interviewees listened to the more sensitive questions via headphones and entered their answers on a laptop without the interviewer's help. By asking people to disclose offences they have committed, the OCJS provides information on offenders and offences that are not necessarily dealt with by the police or courts.

Look at question (f) on page 47 which focuses on self-report studies. Read this question carefully. It tests your knowledge and understanding (AO1) of self-report studies and your ability to compare the data from these with police statistics (AO2). Here is how one student answered this question.

> Self-report studies such as the Offending, Crime and Justice Survey (OCJS) ask a sample of people to disclose any criminal offences that they have committed during the last year. The studies are usually based on interviews but respondents may answer the more sensitive questions via a laptop.
>
> Police statistics only include crimes that are witnessed or discovered by someone, reported to the police and recorded by them. Self-report studies ask people about their own offending so they provide statistical data about offenders and offences that do not necessarily come to the attention of the police or the courts. So the two sources provide different accounts because they are measuring different things.
>
> **5/5**

> You could refer to the OCJS as an example when answering exam questions on longitudinal studies or on secondary sources in Section A of Paper 1, Studying Society.

> The OCJS is a good example to use.

Good points

- The student describes clearly how a self-report study is carried out.
- The answer explains why self-report studies and police statistics provide different accounts of the number of crimes committed.

Task 1

The question below tests your knowledge and understanding (AO1) of the concept of white-collar crime. Write an answer to this question. Try to spend between three and four minutes on it – this is roughly how long you will have for this kind of question in the exam.

Explain what sociologists mean by the term white-collar crime. *(4 marks)*

Task 2

Drawing on the information provided here as well as relevant material in your textbook and class notes, make a list of the advantages and disadvantages of:

a) official crime statistics

b) victim surveys

c) self-report studies.

Examiner's tip

You can draw on relevant information about official statistics from Unit 1, Studying Society, to help you to answer Paper 2 exam questions on official crime statistics.

The social distribution of crime

Key points

- In Section A of Paper 2, you may be asked to **discuss the social distribution of crime**.
- In practice, this is likely to mean that you should be able to:
  - describe the links between involvement in crime and social factors such as age, gender, ethnicity, social class and locality
  - explain these links.

Key concept

chivalry effect

Examiner's tip

You will get much more out of this topic if you read about official statistics of crimes recorded by the police first (see pages 52–3).

When taken at face value, official statistics suggest that members of some social groups are more likely to commit crime than others. You should be aware of the links between involvement in crime and social factors such as age, gender and locality.

Age and crime

Official statistics indicate that younger people, particularly young men, are more likely to engage in crime than older people. Explanations for this include **peer group pressure** and **sub-cultural influences** (see pages 50–1) on young people.

Gender and crime

Official statistics suggest that, in general, more men than women commit crime. Possible explanations for this include **gender socialization processes**, gender differences in **opportunities** to become involved in crime and the **chivalry effect** that operates during reporting, police response, trial and sentencing.

The number of female offenders in the UK, however, appears to be **increasing**. This may be due partly to changes in the social position of women who now have similar opportunities to men to act illegally. Another explanation for the increase relates to changing attitudes to gender. Shifts in attitudes may mean that women no longer receive less harsh treatment than men within the criminal justice system.

Ethnicity and crime

Official statistics show that people from some ethnic groups are **over-represented** in prisons relative to their proportion in the population. Black people, for example, are around five times more likely to be in prison than white people. At face value, such figures could suggest that members of some ethnic groups commit more crime than others.

Many sociologists, however, argue that crime statistics exaggerate crime among some ethnic groups. The statistics are seen as reflecting the way that **policing** is carried out and also bias within the criminal justice system. Research shows, for example, that black people are more likely to be stopped and searched, prosecuted and convicted than people from other ethnic groups.

You can link this to institutional racism within the police force.

Social class and crime

There is evidence that working-class people are **over-represented** in prisons. One view is that working-class people have fewer **opportunities** to succeed via legal routes such as education. As a result, they are more likely than middle-class people to resort to crime for financial gain. Another view suggests that **working-class subcultures** stress deviant and criminal behaviour as a way of achieving status among peers.

Alternatively, working-class people may be over-represented in prisons due to social class **bias** within the criminal justice system. Some sociologists argue that the law is more strictly enforced against working-class people engaging in robbery or benefit fraud than against middle-class people engaging in expense account fraud or tax evasion.

You can link this to white-collar crime.

Locality and crime

In general, the crime rate is higher in **urban areas** than in rural areas and in the **most deprived areas** of Britain compared with the least deprived areas. One view is that urban areas have higher levels of **unemployment** and **poverty**, which provide a context for crimes such as theft. Another view is that, compared with rural areas, there are more **opportunities** to commit crime in urban settings such as city centres. Alternatively, the statistics may reflect differences in **policing** levels and methods between urban and rural areas.

Study question (g)(ii) on page 47, which is an example of an extended-answer question on crime and deviance. Here is how one student answered this question.

A crime is an illegal act. If detected, the offender is usually prosecuted and sentenced. According to police statistics, females are much less likely to commit serious crimes than males. Only around 20 per cent of people found guilty of, or cautioned for, serious offences are women. On the other hand, males may be much more likely to be found guilty.

Some sociologists argue that women are less likely to commit crimes than men because of gender socialization. Males are often under peer pressure to act in masculine ways. This could lead to alcohol-related violence and conflict with the police.

Other sociologists argue that females have fewer opportunities to commit crime. Girls, for example, are often supervised more closely than boys.

Another view is that female offenders who conform to gender stereotypes (e.g. wearing feminine clothes during the trial) are treated less harshly than men within the criminal justice process. This is known as the 'chivalry effect'.

However, official statistics suggest that nowadays females are more likely to commit crimes than thirty years ago. On the other hand, it may be that females are now more likely to be arrested, charged and convicted because the chivalry effect is declining.

To sum up, sociologists do agree that generally females are less likely to commit crimes than males. However, they disagree on how to explain this and also why female crime has increased.

11/12

Examiner's tip

You don't need to memorise the official crime statistics in any detail. However, it is important to be aware of the general patterns. For example, you should know that official statistics indicate that more men than women commit crime.

The concept of crime is explained at the outset.

The student draws on the relevant statistic.

Good points

- The student puts forward and discusses several different views.
- The answer reaches a clear conclusion on the 'how far' aspect of the question.

Good use of key sociological concepts.

The conclusion directly addresses the question.

A brief reference to feminist approaches in sociology would add a more theoretical slant to this answer.

Task

Explain what sociologists mean by the chivalry effect.   (4 marks)

The impact of crime and deviance

Key points

- In Section A of Paper 2, you may be asked to **describe the significance of criminal and deviant behaviour for victims, communities and society in general**. You may also be asked about **the ways in which crime and deviance have generated public debates in recent years** and about **the nature and significance of social problems such as racism and teenage crime**.

- In practice, this is likely to mean that you should be able to:
  - explain how crime and deviance affect victims, communities and society
  - discuss public debates on issues such as teenage crime and knife crime
  - explain why racism and teenage crime are seen as social problems.

Key concepts

antisocial behaviour
corporate crime
folk devil
moral panic
scapegoat

The impact of crime on victims

When you are revising the impact of crime on victims, you should distinguish between three different types of research.

- **Measurement research** examines the type and number of people who are victims of crime. For example, **victim surveys** such as the *British Crime Survey* provide statistical information on the victims of crime, such as their age, gender and ethnicity. Measurement research indicates, for instance, that males are more likely to be victims of crime than females and younger people are more likely to be victims than older people.

You can link this to material about victim surveys on pages 52–3.

- **Studies of the impact of crime** show that crime can impact on victims **physically** (e.g. being injured during an assault), **financially** (e.g. having to replace stolen items that were not insured), **socially** (e.g. affecting victims' relationships with family members and friends) or **psychologically** (e.g. feeling stressed after a burglary).

- **Studies of the role of victims in the criminal justice process** look at victims' role in reporting crime, providing evidence and acting as witnesses in court.

The impact of crime and deviance on society

When writing about the impact of crime and deviance, you should be aware that they also impact on **society** as a whole. **Fear** or **worry about crime** is one way that crime affects everyone to some degree, regardless of whether they have been victims of crime. Sometimes, the level of anxiety about crime (such as credit card fraud) is not in proportion to the actual risk of becoming a victim.

Crime can impact on **local communities** by generating fear of violence, burglary and car crime. It can lead people to worry about antisocial behaviour in their own community and to feel unsafe walking alone after dark. Crime is seen as causing damaging tensions within communities. For example, it can lead people to believe that community ties are breaking down or that community life is being destroyed.

White-collar and corporate crime

White-collar and corporate crime can have **financial**, **physical** and **social costs**. Tax evasion has a financial cost, for example, because it results in loss of government revenue. Physical harm and sickness can result from environmental pollution, the sale of unfit foods or exposure to substances such as asbestos at work. The social costs of corporate crime include mistrust between employers and employees.

Youth crime as a social problem

Crime and deviance generate **media coverage** and **public debate**. These debates focus on wide-ranging issues such as antisocial behaviour, identity theft and knife crime. One view is that media reporting increases public anxieties about law and order.

Drug-taking, binge-drinking, knife crime, involvement in gangs and antisocial behaviour are often front page news in the UK. Such behaviour, when associated with teenagers, can create anxiety and fear of young people among members of the public.

Youth crime generates public debate and is seen as a serious **social problem** because of its negative or harmful consequences. For example, fear of teenage crime is seen as damaging to community life and to community ties. Vandalism and graffiti have financial costs. Teenage knife crime is costly in terms of the loss of young lives and the devastating impact of this on the families of victims.

Some researchers argue that young offenders are cast as society's number one '**folk devil**'. The media's portrayal of young people as folk devils can lead to a **moral panic** or a public outcry about their behaviour. Trivial acts of vandalism are seen as typical of all young people and as a threat to law and order. Young people become **scapegoats** who are blamed for society's problems.

> You can link this to the process of deviancy amplification (see the next chapter on Mass Media).

Governments have designed various **policies** to control youth crime and antisocial behaviour. These include fining parents for their children's misbehaviour, curfews and Antisocial Behaviour Orders (although ASBOs are also issued to adults). However, critics argue that ASBOs have not been entirely successful as a policy to reduce antisocial behaviour because they can be a status symbol or badge of honour among the young.

> Government policies are also relevant to topics such as Education and Families.

Study question (e) on page 47, which focuses on the impact of crime and deviance on communities. Here is how one student answered this question.

> Antisocial behaviour such as vandalizing bus shelters can have a negative impact on a community because it may lead some adults to label all local teenagers as a source of trouble. So crime and deviance could affect communities by causing tension between some adults and some teenagers (for instance those who wear hoodies) and also by generating fear of young people among some adults.
>
> If some people feel that there is tension and conflict in the local community, they may think that community ties are breaking down because of antisocial behaviour. This impact could be seen as a problem because it is divisive and it damages social cohesion.

5/5

Good points

- The student gives an appropriate description and earns the maximum two marks for this description.

- The answer explains why the impact is seen as a problem by some members of the public. It earns the maximum three marks for this explanation.

> Hoodies are a good up-to-date example to use.

Examiner's tip

It is a good idea to keep up to date with current social problems and social policies by reading a quality newspaper or watching the television news.

Task

Match the term in the first column with the correct meaning in the second column.

Term	Meaning
1 Folk devil 2 Moral panic	a) The process of blaming an individual or a group (such as asylum-seekers) for something that is not their fault.
3 Scapegoating	b) A group (such as mods and rockers) that is seen as a threat to society's values.
	c) A media-fuelled over-reaction to a social group (such as 'hoodies'). This process involves the media exaggerating the significance of a social problem. A particular social group is cast as a folk devil.

Paper 2 Section B: Mass Media

Key points

- Paper 2 contains **four** sections (one of which is Mass Media). In the exam, you will choose **three** sections and you must answer all of the questions in each of these three sections.

- Section B of Paper 2 will focus on **Unit 2, Mass Media**.

- It is marked out of 30.

- If you choose to answer the question on Mass Media, it will account for 33 per cent (one third) of your total mark for Paper 2.

- You should spend no more than 30 minutes on each of your three chosen sections. Bear in mind that you may use up time deciding which three questions to answer.

About the Mass Media exam question

Here is an example of the sort of exam question that could be set on the Mass Media option. The question is divided into parts (a) to (g). For each part, the assessment objectives (AOs) have been identified for you. This will help you to recognize which skills each part is testing. The comments are there to give you some guidance on how to go about answering exam questions on Mass Media.

In the exam, the 'Items' could contain material such as written extracts from newspapers or textbooks, charts, bar graphs, tables of statistics or photographs. In the question below, Item C provides information on television viewing and household access to the internet. Item D describes some of the main findings from a research study into men's magazines.

> Paper 2 consists of four sections. Only Section B (Mass Media) is given here.

SECTION B: MASS MEDIA

Answer **all** questions from this section.

Total for this question: 30 marks

2 Study **Items C and D** and then answer parts (a) to (g).

ITEM C

In 2008, almost one quarter of adults in England said that they watched TV for an average of three hours per day. Ownership of a digital television service has grown steadily since the 1990s and in 2007 almost four-fifths of UK homes had a digital television service. Household internet access has increased rapidly and in 2007, 61 per cent of UK households had internet access.

ITEM D

Gauntlett (2008) has carried out research into men's magazines such as *Zoo*, *Nuts* and *Loaded*. He found that these magazines present several key themes of masculinity. One theme was that men like to look at women and another was that men like cars, gadgets and sport. Critics argue that these 'lads' mags' present stereotypical images of gender.

Questions (a) and (b) are asking you to interpret what the Items are saying so you need to make sure that you read the Items carefully. You will get marks for picking out the relevant information from the Items.

(a) From **Item C**, what percentage of households in the UK had internet access in 2007? AO3 *(1 mark)*

(b) From **Item D**, identify one theme of masculinity found in men's magazines. AO3 *(1 mark)*

For questions (c) and (d), you will get marks for your knowledge and understanding.

(c) Identify **two** reasons why people might watch television. AO1 *(2 marks)*

(d) Explain what sociologists mean by the term 'new media'. AO1 *(4 marks)*

Aim to spend around three minutes writing your answers to 4-mark questions, four minutes writing your answers to 5-mark questions and around 10 minutes writing your answers to 12-mark questions.

(e) Describe **one** way in which individuals or groups could use the internet in order to participate in the political process **and** explain how this might give them power. AO1 AO2 *(5 marks)*

(f) Describe **one** way in which the mass media could have a negative effect on turnout in a general election **and** explain why this could be a problem in a democratic society. AO1 AO2 *(5 marks)*

For questions (e) and (f), you will get marks for your knowledge and understanding as well as for your application skills.

(g) **EITHER**

(i) Discuss how far sociologists would agree that the mass media can have a direct and immediate effect on their audiences. AO1 AO2 AO3 *(12 marks)*

OR

(ii) Discuss how far sociologists would agree that the mass media represent gender roles in ways that reflect the reality in modern Britain. AO1 AO2 AO3 *(12 marks)*

Make sure that you understand what the different command words (such as 'describe' and 'explain') are asking you to do.

You should spend a couple of minutes planning your mini-essay. This will help you to put together a well-structured answer with an introduction, a main body and a conclusion. As you write your answer, remember to keep referring back to your plan.

Remember to answer just one of these options. You would not gain any extra marks by answering both – you would just waste valuable time.

As you work through this revision chapter on the Mass Media, you will have the opportunity to read examples of how students have answered questions (c) to (f) and (g)(ii).

You could use relevant information from Item D when answering (g)(ii). However, you should avoid copying from the Items.

These sample student answers have all been given a mark and there is also a written comment about each one. It is important to study all of this information carefully because it will give you further guidance on how to tackle exam questions on the Mass Media and also on what the examiners are looking for in answers.

For question (g), you will earn marks for demonstrating a range of skills including your knowledge and understanding, application, interpretation and evaluation.

Task 1

Answer questions (a) and (b).

Task 2

Once you have worked through this chapter on the Mass Media, you should answer questions (c) to (f) and (g)(ii) and then compare your own responses to the sample student answers provided.

An overview of the mass media

Key points

- In Section B of Paper 2, you may be asked to **identify the mass media and outline the main features of this means of communication**. You may also be asked to **describe technological developments such as the internet**.

- In practice, this is likely to mean that you should be able to:
  - define the term 'mass media'
  - describe the key technological changes (such as digital broadcasting and the internet) that have transformed the mass media.

Key concepts

mass media
new media
traditional media

Good points

- The student gives a clear definition of what the term means and addresses both the 'new' and the 'media' aspects.

- The answer provides good examples of new media.

Defining the mass media

The term **mass media** refers to all forms of communication (media) that reach large (mass) audiences. When revising the mass media, you should distinguish between:

- **traditional media** such as newspapers, books, television and radio
- **new media** such as the internet, cable and satellite TV and digital radio.

One way of making sense of the wide range of media that are available today is to divide them into the press, broadcasting and electronic media.

The press

This includes **newspapers and magazines** that are privately owned and run as profit-making businesses. The press is financed through income from sales and advertising.

Broadcasting

This refers to **television and radio**. Public service broadcasting operates through the British Broadcasting Corporation (the BBC) and is funded by income from the television licence fee. Commercial broadcasting is funded mainly by revenue from advertising. Cable and satellite TV are funded mainly by income from advertising and subscribers.

Electronic media

This refers to the **internet**, which provides the World Wide Web and services such as email.

Study question (d) on page 59. This question tests AO1 and it is marked out of four. It is asking you to define the term 'new media'. To earn full marks, you must ensure that your explanation covers the 'new' aspect as well as the 'media' aspect. When answering questions such as this, it is a good idea to provide examples to support your definitions. Here is how one student answered this question.

> The term mass media refers to the different means of mass communication that reach big audiences. The media can be divided into new and old media. New media include the internet which is an electronic medium and digital television which is interactive. Old media include newspapers and terrestrial television based on old technology. So the term new media refers to the various media that are based on new technology such as digitalization rather than on older technology.

4/4

This effectively addresses the 'media' aspect of the question.

This effectively addresses the 'new' aspect.

Examples of both old and new media are given. However, the question doesn't ask about old media so, strictly speaking, the material on old media is not necessary.

Developments in the technology of the mass media

Over the last 30 years, important changes in **communications technology** have transformed the mass media. As part of your revision, it is a good idea to summarize your notes into key points to make them more manageable. You could summarize your notes on developments in media technology into the following points:

- In 1980, there were just three terrestrial TV channels in Britain (which delivered broadcasts by ground transmitters rather than by satellite). Today, by comparison, viewers can subscribe to numerous **satellite and cable TV** channels.

- **Digital broadcasting** provides multi-channel TV with high quality pictures and sound.

- Digital TV services offer **interactivity**. Viewers can now use their handsets to interact with the TV in order to enter competitions, for example, or to vote on reality shows.

- The technologies of the media, telecommunications and computing can now come together (or converge) in one product. For example, some digital TV services allow people to access the internet, text, email, shop and bank through their TV sets. This development is referred to as **convergence**.

- The **internet** allows people to access electronic versions of newspapers and 24-hour rolling news. It also enables people to **produce content** (e.g. via Wikipedia, Facebook, twittering, websites and blogs) rather than just consume it.

Examiner's tip

The sample student answer shown on page 60 earns full marks. However, there are other ways of writing your answer to this question that would also earn full marks. For instance, you could give different examples of new media from the ones provided here. Your own definition, as long as it is appropriate, will be credited.

Changing patterns of consumption

Sociologists study how much media people consume (i.e. use), and changes in their consumption patterns over time. When writing about changing patterns of consumption, you should be aware of the following points:

- Over the last 25 years in Britain, there has been a **decline in the readership of popular newspapers** such as the *Daily Mail* and *Daily Mirror*.

- **Household ownership of a digital TV service** (including digital, satellite and cable receivers) has grown steadily since the 1990s. In March 2007, over 80 per cent of homes in the UK had a digital TV service. People subscribe in order to get more channels, to get particular channels (e.g. dedicated to music, sport or films) and to get high quality pictures and sound.

- Since the late 1990s, **household internet access** has also grown rapidly in the UK. In 2007, over 60 per cent of UK households had internet access. However, high-income households are much more likely than low-income households to have internet access. People access the internet for many reasons, such as to find information about goods and services, to send and receive email and to shop online.

You don't need to memorize these figures in any detail. However, it is important to be aware, in general terms, of the changes in consumption patterns.

Critics argue that multi-channel TV does not provide viewers with more choice. It just gives them more of the same.

People's use of the internet varies by age. For instance, young people aged 16–24 are more likely than people in other age groups to download games, films or music.

Task

Each of the following definitions contains a highlighted word and you have to decide whether the highlighted text is correct. If it is incorrect, you should replace it with a correct word.

1 Traditional media – older media such as newspapers, radio and digital television.

2 New media – media such as digital television, based on the latest communications technology.

The impact of the mass media

Key points

- In Section B of Paper 2, you may be asked about the **different views of the relationship between the mass media and the audience** or about **contemporary media-related issues**. You may also be asked to **describe the process of deviancy amplification**.

- In practice, this is likely to mean that you should be able to:

  - explain the hypodermic syringe, uses and gratifications and decoding approaches

  - discuss issues such as whether media exposure encourages copycat violence and the possible ill-effects of the internet

  - describe how the media can amplify deviance.

Good points

- The student gets full marks for identifying two appropriate and different reasons why people might watch television.

- These examples are useful because they help to clarify what the student means.

The media's impact on audiences

When you are revising the impact of the mass media on audiences, you should distinguish between three broad approaches. These are the '**hypodermic syringe**' approach, the **uses and gratifications** approach and the **decoding** approach.

The 'hypodermic syringe' approach

This is one of the earliest approaches to studying the impact of the media on the audience. According to this approach, which was popular in the 1930s and 1940s, the audience receives daily injections of messages from television and newspapers. These messages work like a drug and are seen by some commentators as having a **direct** and **powerful effect** on people's behaviour or beliefs.

The uses and gratifications approach

This approach focuses on how members of the audience **use** the media. It examines the individual needs that are **gratified** (met or satisfied) by the media. For example, watching television might meet people's need for information and entertainment or it might provide them with a source of conversation at work.

The decoding approach

This approach sees television viewers as **active decoders** of the contents of TV programmes. In other words, audience members actively interpret or make sense of messages from TV programmes. The content of any particular programme has several different meanings and one section of the audience may interpret it very differently from another. The way in which a particular viewer decodes a programme will depend on factors such as their social and cultural background as well as their age and gender.

Question (c) on page 59 tests AO1 and is marked out of two. Study this question carefully. To earn full marks, you must briefly state two different reasons. Here is how one student answered this question.

> Firstly, as a source of information about current affairs (e.g. TV news broadcasts). Secondly, for entertainment purposes (e.g. reality TV shows). **2/2**

> As you revise these three approaches, it can be helpful to pick out some of the differences between them. For example, while the hypodermic approach views the audience as passively receiving media messages, the decoding approach sees the audience as actively making sense of the messages.

> The answer is well-balanced in that the student has written more or less the same amount about each of the two reasons.

Contemporary media-related issues

The mass media are often seen as having potentially harmful effects on their audiences and this issue has generated **public debates** in recent years. One area of concern is whether media exposure encourages **real-life** or **copycat violence**, particularly among children. The hypodermic syringe approach, for example, sees the media as having the power to influence audiences to commit copycat crimes.

> You can link this material to the public debates that crime and deviance have generated.

Sociologists have informed the debates on the media and violence. Sociological research, for instance, has shown that children can tell the difference between fictional and factual material on television. It has also shown that children actively interpret or make sense of television messages rather than passively accepting them. Researchers such as Gauntlett argue that studies which interview young people who have been involved in violence, fail to show a strong connection between screen violence and real-life violence.

The possible **ill-effects of the internet** are another issue of public concern. For example, people worry about invasion of privacy, fraud and the ease with which undesirable content can be accessed by children. Some sociologists, however, see the anxieties over the internet as an example of a **moral panic**.

The media, moral panics and deviancy amplification

A moral panic refers to a **media-fuelled public outcry** about particular social groups or issues. During a moral panic, the media exaggerate the extent and significance of a social problem. A particular group is cast as a **folk devil** and becomes defined as a threat to society's values. This group is portrayed in **stereotypical** terms by the media.

Using concepts developed by Stan Cohen when he wrote about mods and rockers in the 1960s, sociologists have explored the role of the media in creating moral panics and **amplifying deviance** (that is, creating more of it). For example, there have been moral panics surrounding mugging, youth crime, gun crime, knife crime and hoodies.

Here is how one student answered the question: '**Explain what sociologists mean by a moral panic**'. *(4 marks) AO1*

A moral panic is a public outcry that results from the media's exaggerated reporting of a social problem or a social issue. Stan Cohen argued that the media coverage of clashes between mods and rockers in English seaside resorts in the 1960s led to a moral panic or a public outcry. The media's distortion of events or incidents fuels a moral panic and sets particular groups (e.g. mods and rockers) up as folk devils or threats to society's values. More recently, moral panics have surrounded the internet, hoodies and asylum seekers.

4/4

This answer shows a detailed knowledge of Cohen's work. However, you can earn full marks without referring to the work of particular sociologists.

Sociological concepts (such as folk devils and values) are drawn on to answer the question.

It's good to refer to up-to-date examples.

Examiner's tip

It's a good idea to look out for links between the different topics and units that you have studied. For example, the concept of deviancy amplification links up Crime and Deviance with Mass Media. You could use your knowledge of deviancy amplification, folk devils and moral panics to answer questions on both Crime and Deviance and Mass Media – but only if these concepts are relevant to the question!

Good points

- The student defines a moral panic in clear terms and refers to a key sociological study of a moral panic.

- The answer includes several more recent examples.

- It also draws on relevant sociological concepts.

Key concept

deviancy amplification

Task

Drawing on information in your textbook, your class notes and the material here, answer the following questions.

1 Identify one criticism of the hypodermic syringe approach.

2 Identify one difference between the hypodermic syringe approach and the decoding approach.

3 Describe one media-related issue that has caused public concern and explain why it has caused concern.

The mass media and power

- In Section B of Paper 2, you may be asked about **the media as a source of power for the organizations and individuals that own and/or control them**. You may also be asked about the **possible significance of technological developments such as the internet for the distribution of power**.

- In practice, this is likely to mean that you should be able to:

  - discuss the pluralist and conflict approaches to the issue of how far media owners control content

  - identify other possible influences on content such as consumer demand, news values, the profit motive, advertisers, the state and laws

  - explain the processes of agenda setting and norm referencing

  - discuss how far the internet empowers people by providing opportunities to participate in politics.

Power is a key concept in sociology. You can link the issue of the exercise of power within the media to material in the following chapter on Power.

The mass media can be a source of **power** or influence for particular individuals, such as the owners or the people who hold senior positions within media organizations. For example, it is argued that these individuals have the power to shape public opinion on current affairs and to influence people's voting behaviour. One debate that you must be familiar with focuses on the **ownership** of the media and the potential power of owners to **control content**.

Press ownership

In Britain, press ownership is **concentrated** in a few hands. Potentially, this could give some individuals in a media corporation a lot of **power** to influence public opinion because their family owns the company or because they have controlling shareholdings. For example, particular individuals may have the power to impose their views about politics and the economy on readers. Critics of this concentration of ownership argue that, in order to safeguard **democracy**, the power to communicate should be spread out much more widely. When you are revising the issue of how much power and control the press owners have over content, you should distinguish between the **pluralist** and **conflict approaches**.

The pluralist approach to press ownership

According to the pluralist approach, a **range** of views and interests exists in society and no single group dominates. This range of views is reflected in the wide variety of newspapers and magazines that is available on the market. So all political viewpoints are represented within the varied publications that consumers can choose to buy.

The pluralist approach rejects the idea that press owners control content. Instead, it suggests that newspapers simply give people what they want to read. Companies that fail to do this are unlikely to succeed in a competitive market and may go bankrupt. So in this view it is the **consumers** who influence content through their **market power**.

The conflict approach to press ownership

According to the conflict approach, press owners are in a strong position to put their own political views across. This is because, as **owners**, they are able to **control content** and they do so in their own political and economic interests. Supporters of this approach point to several developments within the media to support their position. These include the **increasing concentration** of press ownership in the hands of a few companies and individuals and the emergence of **multimedia (or cross-media) conglomerates** (such as News Corporation) that operate on a global rather than a national scale. As a result of such developments, much of what people read comes from a few multinational media empires.

The exercise of power within the media

Power may be exercised in selecting and presenting news content on TV and in newspapers. When you are writing about this issue, you should discuss the processes of **agenda setting** and **norm referencing**.

- When writing about this debate, you should bear in mind that the BBC does not have private owners.

- As you revise these approaches, it can be helpful to pick out some of the differences between them.

The news media have the power to 'set the agenda'. In other words, the media focus on some issues and topics and ignore others. In doing so, they direct public discussion and debate onto these issues and affect what people think about. Potentially, this could give the media a lot of influence over people's political views and their voting behaviour.

The news media also have power in relation to norm referencing. In other words, they are able to outline the acceptable boundaries of behaviour. The views and behaviour of some groups or organizations are presented positively while those of others are presented negatively. Through norm referencing, **positive images** of some groups (e.g. nurses) and **negative images** of others (e.g. teenage mothers) are created. In this way, the media have the power to **shape public opinion**.

The internet and the distribution of power

Some sociologists argue that developments in **digital technology** will result in a reduction in the power and influence of media owners. This is because digital technology allows everyone (not just media owners or journalists) to **produce media content** rather than just consume or use it. For example, internet blogs and websites enable individuals and groups to publish their views and join in public debates.

A related view is that the internet could help to **safeguard democracy** by spreading the power to communicate and to exert influence more widely among different individuals and groups. Via the internet, people can access political information, express opinions, communicate with politicians and thereby exert influence. They can also go online to find out about **pressure groups** such as Greenpeace or about issues such as global warming. In this way, the internet could **empower people** and provide them with more opportunities to participate in politics.

Other approaches, however, question how far the internet has increased political participation and empowered people. For example, critics argue that most internet users go online to shop or for entertainment purposes rather than for political purposes. Critics also argue that 'e-democracy' requires expensive technology and funding to start up and maintain so not everyone can participate in it.

Question (e) on page 59 is an example of the sort of question that you could be asked about the internet and power. Read this question carefully. It is marked out of five and tests AO1 and AO2. You will get two marks for a relevant description and an additional three marks for a clear explanation. Here is how one student answered this question.

Pressure groups such as Amnesty International could use the internet by publicising their aims or their cause (e.g. human rights) on their website and organizing protest activities via the internet. The internet could give pressure groups more power to communicate their ideas on a global scale. This could help them to recruit new members, exert influence on politicians and inform public opinion. So pressure groups could use the internet to help bring about social or political change. 5/5

Key concepts

agenda setting
citizens
conflict approach
conglomerate
democracy
digital divide
multimedia (or cross-media) conglomerate
news values
norm referencing
pluralist approach
pressure (or interest) group

Topics such as voting behaviour, democracy, participation and pressure groups are also examined in the next chapter.

Good points

- The student describes one appropriate way in which groups could use the internet to participate in the political process.

- The answer clearly explains how the internet might give power to some groups.

Task

Drawing on relevant information from your class notes or your textbook, make brief notes to explain how each of the following factors can influence the content of newspapers: news values, the profit motive, advertisers, the state and the law.

The mass media and socialization

In previous chapters, you will have come across the concept of **socialization**. This term refers to the process through which people learn the culture of the society that they are born into. The **agencies of socialization** are the social groups and institutions that contribute to the socialization process.

The media as an agency of secondary socialization

The mass media, along with schools, peer groups, workplaces and religions, are an important agency of **secondary socialization**. Feminist sociologists, for example, link the media to the process of **gender socialization**.

The mass media and other agencies of socialization play an important part in the development of people's **identity**. The concept of identity refers to how people see themselves (their self-identity) and how others see them. Sources of identity include gender, age, ethnicity, social class, religion and sexuality. Traditionally, sociologists saw people's social class and gender as key parts of their identity. More recently, however, sociologists have found that music, fashion, leisure and social life are more important to young people's identities than class or gender.

The mass media and identity

In developing their identities, people make choices about their **lifestyles** or their ways of living. They could choose a lifestyle focused on dance-music and clubbing or on success at work. Sociologists argue that the mass media are important in spreading ideas about many modern lifestyles. For example, young people might first learn about dance-music and clubbing via dance-music magazines. In this way, the media play a key role in the development of people's identities.

The mass media and political socialization

During the process of **political socialization**, people acquire their political values and beliefs. These, in turn, affect whether they participate in the political process and how they vote in elections. The mass media are very important in the political socialization process because, for many people, they are the main source of information about current affairs, political parties and politicians.

> You can link this to the discussions about political participation and voting behaviour in the following chapter on Power.

The press and voting behaviour

In a democracy, the media are seen as having a key role during **election campaigns**. In Britain, most newspapers tend to side with one political party over another. Some sociologists argue that a person who regularly reads one particular newspaper is likely to be exposed to a slant on current affairs that could encourage them to vote for one political party rather than another.

> The concept of democracy is also discussed in the chapter on Power.

One view is that the press have **too much influence** over how people vote. Another view is that the negative coverage of politics and criticism of politicians in the press influence **election turnout** by discouraging voters from voting at all.

If the press have the power to influence the outcome of general elections, and are slanted towards one political party, then this could be seen as a major problem in a democracy. This is because elections are supposed to be fair and to give citizens the opportunity to express their preferences. If the press are setting the agenda, or influencing turnout, then this bias may work against some political parties.

Key points

- In Section B of Paper 2, you may be asked about the **mass media and socialization**. You may also be asked about the **part played by the media and other agencies of socialization in the development of people's political and social identities and views**.

- In practice, this is likely to mean that you should be able to:
  - discuss the role of the mass media in the socialization process
  - describe the role of the media, families, the education system and other agencies of socialization in the process through which people develop their political and social identities and views.

Examiner's tip

When revising, look out for any links between the different topics that you have studied. The concept of 'agencies of socialization', for example, links up the mass media, families, the education system, peer groups, work places and religions.

Question (f) on page 59 focuses on the way the media might have a negative influence on turnout in a general election. Read this question carefully. It tests AO1 and AO2 and is marked out of five. You will get two marks for an appropriate description and an additional three marks for a clear explanation. Here is how one student answered this question.

The press's negative coverage of politics and their criticism of all politicians (both government and opposition MPs) could <u>discourage some voters from turning out to vote in a general election</u>.

This could be a problem because <u>democracy</u> works best when there is a high turnout in a general election. A high turnout means that most citizens vote and have a say in electing the politicians who will represent them. If there is a low turnout, and this is partly due to the media coverage, then the media have influenced people against exercising their democratic right to vote.

5/5

> This is a good example to use.

> In this answer, it works well to focus on the description in the first paragraph and the explanation in the second paragraph.

Good points

- The student gives a very clear and appropriate description of one way in which the media could have a negative effect on turnout in a general election. They earn the maximum two marks for this description.

- The answer gives a clear and relevant explanation of why this could be a problem in a democracy.

Key concepts

identity
political socialization
secondary socialization
sexuality

Task

The information below discusses the influence of the mass media and other agencies of socialization. Fill in each gap by selecting the correct answer from the following:

a) age
b) of socialization
c) audience
d) decoding
e) hypodermic syringe approach
f) income
g) peer
h) social and
i) education

Although each person is a unique individual, everyone is influenced, to some extent, by the agencies (1) _____ . The mass media, families, the education system, (2) _____ groups and workplaces are all potentially powerful agencies of socialization. Earlier approaches to the study of the mass media, such as the (3) _____ , suggested that the media could have very powerful effects on audiences. According to these earlier approaches, the (4) _____ accepted and acted upon persuasive media messages. More recent approaches, however, argue that the media have only limited effects on people. The (5) _____ approach, for example, argues that different sections of the audience may interpret the contents of the media in very different ways depending on their (6) _____ cultural backgrounds.

The influence of the different agencies of socialization on particular individuals or groups varies according to how much exposure an individual or group has had to each agent. This will depend on factors such as (7) _____ . For most babies and infants, their families will be more powerful agencies of socialization than the mass media or the education system because they are regularly exposed to this agency. Primary school pupils are unlikely to have much direct experience of workplaces and paid employment but they are likely to have had first-hand experience of families, the mass media and the (8) _____ system.

The influences of factors such as age, gender and social class mean that some individuals will have more access to new media than others. People aged 16–24, for example, are more likely than other age groups to use the internet to play and download games or music. Furthermore, household access to the internet is linked to household (9) _____ .

Media representations

Sociologists study the media **representations** or portrayals of different social groups such as women or black people. When you are revising this topic, you should consider whether the media present **stereotypical** or **realistic images** of such groups.

Key points

- In Section B of Paper 2, you may be asked about **the ways in which the media encourage stereotyping**.

- In practice, this is likely to mean that you should be able to:
  - discuss media representations of different social groups such as women and some minority ethnic groups
  - discuss how far the media present stereotypical images of particular social groups.

Media representations of gender

Research indicates that, in the 1950s, 60s and 70s, media representations of women were stereotypical rather than realistic. The media images of women did not reflect the range of **roles** that they actually played in society.

Since the 1970s, there have been some **changes** in the media's representations of gender. For example, children's books that present women and men in non-stereotyped roles are becoming more widely available and there are now more strong female characters in television dramas.

Research by Cumberbatch, published in 1990, focused on gender stereotyping in TV advertisements. It found, for example, that the majority of voiceovers were male and that women were more likely than men to be young and blond. More recently, researchers point out that some TV advertisements still present stereotyped messages about the role of women. In 2009, for example, TV advertisements for Iceland (the supermarket chain) used the slogan '... so that's why mums go to Iceland!'.

In the 2000s, some women's and men's magazines presented unrealistic images of gender. Today, men's magazines in particular often project stereotypical images of men and men's interests (including cars, drinking and sport). They also tend to present stereotypical images of women (for example, as sex objects). Critics argue that men's magazines present narrow and stereotyped images of both masculinity and femininity.

Some **feminist approaches** argue that men and women are portrayed in very different ways in magazines, films and television shows. Although the media's influences may be subtle, they build up over time and contribute to the process of **gender socialization** (see page 66).

Examiner's tips

- When writing about this topic, bear in mind that it may not be possible to generalize about the mass media as a whole. For example, the images of women presented in the tabloid press or in lads' mags may be very different from the images presented in women's magazines or soap operas.

- It can be useful to refer to relevant research studies in your answers. However, the examiners will not expect you to have a detailed knowledge of particular studies.

Media representations of minority ethnic groups

Research shows that in TV drama productions during the 1950s, 60s and 70s, black people were either absent or under-represented. When they were represented, the media often used negative stereotypes of black people or presented them in a narrow range of roles such as singers, dancers or sportspeople.

Other research suggests that during the 1960s and 70s, news reporting tended to **simplify race issues** and to report on them negatively. The problems facing countries in parts of Africa and Asia (such as war and famine) were over-reported. In Britain, news reporting often linked black people with mugging, conflict and inner-city riots while under-reporting the racism experienced by black people.

Research suggests that, during the 1990s, there were **changes** in the representation of race and ethnicity on television. For example, there were now more black actors playing ordinary characters rather than unrealistic stereotypes.

More recently, some researchers have found evidence that the media still portray people from minority ethnic backgrounds in distorted ways. For example, many stories about British Asians tend to focus narrowly on forced marriage, runaway girls, terrorism and refusal to fit into society.

Question (g)(ii) on page 59 focuses on media representations of gender roles. Read this question carefully. Like the other extended-answer questions that you have considered so far, it is marked out of 12 and tests AO1, AO2 and AO3. Here is how one student answered this question.

'Gender' refers to masculinity and femininity and 'roles' refer to who does what e.g. in families or in workplaces. Some sociologists argue that the mass media (the means of mass communication such as TV) now represent gender roles in realistic ways that reflect the reality.

However, sociologists from the feminist approach argue that the media often present stereotypical images of women's roles. A 'stereotype' is a fixed and distorted view of a social group. It is usually based on prejudice or sexism (e.g. the bimbo stereotype).

Some TV adverts today (for instance, the Iceland ad) give the impression that it is a mother's role to make decisions about grocery shopping. Also, research shows that men's magazines present stereotypical images of women and men.

To sum up, the feminist approach argues that the media often present stereotypical images of women's roles. So the media do not represent gender roles realistically. Other sociologists, however, argue that the media now present many images that reflect the reality of gender in modern Britain.

10/12

It's a good idea to refer to a relevant sociological approach (such as the feminist approach) in your extended answers.

The student has drawn on relevant information from Item D but has avoided the trap of copying directly from the Item.

This is a good point. The question asks about representations of gender (women and men) so it's important to recognize that the media may present stereotyped images of men as well as women.

The conclusion refers back to the set question. However, the first line in this paragraph tends to repeat an earlier point.

Task

Match the term in the first column with the correct meaning in the second column.

Term	Meaning
1 Gender	a) A fixed and distorted view of the characteristics of a particular group – such as women, black people or Muslims – that is usually based on prejudice.
2 Sexism	
3 Stereotype	b) A sociological approach that examines how gender operates in society against the interests of women.
4 Ethnic group	
5 Gender socialization	c) Prejudice (prejudgements) or discrimination (less favourable treatment) based on a person's gender.
6 Feminist approach	d) The cultural differences (rather than biological differences) between men and women that are associated with masculinity and femininity.
	e) A social group whose members share an identity based on their culture, religion or language.
	f) The learning process during which individuals acquire their gender identity and pick up messages about social roles related to gender.

Good points

- The student shows a good understanding of relevant concepts such as the mass media and stereotypes. They also show knowledge of the feminist approach.

- To achieve higher marks, the student could discuss in detail the idea that some media (e.g. lads' mags) represent gender roles in unrealistic and stereotypical ways while others (e.g. some TV advertisements) present realistic or more varied images of gender roles.

Key concepts   ethnic group   prejudice   sexism

Paper 2 Section C: Power

Key points

- Paper 2 contains **four** sections (one of which is Power). In the exam, you will choose **three** sections and you must answer all of the questions in each of these three sections.

- Section C of Paper 2 will focus on **Unit 2, Power**.

- It is marked out of 30.

- If you choose to answer the question on Power, it will account for 33 per cent (one third) of your total mark for Paper 2.

- You should spend no more than 30 minutes on each of your three chosen sections.

Try to get as much practice as you can at writing answers under timed conditions.

Remember that during the exam, you will have to divide your time between studying the Items, reading the questions, thinking about your answers, planning your mini-essays, writing your answers and reading them through.

About the Power exam question

Here is an example of the sort of exam question that could be set on Power. The question is divided into parts (a) to (g). For each part, the assessment objectives (AOs) have been identified for you. This will help you to recognize which skills each part is testing. The comments are there to give you some guidance on how to go about answering exam questions on Power.

In the exam, the 'Items' could contain material such as written extracts from newspapers or textbooks, charts, bar graphs, tables of statistics or photographs. In the question below, Item E provides information on the links between voting behaviour and social factors such as class and gender. Item F contains a photograph showing one form of political participation.

Paper 2 consists of four sections. Only Section C (Power) is given here.

SECTION C: POWER

Answer **all** questions from this section.

Total for this question: 30 marks

3 Study **Items E and F** and then answer parts (a) to (g).

ITEM E	ITEM F

ITEM E

Sociologists are interested in the links between voting behaviour and social factors such as class and gender. In the 2005 general election:

- 37 per cent of professional middle-class voters voted Conservative, while 28 per cent voted Labour

- 25 per cent of manual workers voted Conservative, while 48 per cent voted Labour.

In the same election:

- 34 per cent of men voted Conservative and the same percentage voted Labour

- 32 per cent of women voted Conservative, while 38 per cent voted Labour.

ITEM F

Remember to identify **two** different services.

This question gives you a time frame. It's important to describe changes that have occurred within this time frame rather than describing changes, for example, since the early 20th century.

For questions like this, you will get a maximum of two marks for your description and a maximum of three marks for your explanation.

Remember to answer just **one** of these options.

You can draw on relevant information from the Items when answering extended-answer questions. For example, you could use relevant information from Item E when answering (g)(i). However, don't fall into the trap of copying out chunks from the Items. This won't earn you any extra marks and will waste your time.

Make sure that you understand exactly what the different command words (such as 'identify' and 'discuss how far...') are asking you to do.

(a) From **Item E**, what percentage of manual workers voted Labour in the 2005 general election? AO3   *(1 mark)*

(b) From **Item F**, identify **one** type of participation in the political process. AO3   *(1 mark)*

(c) Identify **two** services that are provided by the welfare state today. AO1   *(2 marks)*

(d) Explain what sociologists mean by power relationships. AO1   *(4 marks)*

(e) Describe **one** way in which governments have tried to tackle discrimination in recent years **and** explain how successful this policy has been. AO1 AO2   *(5 marks)*

(f) Describe **one** way in which school teachers may have authority over their pupils **and** explain the source of this authority. AO1 AO2   *(5 marks)*

(g) **EITHER**

(i) Discuss how far sociologists would agree that age and ethnicity are now more important influences than social class on British people's political attitudes and the way they vote. AO1 AO2 AO3   *(12 marks)*

OR

(ii) Discuss how far sociologists would agree that power is distributed evenly between the different groups in British society today. AO1 AO2 AO3   *(12 marks)*

As you work through this revision chapter on Power, you will have the opportunity to read examples of how students have answered questions (c), (d) and (g)(i) and some other questions. These sample student answers have all been given a mark and there is also a written comment about each one. It is important to study all of this information carefully because it will give you further guidance on how to answer exam questions on Power.

Task 1

Answer questions (a) and (b).

Task 2

Once you have worked through the entire chapter on Power, you should answer questions (c), (d) and (g)(i) and then compare your own responses to the sample student answers provided.

Defining power

Key points

- In Section C of Paper 2, you may be asked about the **definition of power**. You may also be asked about **power relationships in everyday situations**.

- In practice, this is likely to mean that you should be able to:
  - define the term 'power' and explain the difference between coercion and authority
  - discuss how power can operate in relationships between: parents and children; children and peers; teachers and pupils; employers and employees; members of the public and the police.

Key concepts

authority
charismatic authority
citizenship
coercion
government
legal rational authority
political party
representative
  democracy
the state
traditional authority

Power is a key concept in sociology and sociologists study **power relationships** in society. Power can be defined as the ability to get what you want, despite any opposition or resistance you may face from other people. An individual or a group exercises power over someone when they influence the person, even against their will.

The sources of power: coercion and authority

Once you have revised the **sources** of power, you should be able to distinguish between **coercion** and **authority**. Coercive power involves the threat or use of **force** including physical violence, torture or blackmail. People who are coerced into obeying an individual or a group do so because they feel they have no choice in the matter.

Authority is exercised over people when they willingly agree to obey an individual or a group because they see this as the right thing to do. Force is not necessary because people give their **consent**. A teacher, for instance, exercises authority over pupils when they willingly hand in their completed homework for marking.

Power in democracies

In some political systems, power is concentrated in a few hands while in others it is distributed more widely. In many states, such as the United Kingdom, the political system is based on democracy. Literally, **democracy** means government by the people. In a democracy, power is distributed widely and the government's power is based on authority.

> Drawing on Weber's ideas, this is an example of legal rational authority.

Citizenship

When you are writing about the concept of **citizenship**, it is important to bear in mind that the term is used in several different ways. It can refer to:

- **a political and legal status** linked to membership of a particular state. All UK citizens have full legal rights (for example, to be treated equally before the law) as well as responsibilities (such as paying taxes and obeying the law).

- **active involvement in public life** and participation in the political process. The term 'active citizenship' is sometimes used to describe activities such as joining a pressure group or a political party, voting in elections or taking an interest in current affairs.

Active citizenship is seen as a key feature of democracies. For instance, if citizens participate actively in the political process then this can help to make governments more responsive to public opinion.

Power relationships in everyday situations

When you are writing about power, it is important to be aware that power may be exercised in relationships between people in **everyday settings** such as homes, workplaces and classrooms. This is because people enter into power relationships when they try to **control or influence** the behaviour and decisions of others. They also enter into power relationships when other people try to influence their behaviour. This means that all relationships involve power when influence, authority, control, constraint or coercion is exercised.

Power relationships operate in everyday situations when there are **inequalities** in power between individuals and groups. They may operate, for instance, between children and their peers and between employers and employees. Power relationships may also operate between:

- **children, parents or guardians**. Parents exercise power over their children when they influence, control or constrain their children's behaviour against their will.

  > You can link this to material on changing relationships between parents and children in the chapter on Families.

- **pupils and their teachers**. Teachers exercise authority over pupils based on their position within the school's authority structure. Some teachers – exceptionally gifted individuals who inspire their pupils – also exercise authority based on their **charisma**.

  > Drawing on Weber's ideas, this is an example of charismatic authority.

- **members of the public and the police**. The police force operates as an agency of social control on behalf of the state and is responsible for enforcing the law. Police officers exercise power over members of the public based on the position they hold within the police force. For example, they have the power to stop and search, arrest and detain people. Their authority is based on written rules that are laid down by the state and their interaction with the public is governed by codes of practice.

  > You can link this to material about social control in the chapter on Crime and Deviance.

  > This is another example of legal rational authority.

Question (d) on page 71 tests your knowledge and understanding (AO1) of the concept of power relationships and is marked out of four. Read this question carefully. Here is how one student answered this question.

People such as politicians and parents are involved in power relationships with other people when they make decisions about other people's lives.

2/4

Task 1

Drawing on information in your textbook or class notes, write a short definition of each of the following terms:

1 Traditional authority
2 Legal rational authority
3 Charismatic authority
4 The state

Task 2

Drawing on relevant information in your textbook or class notes, copy out and complete the following table to summarize the pluralist and Marxist approaches to the study of power and the state.

	The pluralist approach	The Marxist approach
1 Who holds power in society?		
2 Is power concentrated or spread evenly through society?		
3 Whose interests does the state represent?		

Examiner's tip

It is helpful to distinguish between direct and indirect democracy:

- In a direct democracy, the citizens participate directly in the decision making process. For example, they can vote on policy proposals and the results of the vote will determine whether the proposals become law.
- In an indirect or representative democracy, citizens elect representatives (such as MPs) who make political decisions on their behalf.

Good points

- The answer recognizes that power can be exercised by politicians and also by people such as parents in everyday relationships.
- However, it gives only a partial explanation of what sociologists mean by power relationships. To get full marks, the student needs to give a more detailed explanation by, for example, referring to the different types of power relationships such as those based on authority and coercion.

Ways of participating in the political process

- In Section C of Paper 2, you may be asked about **opportunities for participation in the political process and limitations on participation**. You may also be asked about **factors that might increase or decrease the chances of participation being successful**.

- In practice, this is likely to mean that you should be able to:
  - distinguish between narrow and broad definitions of participation
  - identify barriers to successful participation
  - discuss some of the factors affecting the success of pressure groups.

Opportunities for participation

When revising the opportunities for participation in the political process, you should be clear about the difference between **narrow** and **broad** definitions of participation:

- the narrow definition focuses on **traditional forms** of participation linked to governmental and electoral aspects of politics. Examples include standing for public office in elections, voting in elections and being actively involved in a political party.

- the broad definition focuses on **all forms of involvement in public life** including participation in community organizations, trade unions and other pressure (or interest) groups. It also includes participation in protest activities such as going on demonstrations or signing petitions.

Examiner's tip

When writing about opportunities for political participation, bear in mind that individuals, groups and communities can participate at local, national and international levels. For example, they can vote in local, general and European Union elections.

Changes in political participation

Participation in the political process has changed significantly in the UK over the last 50 years. In general, **traditional forms** of participation – such as voter turnout in general elections and membership of political parties – are declining. However, this does not necessarily mean that people are politically **apathetic** (not interested in politics). For instance, many people participate in the political process by signing petitions, joining protest marches and supporting consumer boycotts.

You can link this to material in the chapter on Education. Citizenship education was introduced into schools partly to encourage interest and participation in the political process.

Here is how one student answered the question: '**Identify two ways in which people can participate in the political process in Britain**'. *(2 marks)* AO1

Good points

- The student clearly identifies two different ways and provides examples to illustrate these.

- The answer earns the full two marks. However, the first paragraph could be reduced to one sentence and still earn the mark.

One way in which people can participate in the political process in Britain is by voting in elections. For example, as UK citizens they have the right to vote in local, general and EU elections.

The second way is by protesting, e.g. against building a proposed third runway at an airport.

2/2

You don't need to repeat the question. Instead, you could write: 'One way is …'.

On these short-answer questions, one example is sufficient. Additional examples won't earn extra marks.

Barriers to political participation

As part of your revision, make sure you understand why some people do not participate in the political process. For instance, research suggests that people are prevented from participating in traditional politics and in activities such as volunteering or becoming a school governor because they:

- lack the necessary **time** or **money**

- have too many work **commitments** or caring **responsibilities**

- lack access to **transport**
- do not have the relevant **information**
- are **not interested** in participating in politics or community issues.

Factors affecting the success of pressure groups

The chances of pressure group activity being successful depend on several factors, such as whether the group is an **insider** or an **outsider** group. Insider groups such as the Automobile Association, the National Trust and the CBI have close links with government networks and they are consulted by government departments, civil servants and ministers when policy proposals are being prepared. So they are in a strong position to influence government policy. By contrast, outsider groups such as Greenpeace are not consulted automatically. This may be because their aims or their tactics are not recognized by government. Other factors include:

- **resources**, such as the finances and staffing that the group can draw on to help them represent their interests or promote their cause effectively
- the **size** of the group's membership
- **public opinion** and whether the public support the group's aims, cause or tactics.

Task 1

Read through the summary about turnout in elections and the reasons for not voting then fill in the gaps numbered 1 to 7 by selecting the correct answer from the following:

a) two main political parties	c) a representative	e) politics	g) satisfied
b) election result	d) real choice	f) the will of the people	

Some commentators see the fall in turnout in recent UK general elections as a cause for concern in (1) _____ democracy. For example, if a large proportion of the electorate does not vote, then it becomes difficult to claim that the government represents (2) _____ .

Research findings highlight several possible reasons why some people abstain (do not vote) in UK general elections. Firstly, some people see few genuine differences between the policies and the politicians of the (3) _____ (Labour and the Conservatives). Consequently, they see no point in voting because there is no (4) _____ on offer. Secondly, some people think that they already know what the (5) _____ will be before the election actually takes place. In this case, they may see voting as a pointless exercise because the result is a foregone conclusion. Thirdly, some commentators see a low turnout as evidence that voters are (6) _____ with the current government and its policies. Fourthly, other commentators see a low turnout as reflecting voters' disillusionment with the government and its policies or with (7) _____ in general.

Task 2

Drawing on relevant information from your textbook or class notes:

a) Explain, with examples, **one** difference between protective (or sectional) and promotional (or cause) pressure groups.

b) Explain **one** difference between the pluralist and the conflict views on the role and significance of pressure groups in representative democracies.

c) Explain **two** problems with using social surveys to measure the levels of participation in the political process.

Sociologists disagree about the role of pressure groups in society. There are two broad approaches to this: the pluralist and conflict views. You can link this to material on the pluralist and conflict approaches to the mass media in the previous chapter.

Key concepts

insider group
outsider group
promotional pressure group
protective pressure group

Examiner's tip

Research on levels of participation is often based on social surveys. However, the results are not always valid because they do not necessarily give a true picture of what they claim to be measuring. For example, a question about political participation may be interpreted differently by different respondents. Some respondents may think of political participation in narrow terms while others may see it more broadly.

Social factors, participation and power

- In Section C of Paper 2, you may be asked about the **social factors that influence the pattern of political participation and the distribution of power**.

- In practice, this is likely to mean that you should be able to explain how and why:
  - social factors such as age, gender, ethnicity and class, influence political participation
  - social factors influence the distribution of power.

Key concept

class dealignment

Examiner's tip

Remember to reach appropriate conclusions when answering extended-answer questions.

Social factors such as **class**, **age**, **gender** and **ethnicity** influence the patterns of **political participation** in Britain. When you are writing about this, you should be aware of the links between social factors and things like voting behaviour, turnout in general elections, interest in politics and protest activity. Social factors also influence who holds power in society. So it is also important to be aware of the links between social factors and the **distribution of power**.

Social factors influencing voting behaviour

Social class and voting behaviour

Up until the 1970s, **social class** was seen as the most important influence on voting behaviour in Britain. Working-class people tended to vote Labour and middle-class people tended to vote Conservative. In 1997, however, the Labour Party won a landslide election victory and received support from both the working class and the middle class.

One view is that social class is no longer a particularly strong predictor of voting behaviour. The term **class dealignment** refers to the weakening of the traditional links between social class and voting behaviour. Some researchers argue that the social class divide in voting was weaker than ever in the 2005 general election.

Another view is that social class remains an important influence on voting behaviour. For example, the 2005 general election results indicated that professional and lower-middle-class voters were still more likely to vote Conservative and working-class voters were still more likely to vote Labour. In this view, the link between class and party support continued along traditional lines in 2005.

> In Britain, there is a north-south divide in voting. The Conservatives are strong in East Anglia and the south outside London. Labour is strong in Wales, Scotland and the north of England.

Age, gender, ethnicity and voting behaviour

Traditionally, young people were more likely to vote Labour and older people were more likely to vote Conservative. This link between **age and voting** persists and in the 2005 general election, Labour led the Conservatives in all age groups except the over-55s.

Traditionally, women were more likely than men to vote Conservative. However, voting patterns based on **gender** seem to be changing. In 2005, a higher proportion of women than men voted Labour and a higher proportion of men than women voted Conservative.

Traditionally, British Asian and black communities were much more likely to vote Labour than Conservative. In the 1992 general election, for example, 81 per cent of **minority ethnic voters** voted Labour while only 10 per cent voted Conservative. There is evidence of some change here. For example, in 2001, 73 per cent of minority ethnic voters voted Labour and 12 per cent voted Conservative.

> Religion may also affect voting behaviour. For example, one view is that Muslim voters were less likely to vote Labour following the Labour government's decision to join the USA in invading Iraq in 2003.

Question (g)(i) on page 71 focuses on some of the social factors influencing political attitudes and voting behaviour. Study this question carefully and underline the command words. It assesses AO1, AO2 and AO3 and is marked out of 12.

Here is how one student answered this question.

Social class is a powerful influence on the way people vote in general elections but in this answer, I will discuss whether age and ethnicity are now more important influences.

Social class is measured by occupation and in Britain, the two main classes are the working class (e.g. bus drivers and cleaners) and the middle class (e.g. nurses and lawyers).

Traditionally, social class was the most important influence on voting behaviour. Most working-class voters voted Labour and most middle-class voters voted Conservative.

More recently, there has been a class dealignment in voting. Other important factors affecting the way people vote today include age and ethnicity. Younger people are more likely to vote Labour and older people are more likely to vote Conservative. People from minority ethnic groups are more likely to vote Labour than Conservative.

Religion, geography, the media, party leaders and policies are also important influences on voting.

7/12

> The student could draw on relevant information from Item E.

> The student refers to 'class dealignment' but does not explain what this term means.

> It's important to link these factors to the question.

> There is no conclusion on whether age and ethnicity are more important influences than class.

Good points

- The answer shows a good understanding of social class and how it is measured.

- The traditional patterns of voting behaviour are outlined clearly in the third paragraph.

- The question asks about political attitudes (e.g. reflected in political party membership or in protest activity). However, these are not discussed.

Social factors influencing the distribution of power

One view is that all citizens can exercise political power, participate in decision making and influence government policy. They can do this, for example, by getting elected to public office, voting, joining pressure groups or political parties or going on marches.

In practice, however, members of some social groups are **more likely to participate** than others. For example, people with higher level educational qualifications, employed people and people in higher income households are more likely to participate in organizations such as pressure groups or political parties than people without qualifications, unemployed people and people in low income households.

Members of some social groups – such as middle-class, middle-aged, white men – are also more likely to become **MPs**. In contrast, women, black people, young people, working-class people and people with disabilities are under-represented among MPs. Women, for example, make up more than 50 per cent of the UK population but they made up fewer than 20 per cent of MPs after the 2005 election.

This under-representation is seen as a problem in a **representative democracy**. This is because the MPs who hold power and exercise it when making decisions on behalf of UK citizens are not a representative cross-section of the population. One view is that women's interests are not represented adequately in the male-dominated House of Commons. A related view is that half of MPs should be female if the political system is to be seen as fair and just.

Task

Drawing on relevant information from your class notes or textbook, identify two differences between a pressure group and a political party.

The welfare state

Key points

- In Section C of Paper 2, you may be asked about the **different political positions in debates about the welfare state**.

- In practice, this is likely to mean that you should be able to:
  - explain the meaning of the term 'welfare state'
  - describe, in basic terms, the different political views about the welfare state and its future.

Means-tested benefits are also discussed on page 81.

Good points

- The student gets full marks – one mark for identifying each service.

- The student has written about each service in more or less the same amount of detail so this answer is well-balanced.

- The answer is an appropriate length for a two-mark question.

Defining the welfare state

When writing about debates on the **welfare state**, it is important to be clear what this term means. The welfare state refers to a system in which the state takes responsibility for many of its citizens' health, welfare and social needs by providing services and benefits.

The welfare state in Britain today

Today, the welfare state provides services related to health, education, housing and welfare benefits. It also provides social services such as child protection.

Through the **National Health Service** (NHS), services such as GPs, hospitals and dentists are provided. These are funded by central government using income from national taxation.

National Insurance (NI) benefits (such as the state retirement pension) are **contributory benefits**. So, to qualify for them, claimants must have paid sufficient contributions into the NI scheme. Many **non-contributory benefits** (such as Income Support) are designed for people in financial need who do not qualify for NI benefits.

Some benefits are **means-tested**. A means test determines whether a person needs the financial help offered by the benefit in question. To receive means-tested benefits, an individual's or family's income and savings must fall below a certain level. One advantage of means-tested benefits is that resources can be **targeted** at those in most need. However, there are problems with means testing. For example:

- the **claims process** can be complicated and intrusive and this discourages people from claiming benefits to which they are entitled

- means-tested benefits may **label** and stigmatize claimants

- means tests may discourage people from **saving**, because savings might disqualify them from receiving benefits

- **the poverty trap** – means tests may trap people in poverty when an increase in their income from employment reduces the benefits to which they are entitled by more than the increase in their earnings.

Most benefits are **selective** or targeted at people in greatest need on the basis of a means test. However, Child Benefit is a **universal benefit** that is available to anyone with responsibility for a child, regardless of income or savings.

Question (c) on page 71 focuses on the services provided by the welfare state today. Study this question and underline the command word. Here is how one student answered this question.

One service is the National Health Service which provides GPs and hospitals to look after people's health. Another is welfare benefits such as means-tested benefits for people in financial need.

This question tests AO1 and is marked out of two. The command word is **identify**.

2/2

When you are revising welfare provision in Britain today, you should bear in mind that welfare services are also provided:

- **informally** through families, friends and neighbours
- **privately** through profit-making businesses such as private nursing homes
- via **voluntary (non-statutory) sector** organizations such as Barnardo's.

Political positions in debates about the welfare state

Welfare policies and issues are **controversial** because:

- they involve important questions about how society tackles **poverty** and **inequality**
- welfare provision is funded by the state using **income from taxation**.

When writing about this topic, it is important to be aware that one key area of debate concerns the role of the state in providing social welfare and how far the state, families, private companies and voluntary agencies should be responsible for welfare provision.

- One view is that **the state** has a responsibility for the welfare and well-being of its citizens and it should take responsibility for citizens' health, welfare and social needs.
- Another view is that, while there is always the need for a 'safety-net', citizens should take more responsibility for their own well-being and that of their families. For example, they could take out private health insurance and private pensions. In this view, welfare state provision should be slimmed down.
- A related view is that **charitable organizations** (such as Age UK or Barnardo's), profit-making businesses within the **private sector** (such as private nursing homes), **families** and neighbours should be more involved in supplying welfare.

The **political parties** agree that the welfare state has an important part to play in society but they differ in their views about how great a part this should be. The Labour Party favours a larger role for the welfare state. For example, help should be provided to people who need it because they have lost their job or because they require advice to get them back into work. The Labour Party believes that these people should accept help from the state but they should also get ready to find a job.

The Conservative Party believes that the welfare state has helped to tackle some serious social and economic problems. However, it has created other problems. For example, the welfare state enables people to choose to live on benefits and it does not encourage everyone who is able to work to find work. The welfare state is linked to the development of a **dependency culture** which involves long-term dependency on welfare benefits and deliberate avoidance of work.

Key concepts

dependency culture
means test
poverty trap

Examiner's tips

- In your answers, don't include information that is not directly relevant to the question. The examiners won't deduct marks if you include this information. However, you will penalise yourself in so far as you will have wasted valuable time.

- Check how many marks are available for each question and use the marks as a guide to how long your answers should be.

Task

Match the term in the first column with the correct meaning in the second column.

Term	Meaning
1 Dependency culture	a) These benefits are the responsibility of central government. Examples include national insurance (NI) benefits.
2 Local benefits	b) To qualify for these benefits, the claimant must have paid enough contributions into the national insurance (NI) scheme.
3 National benefits	c) These benefits are the responsibility of local councils such as Teesside or Lambeth councils. Examples include housing benefit and free school meals.
4 Contributory benefits	d) Some people who claim state benefits are seen as developing a way of life in which they become so reliant on benefits that they lose the motivation to work.

Government attempts to tackle social problems

Key points

- In Section C of Paper 2, you may be asked about the **ways in which British governments have tried to address social problems**.

- In practice, this is likely to mean that you should be able to:

  - describe how governments have tried to tackle discrimination, unemployment and poverty

  - explain how successful these policies have been.

Such policies or reforms are applied to a wide range of areas including families, education and training, the welfare state, crime and justice. Bear in mind that many of these policies are not problem-based.

For example, some employers believe that workers aged over fifty find it hard to adapt to new technology.

You can link this point to material on the different influences on educational achievement.

You can link this point to material on how crime affects local communities.

Social issues and social problems

Social issues such as discrimination, the ageing population, unemployment and poverty reflect people's concerns about particular aspects of society. They are often seen as **social problems** and many people believe that 'something must be done' to deal with them. Discrimination, unemployment and poverty, for example, are all seen as social problems because they are viewed as damaging to society. As a result of their negative effects on society, social problems require tackling through **social policies**.

Social policies are actions or reforms that bodies such as **governments** or **local authorities** put into place to tackle particular social problems or issues in fields such as education, welfare and criminal justice. Each **political party** (such as the Labour Party, the Conservatives and the Liberal Democrats) has its own ideas about, and policies to deal with, particular social problems. If it is elected to form a government, a political party then has the power to make political and legal decisions to try to tackle social problems. For example, it might change existing social policies or introduce new ones.

Tackling discrimination

Discrimination occurs when people are treated differently and less favourably, for example because of their gender, ethnicity or age. Governments have tried to tackle discrimination by introducing new **equality and anti-discrimination legislation**. As a result, it is now unlawful to discriminate on the grounds of gender, race, age, religion, belief, disability or sexual orientation.

Britain's **ageing population** means that older people are an important focus of social policy. Age discrimination in the labour market is a key social policy issue affecting older people today. In 2006, the government introduced regulations against **age discrimination** in employment and training. Although these regulations cover the whole age range, they are more likely to benefit older people.

Tackling unemployment and poverty

Unemployment is seen as a social problem for:

- the **unemployed people** themselves because it is linked to poverty and ill health

- their **children** because, in general, they are less likely to do well at school and to obtain secure, well-paid jobs

- **communities** with high levels of unemployment because they are often more affected by crime, antisocial behaviour and family breakdown than other communities.

Other social issues that you may have looked at include fear of crime, antisocial behaviour, care of the elderly, violence in the media and educational underachievement.

Remember that UK governments consist mainly of MPs who are government ministers. These ministers are selected by the Prime Minister, who is the leader of the political party that is in government. However, governments may also include members of the House of Lords, who are not elected MPs.

A number of equality and anti-discrimination laws have been passed since the 1970s. Examples include the Equal Pay Act 1970 and the Disability Discrimination Act 2005. However, you don't need a detailed knowledge of the contents of these laws.

Governments have tried to address unemployment through **welfare-to-work policies**. Such programmes aim to:

- increase **job opportunities** for benefit claimants for example by job creation schemes
- improve claimants' **skills and motivation** by providing education, training and counselling; the New Deal programme, for example, helps unemployed people on benefits to find employment and includes training and preparation for work
- encourage claimants to **take up paid employment** by increasing the benefits paid to those in work through Tax Credits.

One way in which governments have tried to reduce the number of people in **poverty** is by state provision of financial support through **means-tested benefits**.

Here is how one student answered the question: '**Describe one social problem in society today and explain why this issue is seen as a social problem by many people**'. *(5 marks)* AO1, AO2

One social problem is unemployment. Officially, unemployed people are people aged 16 and over without a job but who want to work and are looking for a job.

Unemployment (particularly long-term unemployment) is seen as a social problem because it affects the life chances of unemployed people who may experience poverty and ill health. Also, unemployed people's children are generally less likely to achieve good results at school and to get high status jobs. Communities that have high rates of unemployment also tend to be affected by antisocial behaviour.

5/5

Examiner's tip

Read the questions carefully. It's a good idea to underline the command words in each question. You should focus on addressing these in your answers.

A clear definition of unemployment is given.

Reference is made to a relevant sociological concept.

Good points

- The student describes an appropriate social problem.
- The student explains clearly why unemployment can be seen as a social problem.

Key concepts

discrimination
unemployment

Task

Read through the summary about government attempts to help families and to tackle poverty and then fill in the gaps numbered 1 to 7 by selecting the correct answer from the following:

| a) stigma | c) enough | e) of childcare | g) poverty |
| b) reduce | d) benefits | f) their savings | |

One way in which governments try to help families is through the (1) _____ system. For example, Child Benefit is paid to people who are responsible for bringing up children, regardless of their income or (2) _____ . There is no social (3) _____ attached to claiming Child Benefit and take-up rates are high. Another way is through schemes such as the Sure Start scheme. This aims to support parents, increase the availability (4) _____ and improve young children's health and emotional development.

Governments have tried to tackle (5) _____ by providing means-tested benefits and through the national minimum wage. Some critics of government efforts to reduce poverty argue that benefit levels are not (6) _____ to meet people's needs and should be increased. Others argue that over time, governments have failed to significantly (7) _____ the high levels of poverty in Britain.

Key points

- Paper 2 contains **four** sections (one of which is Social Inequality). In the exam, you will choose **three** sections and you must answer all of the questions in each of these three sections.

- Section D of Paper 2 will focus on **Unit 2, Social Inequality**.

- It is marked out of 30.

- If you choose to answer the question on Social Inequality, it will account for 33 per cent (one third) of your total mark for Paper 2.

- You should spend no more than 30 minutes on each of your three chosen sections.

Paper 2 consists of four sections. Only Section D (Social Inequality) is given here.

These figures are presented as percentages and relate to 2008. You can see, for example, that around 19 per cent of men and 12 per cent of women were employed as managers and senior officials in 2008.

About the Social Inequality exam question

Here is an example of the sort of exam question that could be set on Social Inequality. The question is divided into parts (a) to (g). For each part, the assessment objectives (AOs) have been identified for you. This will help you to recognize which skills each part is testing. The comments are there to give you some guidance on how to go about answering exam questions on Social Inequality.

In the exam, the 'Items' could contain material such as written extracts from newspapers or textbooks, bar graphs, charts, tables of statistics or photographs. In the question below, Item G presents a bar graph containing data on the links between gender and occupation. Item H contains written information about child poverty.

SECTION D: SOCIAL INEQUALITY

Answer **all** questions from this section.

Total for this question: 30 marks

4 Study **Items G and H** and then answer parts (a) to (g).

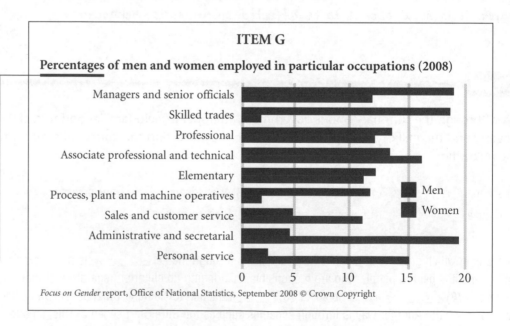

ITEM G

Percentages of men and women employed in particular occupations (2008)

Focus on Gender report, Office of National Statistics, September 2008 © Crown Copyright

ITEM H

Child Poverty

Child poverty generates concern among members of the public, politicians and pressure groups. Poverty has a negative effect on children's life chances, including their life expectancy, health, housing, educational achievements and their job prospects. In 1999, the Labour Government set a target to reduce child poverty by half by 2010 and to end it by 2020.

The AOs have been included here to help you to focus on the relevant skills. Bear in mind that the AOs won't be included on the AQA exam papers.

(a) From **Item G**, what percentage of women was employed in personal service in 2008? AO3 *(1 mark)*

(b) From **Item H**, what did the Labour Government plan to end by 2020? AO3 *(1 mark)*

Remember to give **two** different ways.

(c) Identify **two** ways in which British governments have tried to reduce inequalities between different ethnic groups over the last 50 years. AO1 *(2 marks)*

Make sure that you understand what the different command words (such as 'describe' and 'explain') are asking you to do.

(d) Explain what sociologists mean by social inequality. AO1 *(4 marks)*

(e) Describe **one** way in which ethnicity and social class may be linked **and** explain the possible consequences of this link. AO1 AO2 *(5 marks)*

On 5-mark questions like this, you will get a maximum of two marks for your description and a maximum of three marks for your explanation.

(f) Describe **one** way in which sociologists measure social class **and** explain why this way of measuring class could be criticized. AO1 AO2 *(5 marks)*

Remember to answer just **one** of these options.

(g) **EITHER**

(i) Discuss how far sociologists would agree that poverty is likely to persist from one generation of a family to the next generation. AO1 AO2 AO3 *(12 marks)*

OR

Try to get as much practice as you can at writing answers under timed conditions.

(ii) Discuss how far sociologists would agree that inequality based on gender is a more significant cause of social division than social class in modern Britain. AO1 AO2 AO3 *(12 marks)*

Remember that during the exam you will have to divide your time between studying the Items, reading the questions, thinking about your answers, planning your mini-essays, writing your answers and reading them through.

As you work through this revision chapter on Social Inequality, you will have the opportunity to read examples of how students have answered questions (c), (d), (e), (f) and (g)(i) and some other questions. These sample student answers have all been given a mark and there is also a written comment about each one. It is important to study all of this information carefully because it will give you further guidance on how to answer exam questions on Social Inequality.

Task 1

Answer questions (a) and (b).

Task 2

Once you have worked through this chapter on Social Inequality, you should answer questions (c), (d), (e), (f) and (g)(i) and then compare your own responses with the sample student answers provided.

Defining social inequality and stratification

Key points

- In Section D of Paper 2, you may be asked to **explain the nature of stratification**. You may also be asked about **the main concepts that sociologists use to analyse stratification**.

- In practice, this is likely to mean that you should be able to:
  - explain that stratification involves the unequal distribution of wealth, income, status and power
  - use concepts such as class, status and life chances.

Key concepts

achieved status
ascribed status
income
life chances

Good points

- The student understands what the term social inequality means.

- The explanation is clear. It recognizes that social inequality is linked to the uneven distribution of resources and opportunities.

Defining social inequality

When you are writing about social inequality, it is important to understand that this term refers to the unequal distribution of:

- **resources** such as power, income and wealth
- **opportunities** related – for instance – to education, employment and health.

Social class, gender, ethnicity and age are all sources of inequality in modern British society. In other words, resources and opportunities are distributed unequally between individuals and groups based on their social class, gender, ethnicity and age.

Defining social stratification

The term **social stratification** describes the way society is structured into a hierarchy of strata or layers that are unequally ranked. A social hierarchy is shaped like a pyramid and each layer is more powerful than the one below it. The most privileged group forms the top layer and the least privileged group forms the bottom layer.

Stratification involves **inequalities** between groups in the distribution of economic and social resources such as **wealth**, **income**, **status** and **power**. When revising this topic, it is important to appreciate that these inequalities persist or continue over time.

> You can link this to material on power in the previous chapter.

The group in the top rank of the hierarchy is likely to have much more power, wealth, income and status than the group at the bottom. In modern Britain, class, gender, ethnicity and age are the main criteria by which people tend to be stratified.

Different forms of stratification

The **caste system** in traditional India, **slavery** in the southern states of the USA in the 19th century, **Apartheid** in South Africa (1948–1994) and the **social class** system in modern Britain are all types of stratification.

As you revise the various forms of stratification, bear in mind that they differ according to whether **status** (i.e. social position) is **ascribed** (fixed at birth) or **achieved** (earned on the basis of talent or merit). They also differ in terms of how open or closed they are. In an open system of stratification, status is achieved and **social mobility** (movement up or down between the strata) is possible. In a closed system, status is ascribed so social mobility is highly unlikely.

> Status is used in two ways. It can refer to social position and it can also refer to honour or prestige.

Question (d) on page 83 focuses on the meaning of social inequality. It assesses AO1 and is marked out of four. Here is how one student answered this question.

Social inequality refers to the unequal distribution of resources such as power and money. Some individuals and groups in society have more influence and wealth than others. It also refers to the unequal distribution of life chances or opportunities related to things like

Continued >

health, education and employment. In Britain today, social inequalities are linked to class, gender, ethnicity and age.

4/4

Here is how another student answered the question: '**Identify two forms of social stratification in modern Britain other than social class**'. *(2 marks)* AO1

One form of social stratification is age and the other form is gender.

2/2

Good point

The student identifies two appropriate forms of social stratification.

Ethnicity is another possible answer.

Life chances

When you are writing about **life chances**, it is important to be aware that they are a key aspect of studying social inequality and stratification. Life chances refer to people's chances of having positive or negative outcomes over their lifetime in relation to, for example, their education, health, income, employment and housing.

Life chances are distributed unequally between individuals and groups because they are affected by **social factors** such as class position, gender and ethnicity. For instance, people in higher social classes (such as lawyers and architects) have more chance than those in other classes of accessing good quality healthcare and decent housing. When you are revising life chances, remember that they are shaped by inequalities in wealth, income, power and status.

You can link this to material about the different social influences on educational achievement in the chapter on Education.

Task 1

Match the term in the first column with the correct meaning in the second column.

Term	Meaning
1 Wealth	a) Social positions that are earned on the basis of individuals' talents or abilities.
2 Income	b) Movement up or down between a society's strata.
3 Ascribed status	c) Money held in savings accounts and shares or ownership of assets such as land.
4 Achieved status	d) The resources that individuals and households receive over a specific time period. It could be received in cash (e.g. wages) or in kind (e.g. a company car).
5 Social mobility	e) Social positions that are fixed at birth and unchanging over time, e.g. hereditary titles.

Task 2

The following table compares two different forms of social stratification. Drawing on relevant information from your textbook or class notes, copy out and complete this table.

Term	Social class	Slavery
1 What is stratification based on?		
2 Is status achieved or ascribed?		
3 Is social mobility possible?		

Examiner's tip

When you are writing about life chances, it's important to be aware that research has identified marked inequalities between different social classes in relation to life expectancy at birth, infant mortality and morbidity (having an illness or a disease).

It's also important to appreciate that there are links between life chances and gender, ethnicity and age. For instance, research has shown that the chances of experiencing poverty are linked to age, gender and ethnicity as well as to class (see pages 90–1).

Social class as a form of stratification

Key points

- In Section D of Paper 2, you may be asked about **social class as a form of stratification**.

- In practice, this is likely to mean that you should be able to:
  - explain what the term social class means
  - discuss how sociologists measure social class.

Examiner's tips

- When you are writing about the different social class scales, bear in mind that the Registrar General's classification was the UK's official government social class scale from 1911–98. It was replaced by the NS-SEC in 1998.

- You may have come across people who assume that the term 'working class' refers to people who work or who have a job regardless of what job they do. However, the term 'working class' refers to people who work in working-class jobs. It can include unemployed people or people living on state benefits.

Approaches to social class

Within sociology, there are different approaches to social class. **Karl Marx**, **Max Weber** and sociologists working within the **functionalist approach** have all shaped sociological views on social class.

- Karl Marx (1818–83) identified **two main classes** in capitalist society: the **bourgeoisie** (the capitalist or ruling class) and the **proletariat** (the working class). Class membership was determined by **economic factors** (ownership and non-ownership). The wealthy bourgeoisie owned the property, big businesses, land and factories. In contrast, the proletariat owned no property and were forced to sell their labour to the bourgeoisie to survive. These two classes had very different interests (for example, the bourgeoisie want higher profits whereas the proletariat want higher wages) and this led to **conflict** between them.

- Max Weber (1864–1920) identified **four main classes**: property owners, professionals, the petty bourgeoisie (such as shopkeepers) and the working class. These classes had different **life chances** in the labour market. Like Marx, Weber saw class as based on economic factors such as wealth. However, Weber also stressed the importance of **status** (prestige) and **power** in determining life chances.

> Marx and Weber are regarded as two of the founders of sociology as an academic subject. Their ideas remain influential today.

- According to the functionalist approach, modern society needs a system of unequal rewards. This motivates the most talented people to train for the key occupations that are essential for society to continue. These top positions must provide **scarce rewards** such as high pay and status to attract the most able people. So the stratification system fulfils the function of ensuring that the most important jobs are filled by the most talented and highly qualified people.

> The functionalist approach sees modern societies such as Britain as – to a large extent – meritocratic.

> You can link this to material on the functions of families and the education system.

Measuring social class

Occupation is often used to measure social class because it is linked to factors such as levels of pay, working conditions and social status.

The Registrar General's scale

In the past, many sociologists used the Registrar General's scale to measure social class. This scale allocated people to a class based on their occupation. It distinguished between **manual** and **non-manual occupations**. Manual occupations require some physical effort and they may be skilled, semi-skilled or unskilled. These jobs were seen as **working class** in the Registrar General's scale. In contrast, non-manual occupations do not require physical effort. Skilled non-manual, managerial and technical and professional occupations were seen as **middle class** in this scale.

Problems with the Registrar General's scale

Although the Registrar General's occupation-based scale was used for many years, there were problems with it.

- With a scale based on occupation, it is difficult to place **people without jobs** (such as students, retired and unemployed people) into a social class.
- The class position of a jobless married woman was assessed on the basis of her **husband's occupation**, which might be misleading.
- Wealthy **upper-class** people and **property owners** were difficult to place on a scale based on occupation.
- Two people may have the same occupation or job title (such as lecturer) yet there may be **huge differences** in their wealth, income, status and qualifications.

The National Statistics Socio-economic Classification

The National Statistics Socio-economic Classification (NS-SEC) addresses some of the problems associated with the Registrar General's scale. It uses **occupation** but covers the full population including students and long-term unemployed people.

The NS-SEC groups together the occupations that are similar in:

- the **rewards** they provide – such as pay, career prospects and job security
- **employment status** – this takes into account whether someone is an employer, self-employed or an employee
- **levels of authority and control** – this takes into account whether someone is responsible for other workers or whether they are supervised by others.

Question (f) on page 83 focuses on ways in which sociologists measure social class. Read this question carefully and underline the command words.

Here is how one student answered this question.

> One way is through occupation (e.g. using the Registrar General's scale) because a person's life chances are linked to their job. However, this might not be accurate and could be misleading. For instance, two people with the same job title (e.g. farmer) may have very different amounts of wealth, income, power and status. For example, a 'gentleman farmer' may own acres of land, have a hereditary title and employ 300 people. Another farmer may rent land, scrape a living and have no employees. Yet, if we use occupation alone, they would both be placed in the same social class.

5/5

> The answer draws on relevant sociological concepts.

> The example of farmer is used effectively to highlight a possible inaccuracy in the Registrar General's scale.

Key concept

proletariat

This question tests AO1 and AO2 and is marked out of five. You will get a maximum of two marks for your description and a maximum of three marks for your explanation.

Good points

- The student gives an appropriate description.
- The answer explains clearly why the use of occupation to measure social class can be criticized.

Task

1 Identify one similarity and one difference between Marx' and Weber's views on social class.

2 Identify one similarity and one difference between the Registrar General's scale and the National Statistics Socio-economic Classification (NS-SEC).

Gender, ethnicity and age

Key points

- In Section D of Paper 2, you may be asked about **gender, ethnicity and age**.

- In practice, this is likely to mean that you should be able to:
  - discuss gender, ethnicity and age as forms of social stratification.

Examiner's tip

You can contrast **sociological with biological explanations** for ethnicity and race when answering relevant Paper 1 questions. For example:

- The sociological idea of ethnic group emphasizes the cultural or social differences (and similarities) between ethnic groups. By contrast, the biological idea of race tends to emphasize the biological differences between people in different 'racial groups'.

- Sociologists argue that 'racial differences' are socially constructed. In other words, they are created by society rather than rooted in biology.

When you are writing about stratification, it is important to remember that sources of inequality based on **gender**, **ethnicity** and **age** are significant in class-based societies.

Inequality based on gender

Feminist approaches explore **gender inequalities** in society. Over the last 40 years, reforms in areas such as education and employment have addressed aspects of gender inequality. You should be aware, for example, that governments have introduced **anti-discrimination laws** such as the Equal Pay Act (1970) to reduce gender inequalities.

Today, women are increasingly likely to achieve high level educational qualifications, high status jobs and good salaries. Despite this, feminist approaches argue that gender remains the most significant social division in contemporary society. Some feminist approaches see society as **patriarchal**. A patriarchal society is one in which men:

- have a lot of **power** within families, politics and the workplace

- generally receive a bigger share of **rewards** such as wealth and status.

> You can link the feminist approach to material on sex and gender, education, families, crime and the media.

> You can link this to the discussion of government attempts to tackle discrimination in the chapter on Power.

> You can link this to the material in the chapter on Power about the under-representation of women in the House of Commons.

Inequality based on ethnicity

Over the last 40 years, reforms and policies have addressed inequality based on **ethnicity** in areas such as education, employment and criminal justice. For example:

- many employers have **equal opportunities policies** to support equality and diversity

- the 1976 Race Relations Act outlawed **discrimination** based on ethnicity

- the Equality and Human Rights Commission has powers to **enforce** the equality laws and to **shape public policy** on equality issues

- within organizations, awareness of institutional racism has been raised.

As a result of such changes, some commentators argue that inequalities based on ethnicity are less significant today than they were 40 years ago. However, others argue that there has been little real change in the fields of employment, education and criminal justice. For example, **unemployment rates** in England and Wales are higher among people of Pakistani, Bangladeshi and Black Caribbean heritage than among White British or White Irish people. Research has also found that men and women of Pakistani and Bangladeshi heritage have much worse chances of getting **professional and managerial jobs** than their white peers of the same age and educational level.

Question (c) on page 83 focuses on the ways in which British governments have attempted to reduce inequalities between different ethnic groups over the last 50 years. Read this question carefully. It tests AO1 and is marked out of two. Here is how one student answered this question.

1) Through equality legislation such as the Race Relations Act in the 1970s. 2) By funding bodies such as the Equality and Human Rights Commission which enforces the equality laws.

2/2

> It's a good idea to identify two completely different ways.

Inequality based on age

Sociologists argue that **age** (like gender and ethnicity) is **socially constructed**. This can be seen in the historical and cross-cultural differences in expectations surrounding age. For example, although child labour is now illegal in Britain, it was the norm among working-class families in the 19th century and exists in some parts of the world today.

> Members of an ethnic group share an identity based on their cultural traditions, religion or language.

The status of **older people** can vary between cultures. In some cultures, getting old is seen as something to be avoided. In other cultures, however, older age is seen as something to look forward to and older people have a high status in society.

The term **ageism** (or age discrimination) describes a situation in which someone is treated differently and less favourably based on their age. In Britain, there are now regulations against age discrimination in employment and training.

Here is how one student answered the question: '**Identify two reasons why young people are often more likely than other groups to be in low-paid jobs**'. *(2 marks)* AO1

Young people often have less work experience than older people. Older people with more experience can apply for the well-paid jobs.

1/2

> The question asks for two reasons. In this answer, the second sentence makes the same point as the first.

Task

Read through the summary about gender and employment then fill in the gaps numbered 1 to 8 by selecting the correct answer from the following:

a) promotion	c) full-time paid work	e) nursery nursing	g) women
b) discrimination	d) senior management	f) less	h) part-time

Often, men and women do not work in the same occupations. For instance, fire fighting is male dominated and (1) _____ is female dominated. When men and women do work in the same occupations, (2) _____ are more likely to be in lower-level or middle-level jobs while men tend to hold the higher grade and (3) _____ posts. For instance, in 2007, 19 per cent of men and 11 per cent of women worked as managers or senior officials. Women on average still earn (4) _____ than men. One reason for this is that women are more likely than men to work in low-paid jobs. Women are also more likely than men to be employed (5) _____ rather than full-time. One explanation for the persistence of gender inequality at work focuses on (6) _____ in the workplace. Another explanation suggests that some women are held back when applying for (7) _____ or developing their career because they have the main responsibility for housework and childcare. A third explanation argues that inadequate or expensive childcare provision prevents some women from participating in (8) _____ or staying in employment long enough to progress in their career.

Wealth, income and poverty

Key points

- In Section D of Paper 2, you may be asked about the **unequal distribution of wealth and income** and the **ways in which life chances are influenced by differences in wealth and income**. You may also be asked about **ways of defining and measuring poverty**.

- In practice, this is likely to mean that you should be able to:

  - describe how wealth and income are distributed

  - explain how life chances are influenced by differences in wealth and income

  - discuss absolute and relative definitions of poverty and the different ways of measuring poverty

  - identify groups who are more likely to experience poverty

  - explain what the term 'life cycle of poverty' means.

Social exclusion is also discussed on pages 92–3.

Key concepts

absolute poverty
life cycle of poverty
poverty line
relative poverty

Wealth and income

Stratification involves the unequal distribution of resources such as wealth and income. When you are writing about wealth and income, it is important to be clear about the difference between them.

- **Wealth** refers to the ownership of assets that are valued at a particular point in time. Marketable assets include houses and land that can be sold in order to make money. Wealth also includes savings and shares.

- **Income** refers to the flow of resources which individuals and households receive over a specific time period. People may receive income in cash (e.g. wages, welfare benefits and pensions) or in kind (e.g. petrol allowances).

The distribution of wealth and income

Wealth is distributed unequally in the UK. For example, in 2001 the wealthiest one per cent owned 33 per cent of marketable wealth (excluding the value of their homes). In contrast, the least wealthy 50 per cent owned just three per cent of this wealth.

Income is also distributed unequally in the UK. For example, in 2007, the poorest 10 per cent of people received three per cent of total income while the top 10 per cent received 40 per cent of total income.

> It's important to be aware that wealth and income are distributed unequally. However, you do not need to memorize these figures in detail.

Wealth and income influence **life chances**. For instance, many people on high incomes have a choice between NHS and private healthcare, state and private education or between renting and buying a property. However, most people on low incomes do not have these choices.

Poverty

When you are revising poverty, you should be aware that this term can be defined in more than one way. For example:

- People experience **absolute poverty** when their income is so low that they cannot obtain the minimum needed to survive.

- People experience **relative poverty** when their income is well below average so they are poor compared with others in their society. They cannot afford to have the general standard of living that most other people in their society enjoy.

Poverty can also be defined in terms of **exclusion** from everyday activities and customs. In this case, poverty is not simply about low incomes. It is also about excluding the people who experience poverty from the activities and living patterns that most people take for granted.

Measuring poverty

As part of your revision, you should familiarize yourself with the different ways of measuring poverty. These include:

- **Low incomes** – this is the main official UK Government way of measuring poverty.

- Lack of items that the majority of the population see as **necessities**.

- **Subjective measures** – in which people judge themselves to be living in poverty.

Here is how one student answered the question: '**Identify two ways in which poverty can be measured**'. *(2 marks)* AO1

> 1) Having an income that is low compared to the average income in your society.
>
> 2) Lacking things that most people in your society see as basic necessities (e.g. two meals a day) because you can't afford them.

2/2

Good points

- The student clearly identifies two appropriate ways of measuring poverty.

- The answer shows a good understanding of these different ways of measuring poverty.

Groups at risk of poverty

People from some social groups are more likely to experience poverty than others. Research findings suggest that the proportion of people in poverty is higher among:

- lone-parent households
- single pensioners
- families with a child under 11
- households without paid workers
- people who left school aged 16 or under
- children and young people.

A number of pressure groups (such as the Child Poverty Action Group) campaign against poverty. You can link this to material on pressure groups in the chapter on Power.

Poverty is linked to **ethnicity, gender and age**. People living in households headed by someone of Pakistani or Bangladeshi heritage are at risk of living in low-income households. Women face a greater risk of poverty than men. Children and pensioners are more at risk of poverty than other age groups. This is captured in the idea of the **life cycle of poverty**.

Here is how one student answered the question: '**Explain what sociologists mean by the life cycle of poverty**'. *(4 marks)* AO1

> The life cycle of poverty shows that people may move into and out of poverty at different points during their lives. For example, an individual may live below the poverty line during childhood. As a young adult, they can earn money and move out of poverty. If they have children, the added expense may mean they move back into poverty. When their children leave home, they may escape poverty. During old age, they no longer get a wage so they may move back into poverty. So children and pensioners are more at risk of poverty.

4/4

Good point

The student gives a clear explanation of how the life cycle of poverty may work.

Task

Drawing on relevant information from your textbook and class notes, answer the following questions:

1 Identify two reasons why women are generally more likely than men to experience poverty.

2 Identify two reasons why people from some minority ethnic groups are more likely to experience poverty than other people.

3 Identify two reasons why some older people are at risk of poverty.

Examiner's tip

Remember to include the relevant terms (such as absolute poverty, relative poverty and the poverty line) in your answers.

Different sociological explanations of poverty

Key points

- In Section D of Paper 2, you may be asked about **different sociological explanations of poverty**.

- In practice, this is likely to mean that you should be able to:
  - describe the difference between individual and structural explanations of poverty
  - describe the different explanations such as the culture of poverty, the Marxist approach and the inadequacies of the welfare state
  - identify some of the strengths and weaknesses of these explanations.

This links to material on the welfare state in the chapter on Power.

You can link this to material on participation in the political process in the chapter on Power.

Key concepts

cultural deprivation
cycle of deprivation
material deprivation
social exclusion
underclass
welfare dependency

When writing about explanations of poverty, bear in mind that some approaches focus on **individuals** and **groups** while others focus on **structural factors**.

Individual explanations of poverty

Individual explanations highlight the behaviour or lifestyles of the individuals and groups who experience poverty. They suggest that 'the poor' are responsible in some way for their own situation. Examples of such explanations include:

- **the culture of poverty**. In this account, people from the poorest sections of society are socialized within a subculture of poverty. They develop a way of life and a set of values to cope with their position. For instance, they live for the moment and see no point in planning ahead. However, these values prevent them from taking up educational opportunities or saving for the future and, in this way, escaping poverty.

This gives you another example of the way in which the concept of socialization has been used.

- **the cycle of deprivation**. In this view, poverty involves both **material deprivation** and **cultural deprivation**. It persists from generation to generation, locking families into a cycle of deprivation.

- **welfare dependency** and the '**underclass**'. In the 1980s and 1990s, New Right approaches identified the emergence in Britain of an 'underclass' – a group of 'undeserving poor' whose attitudes and values are different from those of mainstream society. This group remains in poverty because the **welfare state** encourages them to depend on state provision. Generous state provision makes the problem of poverty worse by creating 'welfare dependency' and encouraging an underclass to develop.

The idea of **social exclusion** can be used to criticize individual explanations of poverty. Socially excluded people are shut out from participating in society's social, economic, political and cultural life by factors beyond their control. The idea of social exclusion stresses **society's role** in excluding some people from full participation.

Structural explanations of poverty

Rather than focusing on individuals and groups, **structural approaches** look at the way **society** is structured. They examine how economic, social and political structures create poverty and perpetuate it over time. Examples of structural explanations include:

- **the Marxist approach**. In this view, poverty is the inevitable result of the class-based inequalities that are built into capitalist society. Capitalism is an economic system that generates extreme wealth for the capitalist class while producing poverty among sections of the working class.

- **unemployment and the inadequacies of the welfare state**. Many sociologists see unemployment as a key issue in understanding the causes of poverty. For instance, during economic recessions, unemployment levels (both short-term and long-term) rise and, as a result, the number of people experiencing poverty also increases. Another view is that welfare state benefits are too low. In this view, the solution to the problem of poverty is to give more money to the people in poverty by increasing the value of pensions and welfare benefits.

Question (g)(i) on page 83 focuses on whether poverty persists from one generation to the next. Read this question carefully. It assesses AO1, AO2 and AO3 and is marked out of 12. Here is how one student answered this question.

According to the culture of poverty, poor people are socialized into particular values that make it hard for them to escape poverty. Through socialization in families, these values are passed on from parents to children. So in this view, poverty is likely to persist across the generations of families.

> The student draws on relevant sociological concepts.

The cycle of deprivation also emphasizes how poverty is passed from one generation to the next in families. In this view, children born into poverty experience material and cultural deprivation. As a result, they grow up to be poor and often become parents of deprived children. However, critics argue that such approaches blame the victim and ignore structural factors such as long-term unemployment or class-based divisions in society.

> This directly addresses the question.

> This is a good criticism and shows evaluation skills.

The life cycle of poverty suggests that people may move into and out of poverty at different stages of their lives. So children who are born into poor families may escape poverty as adults.

In a meritocratic society, young people can achieve qualifications that lead to upward social mobility and to a job with a high income. In this way, they can escape childhood poverty.

> Although short, the conclusion addresses the issue of 'how far'.

To conclude, not all sociologists would agree that poverty is likely to persist across the generations of a family. It is possible to escape poverty.

12/12

> Item H on page 82 contains information on child poverty. It's worth thinking about whether you could draw on this material to answer this question.

Good points

- The answer shows a sound understanding of a range of relevant explanations.

- Rather than simply listing the different explanations, they are applied directly to the set question.

- The answer is clearly structured. The discussion begins by supporting the view that poverty persists across the generations of a family before moving on to argue against this view. It ends with a clear conclusion that addresses 'how far'.

Examiner's tip

It's helpful to have some idea of when the different explanations of poverty were most popular. For example, the culture of poverty explanation was most popular in the 1950s and 1960s. The cycle of deprivation explanation was popular during the 1970s. New Right approaches developed during the 1980s and 1990s.

Task

Each of the following statements contains two highlighted words or phrases and you have to decide which of the two is correct.

1 Critics argue that the culture of poverty and cycle of deprivation explanations ignore individual/structural factors and fail to explain why people are poor in the first place.

2 New Right approaches focus on the underclass whose members are seen as dependent on welfare provision. Critics argue that the term 'underclass' is used to label and blame/make excuses for the victims of poverty.

Major debates about social stratification

Key points

- In Section D of Paper 2, you may be asked about **the major debates related to stratification**.

- In practice, this is likely to mean that you should be able to discuss whether:
  - modern Britain is becoming a meritocracy or a classless society
  - class division has become less significant than divisions based on gender, ethnicity or age.

Key concepts

classless society
inter-generational social mobility
intra-generational social mobility
long-range mobility
short-range mobility

Good points

- The student describes one way in which ethnicity and social class may be linked.

- The student explains two possible consequences of this link.

You can link this to material on the factors influencing voting behaviour and political beliefs in the chapter on Power.

When you are revising social stratification, it is important to remember that this topic has generated **major debates** within sociology. One debate focuses on how much **social mobility** there is in modern Britain and whether society is becoming more **meritocratic**. Other debates look at whether **social class** is still a useful concept in the 21st century and whether Britain is now a **classless society**.

Meritocracy and social mobility

Some sociologists argue that, to a large extent, Britain is a **meritocracy**. In a meritocratic society, status is achieved and people are allocated to occupations mainly on the basis of **individual ability**. So social class origins, gender or ethnicity are seen as less significant than talent and motivation in determining an individual's occupation and class position.

High rates of upward and downward **social mobility** are seen as evidence that:

- society is meritocratic
- opportunities are available to everyone, regardless of their social class origins.

When you are revising, it is important to distinguish between **routes** and **barriers** to social mobility. Routes to mobility include educational qualifications, financial windfalls and changes in the occupational structure such as a growth in white collar occupations. Barriers include gender discrimination, lack of skills and lack of qualifications.

Findings from Goldthorpe's 1972–74 mobility study suggested that some **long-range mobility** had occurred. Working-class children did end up in middle-class occupations. However, they were much less likely than middle-class children to do so. More recently, sociologists such as Crompton have noted that social mobility in Britain is in **decline**. This is linked partly to **changes in the occupational structure**. For example, the growth in professional and managerial jobs has slowed down so there is now less room at the top.

Question (e) on page 83 focuses on ethnicity and social class. It assesses AO1 and AO2 and is marked out of five. You will get a maximum of two marks for your description and three marks for your explanation. Here is how one student answered this question.

> Overall, people of African Caribbean heritage are more likely to be in occupations that are classified as working class. This can have consequences for their chances of upward social mobility. It can also have consequences for their children's life chances including their educational opportunities.

5/5

The answer is shorter than some other 5-mark answers and it's a good example of a response that gets straight to the point.

The answer draws on relevant sociological concepts.

The significance of social class

One view is that social class divisions are less clear-cut in Britain today compared with the 1950s.

For example, it is argued that:

- **traditional working-class communities** centred on heavy industry, coal-mining and shipbuilding have declined
- **class identities** have weakened and people no longer strongly identify themselves as working class or middle class
- Britain now operates as a **meritocracy** in allocating individuals to jobs.

> You can link this to the relevant material on class identity in the chapter on Mass Media.

Another version of the 'decline of class' view suggests that class divisions have become less significant than those based on **gender, ethnicity and age**. For example:

- women, some minority ethnic groups, children and older people are more at risk of **poverty** than other groups
- divisions based on gender can be seen in the **gender inequalities** in the workplace, the gender pay gap and the under-representation of women in political life
- divisions based on **ethnicity** can be seen in the over-representation of some minority ethnic groups among low income households, the under-representation of some minority ethnic groups among MPs and in the professions.

Other sociologists argue that inequalities based on class, gender, ethnicity and age are all significant in modern Britain. In this view, class, gender, ethnicity and age are seen as **interlinked aspects of inequality** rather than as completely separate aspects.

Despite social changes, many sociologists argue that social class remains a **central concept** in sociology because social class still impacts on people's daily lives. Class-based inequalities in **life chances** (linked, for instance, to income, housing, education, social mobility, life expectancy and health) persist in the 21st century. So while class may have changed, it has not declined.

> You can link this to material on the social influences on educational achievement in the chapter on Education.

Task 1

Read through the summary of some of the debates on stratification then fill in the gaps numbered 1 to 8 by selecting the correct answer from the following:

a) examination results	c) Sex Discrimination Act	e) age	g) at school
b) division	d) Marxist	f) professional careers	h) feminist

Sociologists working within the (1) _____ approach argue that gender inequality is the most important cause of social division in modern Britain. Gender inequality can be found in the workplace today despite equality laws such as the (2) _____ . On the other hand, many girls are now achieving better (3) _____ at GCSE and A-Level than boys. Also, increasing numbers of females are going into higher education and entering (4) _____ such as medicine.

Other sociologists see inequality based on ethnicity as the most important cause of social (5) _____ in contemporary Britain. For instance, members of some minority ethnic groups underachieve (6) _____ and experience higher levels of unemployment compared with other groups.

Sociologists from the (7) _____ approach see social class divisions as key to understanding capitalist society. Some sociologists, however, argue that inequalities based on gender, ethnicity, class and (8) _____ are interlinked rather than separate categories. Such sociologists explore the ways these inequalities are all linked together.

Task 2

Describe one difference between inter-generational and intra-generational social mobility.

Examiner's tip

When you are revising, it can be helpful to work with a partner. For example, you could take it in turns to test each other in order to check that you understand the key concepts. Make a note of any terms that you do not fully understand and then refer to your textbook, class notes or teacher for help.

How to raise your Unit 2 exam paper grade

Key point

The advice and tips provided here are designed to help you to **maximize your mark in the Unit 2 exam paper**. They cover:

- the assessment objectives (AOs) and skills that you need to demonstrate in the exam
- the command words that you need to respond to.

If you are taking the **GCSE Sociology Full Course**, you will study both Unit 1 and Unit 2. You will sit the Paper 1 and the Paper 2 exams. When the examiner marks your exam scripts, they will add up your marks for the six questions and calculate your total mark out of 180. This is referred to as your raw mark. They will convert your raw mark into a uniform mark out of 200 and then convert your uniform mark into a grade. To achieve a good grade in the Full Course, you should focus on getting as high a mark as you can in the Paper 1 and Paper 2 exams.

The information on pages 44–5 relates to Unit 1: the GCSE Sociology Short Course. If you are doing the Full Course, you should read this information as well.

The assessment objectives

To achieve an A or A* grade in the Full Course, you need to maximize your marks by demonstrating the **skills** that the examiners are looking for. These skills are:

- **Knowledge and understanding** (AO1)
  You need to demonstrate a thorough knowledge and understanding of the relevant topics (including the social structures, social processes and social issues) that you have studied. So it is essential to revise the subject content carefully in order to maximize your AO1 marks.

- **Application of knowledge and understanding** (AO2)
  You need to apply the appropriate concepts, terms and explanations effectively.

- **Interpretation, analysis and evaluation** (AO3)
  You need to interpret data from the Items accurately. In your extended answers, you should aim to evaluate the different explanations and outline appropriate conclusions.

The command words on Paper 2

The exam questions are carefully worded to test your sociological skills. The command words are very important because they make it clear exactly what you are required to do when answering a particular question. So to maximize your chances of getting high marks and a good grade, you should ensure that you understand what the different command words are asking you to do. This will help you to respond directly and appropriately to them.

It is important to study the Exam 'Dos and Don'ts' on page 45. These apply to the Paper 2 exam as well as the Paper 1 exam.

Examiner's tips

- Remember to study the command words in the questions and respond directly to them.

- It's very important to use your time appropriately during the exam. Check how many marks are available for a particular question and write answers of the right length for the marks available.

- Remember that you won't get any marks for copying out chunks from the Items or for writing everything you know about a particular topic.

- Bear in mind that the examiner is not looking for perfect answers. The examiner appreciates that you are writing your answers under exam conditions and will allow for this when awarding marks.

Command words	Examples of questions from Paper 2	What you are required to do
Identify	From Item A, what percentage of women were employed in personal services in 2008? *(1 mark)*	This question is asking you to **pick out relevant information** from a particular Item. This type of question is encouraging you to demonstrate your interpretation skills.
	Identify **one** advantage and **one** disadvantage of police recorded crime statistics. *(2 marks)*	This question is asking you to **briefly state** an advantage and a disadvantage.
	Identify **two** ways in which people are encouraged to conform to formal social rules. *(2 marks)*	The question is asking you to briefly state two ways. Remember to give two completely different ways.
Explain	Explain what sociologists mean by social inequality. *(4 marks)* Explain what sociologists mean by new media. *(4 marks)*	These questions are testing your knowledge and understanding of a sociological concept. To get high marks on questions like these, you need to define the term clearly and give examples to support your definition.
Describe ... and explain why ...	Describe **one** way in which the mass media could have a negative effect on turnout in a general election **and explain why** this could be a problem in a democratic society. *(5 marks)*	In this question, you need to give a description and an explanation. You need to briefly outline one way (**describe**) and then discuss the reasons why (**explain why**) this could be a problem.
	Describe **one** way in which sociologists measure social class **and explain why** this way of measuring social class could be criticized. *(5 marks)*	In this question, you need to give a description and an explanation. You need to briefly outline one way (**describe**) and then discuss the reasons why (**explain why**) this could be criticized.
Discuss how far sociologists would agree ...	Discuss how far sociologists would agree that inequality based on gender is a more significant cause of social division than social class in modern Britain. *(12 marks)* Discuss how far sociologists would agree that power is distributed evenly between the different groups in British society today. *(12 marks)*	In your answers to extended-answer questions such as these, you need to: • put forward relevant arguments in favour of the statement for discussion, drawing on sociological explanations, concepts and evidence • put forward relevant arguments against the statement for discussion • come to a clear conclusion that directly addresses the issue of 'how far'.

GCSE
Sociology
AQA

Answers to revision guide tasks

Answers to revision guide tasks

Studying Society

Page 7

a) 63 per cent

b)(i) Either a questionnaire or an interview.

Page 9

1 c

2 g

3 h

4 f

5 d

6 a

7 b

8 e

Page 11

Task 1

1 c

2 a

3 d

4 e

5 b

Task 2

1 b

2 d

3 a

4 c

Page 12

Task 1

Advantages of using open-ended questions include:

- The respondent is not restricted to choosing pre-set answers and can give their own answers in their own words.

- Compared to closed questions, the respondent can develop their answers in more depth.

Disadvantages of using open-ended questions include:

- Open-ended questions take longer to complete than closed questions.

- Respondents' answers are likely to vary so it will take more time for the researcher to analyse them.

Page 13

Task 2

1 Disadvantage

2 Advantage

3 Disadvantage

4 Advantage

5 Disadvantage

6 Advantage

7 Advantage

8 Disadvantage

Page 15

Task 1

1 e

2 d

3 h

4 g

5 c

6 i

7 f

8 a

9 j

10 b

Task 2

Advantages of participant observation

- A participant observer can study a group in its natural setting so participant observation (PO) is less artificial than standardized methods.

- PO can provide rich and detailed qualitative data.

- By participating, the researcher can see the world through the group member's eyes and develop a deeper understanding of the group and its behaviour.

- PO enables the researcher to develop a more valid or authentic picture of the topic.
- In some cases, PO may be the only method that could be used. For example, violent football supporters may not agree to be interviewed.

Disadvantages of participant observation

- It can be difficult for the researcher to gain entry to a group at the outset.
- It may be difficult to be accepted by the group members and to gain their trust.
- The researcher may find it difficult to make notes or record information and may have to rely on memory.
- The researcher may become too involved with the group. This could invalidate the findings if they are biased or one-sided.
- If the observer's known presence influences the group (the observer effect), this may invalidate the findings.
- PO can be relatively time consuming and expensive for the amount of data gathered.
- It would be difficult to repeat a PO study in order to check the reliability of the findings.

Task 3

a) Two advantages of non-participant observation are:

- As a non-participant, the researcher is less likely to be drawn into the group's activities (e.g. they would not be expected to take part in illegal activities).
- The researcher may be less influenced by their personal views on the group and its activities.

Two disadvantages of non-participant observation are:

- The researcher is less likely to see the world through the group's eyes.
- If group members change their behaviour because they know they are being observed (the observer effect), this may invalidate the findings.

b) Advantages of group interviews include the following:

- Through group interviews, the researcher can gather a wide range of views and experiences and build up a lot of rich information about a topic.

- Participants in group interviews can sometimes be recruited to take part in individual interviews at a later point in the research.
- Some interviewees may feel more comfortable when discussing their experiences in a group setting because they are supported by others in the group.

Disadvantages of group interviews include the following:

- Group interviews require a skilled interviewer who can keep the discussion going, encourage interviewees to 'open up' but be aware that the topics may be sensitive for some people.
- Some interviewees may dominate the discussion and, in this case, not everyone's voice will be heard. Others may feel intimidated in a group setting and prefer a one-to-one setting.
- In a group setting, the researcher cannot guarantee confidentiality or anonymity to the interviewees.

Page 17

Task 1

Sources of quantitative primary data: d), f).

Sources of qualitative primary data: a), h).

Sources of quantitative secondary data: e), g).

Sources of qualitative secondary data: b), c).

Task 2

1 b
2 c
3 f
4 d
5 a
6 g
7 e

Page 19

The following responses are all examples of answers that earned full marks.

(i) One ethical issue is ensuring that the welfare and wellbeing of research participants is taken into account when carrying out this research. Divorce is a sensitive topic for some people (e.g. people who have experienced divorce themselves and their family members). It would be important not to ask insensitive questions or questions that are too personal. Insensitive questions run the risk of upsetting or annoying the participants.

(ii) The secondary source I would use is official statistics on the numbers and rates of divorce in the United Kingdom since 1945. I would use this source because the information is reliable and up to date. Having statistical information about divorce would help to put my study into context and I could relate my study to what is happening in society. From this information, I could work out trends in divorce and then devise questions about social attitudes to these changes. So my questions would be informed ones rather than just off the top of my head.

(iii) I would use a questionnaire mainly because questionnaires are a good way of measuring people's attitudes towards issues like divorce. Questionnaires would be better than informal interviews for several reasons. Questionnaires would be cheaper and quicker for the amount of data collected. I could devise clearly worded, closed questions about attitudes to divorce and then survey a large representative sample of respondents. If I ask exactly the same questions, I could then compare the responses of men and women. By comparing, I could identify any similarities and differences in attitudes according to gender.

If I wanted to explore how people experience divorce, then informal interviews would be a good method to use. However, they would not be the best choice for measuring attitudes as they are usually used on a small sample, they cannot be replicated to check the reliability of findings and you cannot generalize from them.

Education

Page 21

Task 1

a) Home education.

b) Children from less-advantaged backgrounds.

Task 2

The student answer (on page 23) to question (d) earned 3 marks out of 4. The following is an example of a full-mark answer to this question.

Social cohesion refers to the 'glue' or the social bonds that unite the people in a particular society. In a society based on social cohesion, there may be different social groups (e.g. different classes, religious or ethnic groups) but these groups are likely to share an identity (e.g. all seeing themselves as British citizens). Without social cohesion, society could have more conflict between different groups.

The student answer (on page 25) to question (e) earned full marks so it should give you a good idea of the sort of information you would need to include in your own answer in order to get full marks.

The student answer (on page 24) to question (f) earned 3 marks out of 5. The following is an example of a full-mark answer to this question.

One type of school is a grammar school. Grammar schools are selective. Supporters say that they have advantages over comprehensive schools because they provide a challenging education that is suited to their pupils' ability and aptitudes. Grammar schools generally have an academic ethos and their exam results are, on average, better than those of non-selective schools. There is a strong emphasis on academic achievement and many pupils progress from grammar schools to universities.

Page 23

Task 1

1   d

2   f

3   a

4   c

5   b

6   e

Task 2

1　b

2　d

3　a

4　c

Page 25

Task 1

Reasons why some parents and carers want their children to attend faith schools

- Faith schools provide an education that complements the pupils' religion.
- Many faith schools have above average exam results.
- Parents may prefer the religious ethos and teaching in a faith school.
- Some supporters argue that faith schools produce individuals who have a strong sense of identity and self worth.

Criticisms of faith schools

- Faith schools segregate or divide children from different religions and discourage mixing.
- They work against social cohesion.
- The intake of many faith schools is not representative of the local population.
- Some may discriminate in their employment or promotion of staff on religious grounds.

Task 2

Reasons why some people support private education

- Private schools have an academic ethos and pupils tend to achieve exam results that are well above the national average.
- They offer good teaching and learning resources and small classes.
- They offer a wide range of extra-curricular activities e.g. related to music, sport or drama.
- There is a strong focus on careers guidance and progression to university.

Criticisms of private education

- Private schools are selective and only admit pupils who pass an entrance exam and/or whose parents can afford the school fees.
- They tend to recruit pupils from similar backgrounds and help to reproduce social inequality and class divisions.
- They can put pupils under a lot of pressure to compete and to perform well academically.
- Many of the teachers in private schools have been trained at the state's expense.

Page 29

Task 1

1 **Equal opportunities policies in education**

During the 1980s, many schools developed equal opportunities policies to try to address gender inequalities and discrimination in schools. This raised awareness of gender issues in education.

2 **Anti-discrimination laws**

Legislation such as the Sex Discrimination Act (1975) meant that schools could no longer discriminate on the basis of gender. Practices such as lining up girls and boys separately and having separate lists of girls' and boys' names on school registers were phased out.

3 **The impact of feminism**

Attitudes to gender roles generally and to girls' education in particular have changed. Girls are no longer expected to see marriage and motherhood as their main goals in life.

4 **The National Curriculum**

Before the introduction of the National Curriculum, girls tended to specialize in some subjects and boys in others at 14 and beyond. With the introduction of the National Curriculum in the late 1980s, pupils could no longer opt out of science subjects at 14. This helped to raise girls' achievements in science and opened up career opportunities for females.

Task 2

1　b

2　c

3　a

Task 3

The following responses are examples of answers that earned full marks.

a) Some pupils may belong to a peer group that celebrates laddish or ladette culture and that sees working hard at school as 'uncool'. This may discourage group members from making a visible effort to work or to revise for exams. These pupils may develop anti-learning attitudes in order to fit in with the peer group and, as a result, they could underachieve in their GCSEs.

b) Institutional racism occurs when an institution (such as a school or a hospital) does not provide an appropriate service to people (e.g. some pupils, parents or patients) because of their ethnicity, culture or colour. It is an unintentional result of the way the institution is organized.

Page 31

The following response is an example of an answer that earned full marks.

The education system in Britain today has several important functions or roles. According to the functionalist approach, one of its functions is to serve the needs of the economy. In this answer, I will discuss whether serving the needs of the economy is the most important function.

The global economy today is very competitive and needs a highly skilled and well-educated workforce. The education system serves this need by teaching young people the academic and vocational skills they will require when they join the workforce.

The education system is increasingly involved in trying to develop social cohesion and encouraging a sense of 'Britishness' among pupils. It does this, for example, through citizenship education which is now taught in schools.

The education system also performs the function of secondary socialization and is expected to facilitate social mobility. However, some critics argue that young people are not being adequately socialized in schools and that there is little long-range social mobility in Britain today.

The Marxist approach sees the role of the education system differently. Education is seen as serving the needs of capitalism by breeding competition and operating in the interests of the ruling class.

To conclude, some functionalist sociologists would agree that the economic function is the most important. Others would emphasize the increasing importance of promoting social cohesion or social mobility. However, Marxist approaches would see the education system as serving the needs of the capitalist economy. So this means that sociologists do not agree on this issue.

Families

Page 33

Task 1

   a) 37 116

   b) 71 per cent

Task 2

The student answer (on page 35) to question (c) earned 1 mark out of 2. The following is an example of a full-mark answer to this question.

One reason is that people are living longer so there are now more households containing older people (often widows) living alone. Another reason is that there are now more households containing younger people under retirement age who live alone e.g. in a flat.

The student answer (on page 41) to question (e) earned full marks.

The student answer (on page 43) to question (g)(i) earned 7 marks out of 12. The following is an example of a full-mark answer to this question.

There are several reasons for the increase in divorce (the legal termination of a marriage) since the end of the Second World War. In this answer, I will discuss whether the most important reason is changing attitudes.

Social attitudes have changed to a great extent since 1945. For example, there is now less social stigma attached to divorce and it is much more acceptable to divorce, remarry and divorce again.

Changing attitudes have gone hand in hand with changes in divorce laws. Today, people can get a divorce based on irretrievable breakdown of marriage and divorce is now a lot easier, cheaper and quicker to obtain. At the same time, secularization (the decline in the influence of religion in society) has removed the religious barrier to divorce for many people. On the other hand, people who follow a religion may disapprove of divorce so it is difficult to generalize about changing attitudes in a culturally diverse society such as Britain.

One key reason is the impact of the feminist movement since the 1960s. Attitudes to gender have changed and many women are now financially independent. As a result, they are no longer prepared to stay in an unhappy marriage.

However, feminist approaches question how far women have achieved financial independence. For example, after divorce, many female headed lone-parent families are at risk of poverty.

In conclusion, this discussion has identified several important reasons for the general increase in divorce since 1945. The different factors are linked together and it is difficult to say which, if any, is the most important.

Page 35

1. Incorrect. Correct = unrelated
2. Correct
3. Incorrect. Correct = together
4. Correct
5. Incorrect. Correct = homosexual/gay couple
6. Correct
7. Incorrect. Correct = one parent lives
8. Correct

Page 37

Task 1

1. Similarities between the functionalist and the New Right approaches include the following:
   - Both approaches see the nuclear family as the family type that works best in meeting the needs of society.
   - Both see the nuclear family as the family type that works best in meeting the needs of children.
   - Both approaches tend to support the idea of traditional gender roles with women performing the caring role and men performing the breadwinner/main earner role.

2. Similarities between the Marxist and feminist approaches include the following:
   - Both approaches are critical of the role of the family in society.
   - Both see the family as a source of oppression.

3. Differences between the functionalist and Marxist views include the following:
   - The functionalist approach sees the nuclear family as playing a positive role in society while the Marxist approach is critical of the nuclear family.
   - The functionalist approach sees the family as meeting the needs of its members while the Marxist approach sees the family as oppressing its members.

4. Differences between the New Right and the feminist views include the following:
   - The New Right view tends to support the idea of having traditional gender roles in the family while the feminist approach challenges traditional gender roles.
   - The feminist approach is critical of the nuclear family while the New Right approach supports the nuclear family and family values.

Task 2

The following is an example of a full-mark answer to this question.

The term gender refers to masculinity and femininity. Gender socialization describes the process through which people acquire their gender identity and learn how society expects them to behave in order to conform to masculine and feminine behaviour. The family is a key agency of gender socialization. For example, from birth, babies are dressed differently, given different toys and names according to their gender.

Page 39

Task 1

The following is an example of a full-mark answer to this question.

The term 'family' refers to a couple who are married, civil partners or living together, with or without any children, or a lone parent with a child or children. When sociologists study the roles of men and women in families, they look at who does tasks such as housework and childcare.

In the 1960s, gender roles in families were more traditional than they are today. Men were more likely to be the breadwinner or main earner while women had the main responsibility for housework and childcare, even if they had paid employment.

In the 1970s, Young and Willmott found that the symmetrical family was typical in Britain. In this family type, conjugal roles were becoming more equal. Decision making was also more likely to be shared. However, feminist sociologists disagreed with the way Young and Willmott interpreted their findings and argued that they exaggerated the changes.

In 2008, Gatrell's research showed that many fathers in dual-worker couples now played a bigger role in their children's lives compared with the past. So the role of fathers in families has changed.

Some sociologists suggest that gender roles in families have changed due to factors such as the availability of contraception. This gives women control over their fertility and helps them to combine motherhood and a career. Other factors are the impact of the women's movement since the 1960s.

Feminist sociologists question whether gender roles in families have changed significantly since the 1960s. Crompton and Lyonette argue that attitudes to gender roles have changed but men's actual participation in household tasks has not changed much.

To conclude, sociologists would agree that gender roles in families have changed since the 1960s. However, they would not necessarily describe the changes as significant. It may be that attitudes to gender roles have changed significantly but men's participation has lagged behind.

Task 2

1 d

2 h

3 e

4 g

5 a

6 j

7 b

8 i

9 c

10 f

Page 41

Task 1

The following is an example of a full-mark answer to this question.

In a population that is ageing, the proportion of people over retirement age is gradually increasing over time. In 2007, the proportion of the UK population aged under 16 dropped below the proportion over state pension age (60 for women and 65 for men) for the first time. This ageing of the population is linked to past changes in birth rates and death rates.

Task 2

The social consequences of an ageing population include the following:

- An increase in one-person households containing older females who have outlived their husbands.
- An increase in multigenerational or 'beanpole' families.
- The need to provide support to some older people e.g. help with daily tasks. In practice, female relatives and neighbours are most likely to supply this informal support.
- The need to provide local authority care home services e.g. to older people who are frail.
- A possible rise in social exclusion among older people.

Page 43

1 increased

2 increased

3 increased

4 increased

5 decreased

6 decreased

7 increased

8 increased

9 increased

10 decreased

Crime and Deviance

Page 47

Task 1

   a) 1 per cent
   b) 10 200 000

Task 2

The student answers to questions (c), (d), (e) and (f) (on pages 49, 48, 57 and 53 respectively) earned full marks.

The student answer (on page 55) to question (g)(ii) earned 11 marks out of 12. The following is an example of a full-mark answer to this question.

A criminal offence is any act (such as shoplifting or fraud) that breaks the criminal law. According to police recorded crime statistics, females are much less likely to commit crimes than males. For example, in 2007, 1 per cent of females and 5.2 per cent of males aged 20 were found guilty of, or cautioned for, serious criminal offences in England and Wales.

One explanation for why females appear less likely than males to commit crime is gender socialization. Females are socialized to be passive so they are less likely than young males to engage in violent crime. Other explanations include the view that females experience less peer pressure than males to engage in criminal or antisocial behaviour or they have fewer opportunities to offend because they are supervised by parents more closely than boys.

Some sociologists argue that due to the chivalry effect, women are treated less harshly than men within the criminal justice system. So it may be that females who conform to gender stereotypes (e.g. dressing in a feminine way and appearing upset) are less likely to be arrested, charged, prosecuted and found guilty than males.

Some sociologists question the validity of the official statistics and argue that they do not give a true account of female and male involvement in crime. Also, sociologists argue that the official statistics are socially constructed and reflect the actions of witnesses, police officers and jurors. These people may unintentionally respond in sexist ways e.g. assuming that a female is unlikely to be involved in gang-related violence.

The recent statistics show that females are increasingly likely to be found guilty of, or cautioned for, criminal offences. This may be because the chivalry effect is not so widespread today.

In conclusion, most sociologists would accept that females are less likely to commit criminal offences than males, but they would also agree that women are increasingly likely to commit offences. At the same time, sociologists would not take the official statistics at face value.

Page 49

Task 1

   1 c
   2 a
   3 b

Task 2

The following is an example of a full-mark answer to this question.

One way is through peer pressure when a group exerts social pressure on its members to conform to the group's norms. Another way is through the rewards and punishments that some parents use to encourage their children to behave appropriately.

Page 51

The following is an example of a full-mark answer to this question.

Deviance refers to behaviour that does not conform to social norms while criminal behaviour refers to illegal activities. The term 'peer group pressure' refers to the social pressure that a group puts on its members to encourage them to conform to group norms.

Subcultural theories explain crime and deviance among young people in terms of peer pressure. For example, research has shown that boys and young men get involved in vandalism or 'joy riding' after joining a group in which this is done. Some sociologists argue that working-class boys are denied status within the school system and join a deviant subculture to gain status and a sense of identity.

Other sociologists explain deviant and criminal behaviour among young people in terms of inadequate socialization within families. In this view, young people's involvement in crime and deviance is linked to parental failure to take responsibility for teaching the norms of society.

Schools are also seen as failing to socialize young people into society's norms. Pupils who experience peer pressure to conform to the norms of a street culture may behave in deviant ways at school.

Labelling theory puts more emphasis on the labelling of working-class youth within the criminal justice system. In this view, being labelled a criminal or deviant may not be entirely due to the behaviour of the members of a peer group. It is also linked to the reaction of the police and other officials to particular peer groups such as hoodies.

To sum up, some sociologists see deviant and criminal behaviour as due to peer group pressure and this research tends to focus on crime and deviance among young working-class males. Feminist approaches argue that girls are often left out of such research. Sociologists recognize that the causes of youth crime and deviance are complex and that, although peer pressure is an important factor, it is important to consider a range of factors such as socialization and labelling processes.

Page 53

Task 1

The following is an example of a full-mark answer to this question.

The term white-collar crime refers to criminal offences that are carried out at work by middle-class people in white collar or professional jobs. White-collar crime is non-violent and is usually done for personal gain. Examples include expense account fraud, using your position within a bank to steal money or using your position within a business for money laundering.

Task 2

a) Advantages of official police-recorded crime statistics include:

- They are a readily available and cheap source of secondary data.
- They provide a wealth of statistical information on recorded crime rates.
- It is possible to identify long-term trends in recorded crime rates.

Disadvantages of official police-recorded crime statistics include:

- They are based on recorded crimes and exclude crimes that are not discovered, not reported or not recorded.
- They are the end result of a series of decisions made by people such as witnesses, victims and police officers. As such, they do not provide a valid or true picture of crime levels.

b) Advantages of victim surveys include:

- They provide statistical information on some crimes that are not reported to the police.
- They provide valuable information about people's experiences of crime.
- The British Crime Survey (BCS) is carried out each year so it provides useful information on trends over time.

Disadvantages of victim surveys include:

- Surveys such as the BCS do not cover all crimes recorded by the police. For example, they exclude 'victimless' crimes.
- The BCS is a household survey so it does not question any homeless people or those who live in institutions such as prisons.
- Respondents may not tell the truth about their experiences of being a victim of crime.

c) Advantages of self-report studies include:

- They provide information on offenders who are not necessarily dealt with by the police or courts.
- They provide information on offences that are not necessarily dealt with by the police or courts.

Disadvantages of self-report studies include:

- The Offending, Crime and Justice Survey (OCJS) is a household survey so it does not question homeless people or those who live in institutions such as prisons.
- Respondents may not tell the truth about their involvement in crime e.g. they may exaggerate or they may not admit to some offences.

Page 55

The following is an example of a full-mark answer to this question.

The chivalry effect refers to the more lenient treatment of women within the criminal justice system. The idea behind it is that female offenders who conform to gender stereotypes (e.g. by wearing a dress and some – but not too much – make-up in court) are treated less harshly than men. The chivalry effect is said to apply during the reporting of crimes, police response, trial and sentencing.

Page 57

1 b

2 c

3 a

Page 59

Task 1

a) 61 per cent

b) Either men like to look at women or men like cars, gadgets and sport.

Task 2

The student answers to (c), (d), (e) and (f) (on pages 62, 60, 65 and 67 respectively) earned full marks.

The student answer (on page 69) to question (g)(ii) earned 10 marks out of 12. The following is an example of a full-mark answer to this question.

The 'mass media' refer to the means of mass communication such as television and magazines. The term 'gender roles' refers to the social roles that are associated with masculinity and femininity.

One view is that while the media presented stereotypical images of gender roles in the 1960s and 1970s, gender roles are presented realistically today. However, feminist approaches question how far the media present gender roles in ways that reflect the reality. Men's magazines, for example, project unrealistic images of women and men that are often narrow and stereotypical. Other media, such as the quality press, may present more realistic images of gender roles that reflect the reality of people's lives today.

Recent research by Cumberbatch and his colleagues shows a gap between gender as represented on television and the reality in modern Britain. The findings show that women are under-represented on television today with only one female appearing on the screen for every two males. Men have 65 per cent of all possible roles that are broadcast on TV and they are much more likely than women to participate in factual and news programmes. This finding suggests that women are seen as less suited to appearing on serious programmes. By contrast, almost half of the roles in soap operas are female roles.

This research also identifies a link between ageism and sexism in that 60 per cent of men but only 40 per cent of women shown on TV are aged over 40.

Although it is difficult to generalize about all media, the recent research evidence suggests that some media (e.g. television and 'lads' mags') continue to represent gender roles in unrealistic ways and that there is a gap between what we see on the TV screen and the reality.

Page 61

1 Incorrect. Correct = terrestrial.

2 Correct.

Page 63

1 Possible criticisms include:

- It views the audience members as more passive than they are.

- Much of the early research was based on laboratory experiments on people but labs are artificial environments so the findings will not necessarily tell us how people behave in the real world.

2 Possible differences include:

- The hypodermic syringe approach sees audience members as passively accepting messages from the media while the decoding approach sees audience members as actively interpreting these messages.

- The decoding approach sees people as members of social and cultural groups while the hypodermic syringe approach sees them more as isolated individuals.

3 Possible issues are:

- Whether the media can provoke copycat violence – this has caused public concern because: adults worry about the effect of media violence on children; some films have been directly associated with real-life violence; the media itself may fuel a moral panic about this issue.

- Young people's use of social networking sites – this has caused concern because: parents worry about children and young people being taken in by adults who pose as teenagers; media reporting may fuel a moral panic about this issue.

Page 65

News values – news values (ideas about what topics are considered newsworthy) influence the content of newspapers because editors allocate more staff, space and time to cover topics that are seen as newsworthy.

The profit motive – newspapers operate in a competitive environment and, if they do not generate sufficient profits, they risk bankruptcy. So the content will reflect the desire to maximize sales figures and profits.

Advertisers – advertisers are a key source of income for newspapers. Advertisers may influence the content of the press in that they could switch to another newspaper if they disagree with a newspaper's stand on a particular issue.

The state – in Britain, freedom of the press is highly valued and state censorship does not take place. However, during national emergencies and wars, governments may try to influence media coverage.

The law – the laws of libel apply to the content of newspapers.

Page 67

1 b

2 g

3 e

4 c

5 d

6 h

7 a

8 i

9 f

Page 69

1 d

2 c

3 a

4 e

5 f

6 b

Power

Page 71

Task 1

a) 48 per cent

b) A demonstration/rally/protest.

Task 2

The student answer (on page 78) to question (c) earned full marks.

The student answer (on page 73) to question (d) earned 2 marks out of 4. The following is an example of a full-mark answer to this question.

Individuals or groups enter power relationships with other people when they try to influence or control the way other people behave. A power relationship may be based on authority in which case one person is authorized to exercise power over another, e.g. a senior manager in the workplace. A power relationship may also be based on coercion in which case one person (e.g. a kidnapper) uses threats or force to get someone to do something.

The student answer (on page 77) to question (g)(i) earned 7 marks out of 12. The following is an example of a full-mark answer to this question.

One view is that social class is becoming less important in influencing voting behaviour and political attitudes such as views on trade union membership. In this answer, I will discuss whether age and ethnicity are now more important influences than class.

Traditionally, there was an alignment between class, voting behaviour and attitudes. People in working-class jobs were more likely to vote Labour and support trade unions while people in middle class occupations were more likely to vote Conservative. However, there were always exceptions to this such as 'working-class Tories' and middle-class trade union supporters.

Some sociologists argue that social class is no longer a good predictor of voting behaviour and political attitudes. The terms 'class dealignment' refers to the weakening of the ties between class and voting behaviour. In the 2005 general election, for example, Labour gained support from a large section of what used to be the Conservative core vote.

Another view is that not much has changed and in 2005, a higher proportion of the working class voted Labour rather than Conservative and a higher proportion of the middle class voted Conservative rather than Labour.

Traditionally, younger people have been more likely to vote Labour and older people have been more likely to vote Conservative. In 2005, the link between age and voting persisted as Labour led the Conservatives in all age groups except people over 55. Young people are traditionally seen as more likely to have radical political attitudes than older people.

The Labour party has traditionally received support from minority ethnic voters. However, some sociologists explain this support in terms of social class.

In summary, sociologists disagree on whether social class now has less influence on political attitudes and voting. Marxists approaches, for example, would see social class as influential. Sociologists would not necessarily agree that age and ethnicity are now more influential than class.

Page 73

Task 1

1 **Traditional authority**

In some cases, people accept an individual or group's authority because it is customary to do so. In the UK, for example, the monarch (king or queen) exercises authority based on hundreds of years of tradition.

2 **Legal rational authority**

In this case, people obey an individual or a group (such as an elected president or the senior managers in a workplace) because of the position they hold within an organization.

3 **Charismatic authority**

With this form of authority, people obey an inspirational individual with extraordinary personal qualities who can get others to go along with his or her wishes.

4 **The state**

The various institutions (such as Parliament, the civil service, the police force and the courts) that organize and regulate society by making, implementing and enforcing laws.

Task 2

1 **Who holds power in society?**

The pluralist approach:
A range of groups with different interests exists in society. Political power is shared between these groups. No single group gets its own way on every issue.

The Marxist approach:
The people who hold powerful positions within the state and in society come from a narrow range of social and educational backgrounds. Typically, they are from privileged backgrounds.

2 **Is power concentrated or spread evenly through society?**

The pluralist approach:
Power is spread evenly throughout society.

The Marxist approach:
Power is concentrated in the hands of the bourgeoisie/ruling class.

3 **Whose interests does the state represent?**

The pluralist approach:
The state acts as a neutral referee and represents the interests of all social groups without taking sides.

The Marxist approach:
The state represents and protects the interests of the bourgeoisie/ruling class.

Page 75

Task 1

1 c

2 f

3 a

4 d

5 b

6 g

7 e

Task 2

a) Protective groups want to protect or defend their members' interests. Examples include trade unions such as the National Union of Teachers and professional associations such as the Law Society. Promotional groups want to promote a particular cause rather than represent their members' interests. Examples include the Child Poverty Action Group and Greenpeace.

b) According to the pluralist approach, pressure groups ensure that the different interests in society are all represented in the decision-making process and that power is spread out widely in society. The conflict view argues that some groups are able to dominate the decision-making process and that power is concentrated in a few hands rather than spread out widely.

c) One problem is that when the term 'political' is used in social surveys, it may mean different things to different respondents. Some people think of politics in terms of official party politics rather than in terms of involvement in consumer boycotts or pressure groups.

Another problem is that some surveys focus on involvement in trade unions or parents' associations and do not ask about the sorts of activities that young people are likely to be involved in. As a result, these surveys may underestimate young people's participation in the political process.

Page 77

Pressure groups aim to influence government policy but they do not aim to form a government. Political parties aim to form a government and govern the country.

Pressure groups tend to focus on one issue or a set of related issues (e.g. the environment and global warming). Political parties have policies on a wide range of issues including defence, the economy, education and criminal justice.

Page 79

1 d

2 c

3 a

4 b

Page 81

1 d

2 f

3 a

4 e

5 g

6 c

7 b

Social Inequality

Page 83

Task 1

a) 15 per cent

b) Child poverty

Task 2

The student answers to these questions all earned full marks so they should give you a good idea of the sort of information you would need to include in your own answers in order to get full marks.

Page 85

Task 1

1 c

2 d

3 e

4 a

5 b

Task 2

1 **What is stratification based on?**

Social class: Economic factors such as occupation and income (how people earn a living).

Slavery: Some individuals claim that they have the right to own and sell other people, to treat them as property and to deny them their human rights.

2 **Is status achieved or ascribed?**

Social class: Achieved

Slavery: Status was ascribed in the southern states of the USA for the people who were born into slavery.

3 **Is social mobility possible?**

Social class: Yes

Slavery: For many slaves in the southern states of the USA, social mobility was unlikely unless, for example, they escaped to safety or until slavery was abolished.

Page 87

1 Similarities include:

- they both saw class as an important division in society
- they both saw class as based on economic factors such as wealth.

Differences include:

- Marx identified two main social classes in society (the bourgeoisie and the proletariat) while Weber identified four main classes (property owners, professionals, the petty bourgeoisie and the working class).
- Marx stressed the importance of class while Weber stressed the importance of status and power as well as class.

2 One similarity is that they both take account of occupation when allocating people to a social class.

One difference is that the NS-SEC takes into account rewards (such as pay), employment status (such as whether someone is an employer, self-employed or an employee) and levels of authority and control (such as whether someone supervises other workers). The Registrar General's scale does not take these factors into account when allocating individuals to a social class.

Page 89

1 e

2 g

3 d

4 f

5 h

6 b

7 a

8 c

Page 91

1 Possible reasons include: women, on average, earn less than men because they are more likely to work in low paid jobs and to work part-time; in general, women live longer than men so there are more older female pensioners living alone; women are less likely than men to have an income from an occupational pension;

women are more likely than men to head lone-parent families which often have to live on low incomes.

2   Possible reasons include: racism and discrimination in the labour market; members of some minority ethnic groups are more likely to experience unemployment; members of some minority ethnic groups are less likely to take up the welfare state assistance to which they are entitled; members of some minority ethnic groups are more likely to live in low income households.

3   Possible reasons include living on a low income such as a state retirement pension and not claiming the benefits to which they are entitled.

Page 93

1   structural = correct

2   label and blame = correct

Page 95

Task 1

1   h

2   c

3   a

4   f

5   b

6   g

7   d

8   e

Task 2

Inter-generational mobility occurs when an individual enters a different strata from his or her parents (e.g. they end up in a different social class to their parents); it refers to movement between the generations of a family rather than over the course of an individual's life.

Intra-generational mobility occurs when an individual moves up or down between the layers of a stratification system (e.g. between social classes) over the course of their life.

GCSE
Sociology
AQA

Exam practice workbook

Pauline Wilson

How to use this workbook

How the workbook is organized

This exam practice workbook is designed to help you to prepare for the AQA GCSE Sociology exam. It gives you lots of practice at answering questions that are written in a similar style to the AQA exam questions. Hopefully, the workbook will show that you are 'on the right lines' as well as highlight some areas in which you might be able to improve.

The workbook contains exam-style questions covering both Unit 1 and Unit 2 of the AQA GCSE Sociology specification. It links closely to the pattern of the exam. If you are taking the Short Course, you will sit Paper 1. If you are taking the Full Course, you will sit both Paper 1 and Paper 2.

Sociology (Short Course) Unit 1

Paper 1   Section A: Studying Society

  1 hour and 30 minutes   Section B: Education

  100% of the total marks   Section C: Families

Answer all questions in all three sections.

Sociology (Full Course) Unit 1 plus Unit 2

Paper 1   Section A: Studying Society

  1 hour and 30 minutes   Section B: Education

  50% of the total marks   Section C: Families

Answer all questions in all three sections.

Paper 2   Section A: Crime and Deviance

  1 hour and 30 minutes   Section B: Mass Media

  50% of the total marks   Section C: Power

                              Section D: Social Inequality

Choose three sections from the four options and answer all questions in each of the three chosen sections.

There are seven sets of questions in the exam practice workbook. Each set of questions covers one area of the AQA GCSE Sociology specification:

Paper 1: Studying Society (pages 120–127)

          Education (pages 128–135)

          Families (pages 136–143)

Paper 2: Crime and Deviance (pages 144–151)

          Mass Media (pages 152–159)

          Power (pages 160–167)

          Social Inequality (pages 168–175)

Each set of questions contains two exam-style questions.

If you are doing the Short Course, you should answer the questions relating to Paper 1. If you are doing the Full Course, you should answer the questions relating to Paper 2 as well as those relating to Paper 1.

How to get the most from this workbook

Once you have revised a particular area of the specification (such as Studying Society or Crime and Deviance), test yourself by working through the workbook questions on this area.

You will get the most from the workbook by answering as many questions as possible under timed conditions. If you practise answering complete questions in 30 minutes, this will give you valuable experience of managing your time to:

• read the Items and the questions carefully

• plan your extended answers

• write answers of the right length for the marks available

• read through and, if necessary, improve your answers.

Try to remember the examiner's tips and the other advice contained in the revision guide and apply them when answering the questions in the workbook. For example, remember to study the command words in a question and respond to them in your answer.

When you have answered a complete question, read through your answers and make any necessary changes to them. Then check your answers using the Answers section at the back of this book (see pages 193–208). In this section, different types of answer are provided depending on the question:

• Some questions require you to pick out information from the Items. There are usually only one or two possible answers to this type of question and these are provided so that you can check whether your own response is correct.

• Other questions have several possible answers. The answers to these are presented as a checklist of the points that you could include in your responses.

• An extended-answer question can be addressed in several different ways, although good responses to this type of question should contain an introduction, a main body and a conclusion. The answers to extended-answer questions are presented as a checklist of the points that you could include in your own introduction, main body and conclusion.

As you work through the questions, you can check how well you are doing by referring to the Answers. Try not to look at the answer to a particular question before you have completed it. You will get much more from the workbook by writing your own responses to the questions and checking them against the answers provided rather than by just reading through these answers.

As you check your own responses, it is important to ensure that you understand how you could improve them. For example, you may have identified some gaps in your knowledge and understanding of a particular topic. If this is the case, then you should make a note of any gaps in your knowledge and revise this topic again.

Remember that the examination is not simply a test of your knowledge of the subject content (AO1). It also tests your skills of application (AO2) and interpretation, analysis and evaluation (AO3). For example, you may have noted that you did not fully demonstrate your evaluation skills in one of your responses to an extended-answer question. If this is the case, you should aim to develop your evaluation skills when you work on other extended-answer questions in the workbook. In your subsequent answers, try to assess sociological explanations more fully, identify criticisms of these explanations and try to reach a balanced conclusion to your discussion.

In this section of the Workbook, there are two exam-style questions on Studying Society. Once you have worked through the revision chapter on Studying Society, you should be ready to answer these questions. You could start by answering Question 1, and then check your answers before moving on to Question 2.

When you are answering each question, give yourself 30 minutes to complete your response because this is the amount of time you should spend on the Studying Society question in the exam. Answering these questions under timed conditions will help you to prepare for the exam by giving you practice in managing your time.

Studying Society Question 1

Answer **all** questions from this section.

Total for this question: 30 marks.

Study **Items A**, **B** and **C** and then answer parts (a) to (e).

ITEM A

Percentage of pupils aged 16 who had finished Year 11 and who stayed on in full-time education in 2007: according to their parents' occupations.

England *Occupations of parents*	*Stayed on in full-time education (%)*
Higher professional occupations	86
Lower professional occupations	81
Intermediate occupations	71
Lower supervisory occupations	63
Routine occupations	62

Source: adapted from Table 3.8, *Social Trends 39*, 2009, page 34. Office for National Statistics © Crown Copyright

ITEM B

ITEM C

Psychology is sometimes referred to as the 'science of the mind'. Some of the differences between sociology and psychology can be seen in the ways they study prejudice. Psychologists might explain prejudice in terms of factors related to an individual, such as their personality. By contrast, sociologists would focus on the role of social structures (such as families and peer groups) and social processes (such as primary socialization or peer group pressure).

(a) From **Item A**, what percentage of pupils with parents in routine occupations stayed on in full-time education in 2007?

_____

_____ *(1 mark)*

(b) (i) From **Item B**, identify **one** method of research that is shown in the photograph.

_____

_____ *(1 mark)*

(ii) Outline **one** strength and **one** limitation of the method of research that you have identified from Item B.

_____

_____

_____

_____ *(2 marks)*

(c) (i) Study **Item C**. Describe how the sociological approach to studying people differs from the psychological approach.

_____

_____

_____

_____

_____

_____

_____ *(4 marks)*

(ii) Explain what sociologists mean by peer group pressure.

_____

_____

_____

_____

_____

_____

_____ *(4 marks)*

(d) Explain **one** way in which the findings from sociological research might help governments to develop policies to reduce racial discrimination in Britain.

_____

_____

_____

_____

_____

_____

_____ *(4 marks)*

(e) As a sociologist, you have been asked to carry out a study to investigate young people's experiences of transferring from their secondary school to a local sixth form college.

Continued

(i) Identify and explain **one** possible ethical issue that you might need to address while you are carrying out your research.

_____

_____

_____

_____

_____

_____

_____ *(4 marks)*

(ii) Identify **one** secondary source of information that you would use in your study **and** explain why you would use this source.

_____

_____

_____

_____

_____

_____

_____ *(4 marks)*

(iii) Identify **one** primary method of research that you would use in your study **and** explain why this method would be better than another primary method for collecting the data that you need.

_____

_____

_____

_____

_____

_____

_____

_____

_____ *(6 marks)*

Answer **all** questions from this section.

Total for this question: 30 marks.

Study **Items D**, **E** and **F** and then answer parts (a) to (e).

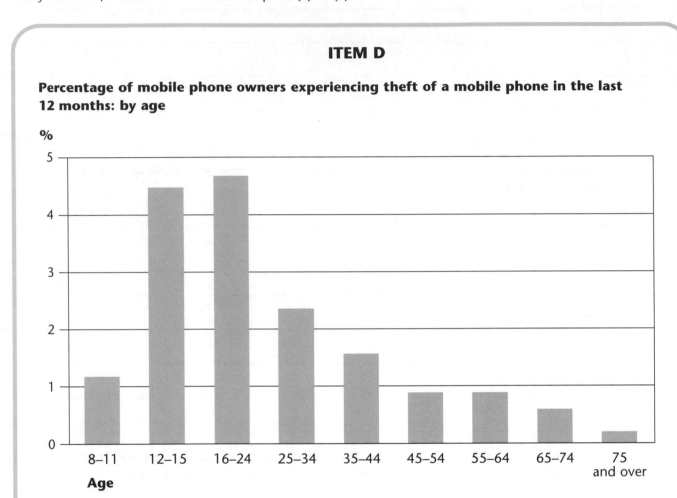

ITEM D

Percentage of mobile phone owners experiencing theft of a mobile phone in the last 12 months: by age

Source: adapted from Figure 9.5, *Social Trends 39*, 2009, page 131. Office for National Statistics © Crown Copyright

ITEM E

In a sociological study, data may be collected by using one or more primary methods of research such as structured interviews and postal questionnaires. Rather than carrying out interviews with, or sending questionnaires to, the whole population, researchers often select a sample. Simple random sampling and snowball sampling are examples of the different sampling techniques that researchers might use.

ITEM F

Some journalists write for newspapers or for the internet. Others report the daily news on television broadcasts. As part of their work, journalists may undertake research in order to report on social issues such as unemployment, girl gangs, changes in families or the impact of crime on communities. Sociologists are also interested in social issues such as these and carry out research to explore these issues. However, there are important differences between sociologists and journalists in the way they approach their research.

(a) From **Item D**, which age group was most likely to experience mobile phone theft?

_____

_____ *(1 mark)*

(b) (i) From **Item E**, identify **one** example of a sampling technique.

_____

_____ *(1 mark)*

(ii) Outline **one** advantage and **one** disadvantage of the sampling technique that you have identified in question (b) part (i).

_____

_____

_____

_____ *(2 marks)*

(c) (i) Study **Item F**. Describe the difference between sociological and journalistic approaches to gathering information about social issues.

_____

_____

_____

_____

_____

_____

_____

_____ *(4 marks)*

(ii) Explain what sociologists mean by age discrimination.

_____

_____

_____

_____

_____

_____

_____ *(4 marks)*

(d) Explain **one** way in which the findings from sociological research might help governments to develop policies to reduce antisocial behaviour in Britain.

_____

_____

_____

_____

_____

_____

_____

_____ *(4 marks)*

(e) As a sociologist, you have been asked to carry out a study to investigate attitudes towards faith schools among parents from different ethnic groups in one local authority.

(i) Identify and explain **one** possible ethical issue that you might need to address while you are carrying out your research.

_____

_____

_____

_____

_____

_____

_____ *(4 marks)*

(ii) Identify **one** secondary source of information that you would use in your study **and** explain why you would use this source.

_____

_____

_____

_____

_____

_____

_____

_____ *(4 marks)*

(iii) Identify **one** primary method of research that you would use in your study **and** explain why this method would be better than another primary method for collecting the data that you need.

_____

_____

_____

_____

_____

_____

_____

_____

_____

_____

_____ *(6 marks)*

Paper 1 Section B: Education

In this section of the Workbook, there are two exam-style questions on Education. Once you have worked through the revision chapter on Education, you should be ready to answer these questions. You could start by answering Question 1, and then check your answers before moving on to Question 2.

When you are answering each question, give yourself 30 minutes to complete your response because this is the amount of time you should spend on the Education question in the exam. Answering these questions under timed conditions will help you to prepare for the exam by giving you practice in managing your time.

Education Question 1

Answer **all** questions from this section.

Total for this question: 30 marks.

Study **Items A** and **B** and then answer parts (a) to (g).

ITEM A

Types of school	Number of schools (United Kingdom 2007–08)
Public sector mainstream schools	
Nursery schools	3 273
Primary schools	21 768
State-funded secondary schools	
Comprehensive	3 304
Selective	233
Modern	172
City technology colleges	5
Academies	83
Special schools (maintained and non-maintained)	1 378

Source: adapted from Table 3.3, *Social Trends 39*, 2009, page 30. Office for National Statistics © Crown Copyright

---

ITEM B

Pupils' achievements at GCSE tend to vary according to the occupations of their parents. In England, for example:

- 81 per cent of pupils whose parents worked in higher professional occupations (such as doctors and lawyers) achieved five or more GCSE grades A* to C in 2006.
- 42 per cent of pupils whose parents worked in routine occupations achieved five or more GCSE grades A* to C in 2006.

However, the achievements of pupils with parents in routine occupations increased by 16 percentage points between 1999 and 2006. By contrast, the achievements of pupils with parents in higher professional occupations increased by only six percentage points.

(a) From **Item A**, identify **one** type of secondary school.

_____

_____ *(1 mark)*

(b) From **Item B**, what percentage of pupils with parents in routine occupations achieved five or more GCSE grades A* to C in 2006?

_____

_____ *(1 mark)*

(c) Identify **two** reasons why some parents of children with special educational needs (SENs) may want their children to be educated in a special school rather than a mainstream school.

_____

_____

_____

_____ *(2 marks)*

(d) Explain what sociologists mean by the hidden curriculum.

_____

_____

_____

_____

_____

_____

_____ *(4 marks)*

(e) Describe **one** way in which British governments have tried to increase competition between schools over the last 30 years **and** explain why they have tried to do this.

_____

_____

_____

_____

_____

_____

_____

_____

_____ _(5 marks)_

(f) Describe **one** feature of a school's ethos **and** explain how this might influence the educational achievements of the pupils who attend that school.

_____

_____

_____

_____

_____

_____

_____

_____

_____ _(5 marks)_

(g) **EITHER**

(i) Discuss how far sociologists would agree that gender is the most significant influence on pupils' educational achievements in Britain today.

OR

(ii) Discuss how far sociologists would agree that the most important function of the education system in Britain today is to encourage social cohesion.

_____

_____

_____

_____

_____

_____

_____

_____

_____

_____

_____

_____

_____

_____

_____

_____

_____

_____

_____

_____

_____

_____ *(12 marks)*

Continue on lined paper if necessary

Answer **all** questions from this section.

Total for this question: 30 marks.

Study **Items C** and **D** and then answer parts (a) to (g).

ITEM C

The percentage of pupils who are entitled to receive free school meals and the percentage who actually take up free school meals. United Kingdom 2007–08

State-funded nursery and primary schools	%
Pupils entitled to have free school meals	15.8
Pupils taking free school meals	13.2

State-funded secondary schools	%
Pupils entitled to have free school meals	13.3
Pupils taking free school meals	9.8

Source: adapted from Table 3.7, *Social Trends 39*, 2009, page 33. Office for National Statistics © Crown Copyright

---

ITEM D

In the UK, the majority of schoolchildren attend state-funded schools. However, the independent (or private) sector educates approximately 628,000 children in around 2,550 schools.

- Around 6.5% of all schoolchildren in the UK are educated in independent schools.
- Around 18% of pupils over the age of 16 are educated in independent schools.

(a) From **Item C**, is the percentage of pupils taking free school meals higher in nursery and primary schools or in secondary schools?

_____

_____ *(1 mark)*

(b) From **Item B**, what percentage of all pupils in the United Kingdom attend independent schools?

_____

_____ *(1 mark)*

(c) Identify **one** advantage and **one** disadvantage of testing in primary schools.

_____

_____

_____

_____ *(2 marks)*

(d) Explain what sociologists mean by the term 'differential educational achievement'.

_____

_____

_____

_____

_____

_____

_____

_____ *(4 marks)*

(e) Describe **one** way in which British governments have tried to increase the number of pupils who stay on in education and training after Year 11 **and** explain why they have tried to increase the staying-on rates.

_____

_____

_____

_____

_____

_____

_____

_____

_____

_____ *(5 marks)*

(f) Describe **one** function that education is expected to fulfil in Britain today **and** explain how it is expected to fulfil this function.

_____

_____

_____

_____

_____

_____

_____

_____

_____

_____ _(5 marks)_

(g) **EITHER**

(i) Discuss how far sociologists would agree that ethnic background is the most significant influence on pupils' educational achievements in Britain today.

OR

(ii) Discuss how far sociologists would agree that school-based factors are the most important influence on pupils' educational achievements in Britain today.

_____

_____

_____

_____

_____

_____

_____

_____

_____

_____

(12 marks)

Paper 1 Section C: Families

In this section of the Workbook, there are two exam-style questions on Families. Once you have worked through the revision chapter on Families, you should be ready to answer these questions. You could start by answering Question 1, and then check your answers before moving on to Question 2.

When you are answering each question, give yourself 30 minutes to complete your response because this is the amount of time you should spend on the Families question in the exam. Answering these questions under timed conditions will help you to prepare for the exam by giving you practice in managing your time.

Families Question 1

Answer **all** questions from this section.

Total for this question: 30 marks.

Study **Items A** and **B** and then answer parts (a) to (g).

ITEM A

Percentage of dependent children: by family type and ethnic group 2008, United Kingdom

Ethnic group	Dependent children living in families headed by a:		
	Married couple	*Cohabiting couple*	*Lone parent*
White	63%	14%	23%
Asian or Asian British	87%	1%	13%
Black or Black British	46%	6%	48%

Source: adapted from Table 2.5, *Social Trends 39*, 2009, page 16. Office for National Statistics © Crown Copyright.

ITEM B

(a) From **Item A**, which ethnic group had the lowest percentage of dependent children living in lone-parent families?

_____

_____ *(1 mark)*

(b) From **Item B**, identify the family type that is shown in the photograph.

_____

_____ *(1 mark)*

(c) Identify **two** reasons for the increase in the number of households containing lone-parent families over the last 30 years.

_____

_____

_____

_____ *(2 marks)*

(d) Explain what sociologists mean by the term 'ethnic group'.

_____

_____

Continue overleaf

_____

_____

_____

_____

_____

_____ *(4 marks)*

(e) Describe **one** way in which authority relationships in families have changed over the last 50 years **and** explain why this change has occurred.

_____

_____

_____

_____

_____

_____

_____

_____

_____

_____ *(5 marks)*

(f) Describe **one** way in which the patterns of fertility have changed in Britain over the last 30 years **and** explain the reasons for this change.

_____

_____

_____

_____

_____

_____

_____

_____

_____

_____ *(5 marks)*

(g) **EITHER**

(i) Discuss how far sociologists would agree that the nuclear family is the typical family type in Britain today.

OR

(ii) Discuss how far sociologists would agree that families are a more important agency of socialization in modern Britain than schools.

_____

_____

_____

_____

_____

_____

_____

_____

_____

_____

_____

_____

_____

_____

_____

_____

_____

_____

_____

_____

(12 marks)

Continue on lined paper if necessary

Families Question 2

Answer **all** questions from this section.

Total for this question: 30 marks.

Study **Items C** and **D** and then answer parts (a) to (g).

ITEM C

A 'family' can be defined as a lone parent with a child (or children) or a couple (with or without children). This means that while some families in modern Britain are headed by a lone parent, others are headed by a couple. In some of the families that are headed by a couple, the partners are married to each other or in civil partnerships. In others, the partners are cohabiting (that is, living together outside marriage or civil partnership).

ITEM D

Percentage of men and women living alone: by age Great Britain 2007		
Age	*Men (%)*	*Women (%)*
75 and over	35	61
65–74	20	30
45–64	15	14
25–44	14	8
16–24	3	2

Source: adapted from Figure 2.7, *Social Trends 39*, 2009, page 17. Office for National Statistics © Crown Copyright

(a) From **Item C**, identify **one** example of a type of family.

_____

_____ *(1 mark)*

(b) From **Item D**, which age group had the highest percentage of both men and women living alone?

_____

_____ *(1 mark)*

(c) Identify **two** possible consequences of divorce for the people involved.

_____

_____

_____

_____ *(2 marks)*

(d) Explain what sociologists mean by family diversity.

_____

_____

_____

_____

_____

_____

_____

_____ *(4 marks)*

(e) Describe **one** way in which life expectancy has changed over the last 50 years **and** explain why this change has occurred.

_____

_____

_____

_____

_____

_____

Continue overleaf

_____

_____

_____

_____ *(5 marks)*

(f) Describe **one** way in which gender relationships between adult partners have changed over the last 50 years **and** explain why this change has occurred.

_____

_____

_____

_____

_____

_____

_____

_____

_____

_____ *(5 marks)*

(g) **EITHER**

(i) Discuss how far sociologists would agree that people's relationships with members of their wider or extended family have become less important over the last 50 years.

OR

(ii) Discuss how far sociologists would agree that families are necessary in modern Britain because they perform important functions for individuals and for society.

_____

_____

_____

_____

_____

_____

(12 marks)

Paper 2 Section A: Crime and Deviance

In this section of the Workbook, there are two exam-style questions on Crime and Deviance. Once you have worked through the revision chapter on Crime and Deviance, you should be ready to answer these questions. You could start by answering Question 1 and then check your answers before moving on to Question 2.

When you are answering each question, give yourself 30 minutes to complete your response. This is the amount of time you should spend on the Crime and Deviance question if you choose this option in the Paper 2 exam. Answering these questions under timed conditions will help you to prepare for the exam by giving you practice in managing your time.

Crime and Deviance Question 1

Answer **all** questions from this section.

Total for this question: 30 marks

Study **Items A** and **B** and then answer parts (a) to (g).

ITEM A

**Crimes recorded by the police: by type of offence
England and Wales, 2007–08**

Type of offence	Percentage
Theft and handling stolen goods	36
Criminal damage	21
Violence against the person	19
Burglary (e.g. housebreaking)	12
Drugs offences	5
Fraud and forgery	3
Robbery	2
Sexual offences	1
Other offences	1
Total	**100%**

Source: adapted from Table 9.1, *Social Trends 39*, 2009, page 128. Office for National Statistics © Crown Copyright

ITEM B

Liverpool Crown Court

(a) From **Item A**, what percentage of all crimes recorded by the police were drugs offences?

_____

_____ *(1 mark)*

(b) From **Item B**, identify **one** agency of formal social control that is shown in the photograph.

_____

_____ *(1 mark)*

(c) Identify **two** ways in which crime may affect the people who are victims of a crime.

_____

_____

_____

_____ *(2 marks)*

(d) Explain what sociologists mean by deviant behaviour.

_____

_____

_____

_____

_____

_____

_____

_____ *(4 marks)*

(e) Describe **one** way in which informal rules may operate within a social group **and** explain why the group's members might conform to these rules.

_____

_____

_____

_____

_____

_____

_____

_____

_____

_____ *(5 marks)*

(f) Describe **one** example of a crime that has generated public debate in recent years **and** explain why this crime is seen by some people as a social problem.

_____

_____

_____

_____

_____

_____

_____

_____

_____

_____

_____ *(5 marks)*

(g) **EITHER**

(i) Discuss how far sociologists would agree that deprivation is the main cause of most crime in modern Britain.

OR

(ii) Discuss how far sociologists would agree that official statistics of crimes recorded by the police provide a complete picture of the extent of crime in Britain.

_____

_____

_____

_____

_____

_____

_____

_____

_____

_____

_____

_____

_____

_____

_____

_____

_____ *(12 marks)*

Continue on lined paper if necessary

Answer **all** questions from this section.

Total for this question: 30 marks

Study **Items C** and **D** and then answer parts (a) to (g).

ITEM C

A social problem is a problem that a particular society faces. Examples of social problems in Britain include teenage crime, domestic violence and poverty. Racism and racially motivated crime are also social problems. This is because they are harmful to their victims, to the communities in which they occur and to society in general. Social problems require solutions. So governments introduce social policies in order to address particular social problems in fields such as criminal justice, health and welfare.

ITEM D

Crimes reported by the British Crime Survey: by type of offence England and Wales 2007–08	
Household crime	**Millions**
Vandalism	2.7
Vehicle-related theft	1.5
Burglary	0.7
Bicycle theft	0.4
Other household theft	1.1
Personal crime	
Theft from the person	0.6
Other thefts of personal property	1.0
Assault with minor injury	0.5
Assault with no injury	0.9
Wounding	0.5
Robbery	0.3

Source: adapted from Table 9.3, *Social Trends 39*, 2009, page 130. Office for National Statistics © Crown Copyright

(a) From **Item C**, identify one example of a social problem.

_____

_____ *(1 mark)*

(b) From **Item D**, how many incidents of vehicle-related theft were reported by the British Crime Survey?

_____

_____ *(1 mark)*

(c) Identify **two** differences between formal and informal rules.

_____

_____

_____

_____ *(2 marks)*

(d) Explain what sociologists mean by a stereotype.

_____

_____

_____

_____

_____

_____

_____

_____ *(4 marks)*

(e) Describe **one** example of antisocial behaviour **and** explain how recent British governments have tried to address this behaviour.

_____

_____

_____

_____

_____

_____

Continue overleaf

_____

_____

_____

_____

_____ *(5 marks)*

(f) Describe **one** agency of informal social control **and** explain how it can influence people's behaviour.

_____

_____

_____

_____

_____

_____

_____

_____

_____

_____ *(5 marks)*

(g) **EITHER**

(i) Discuss how far sociologists would agree that official statistics of police-recorded crime exaggerate crime levels among young people.

OR

(ii) Discuss how far sociologists would agree that official statistics of police-recorded crime exaggerate crime levels among some ethnic groups.

_____

_____

_____

_____

_____

_____

_____

(12 marks)

Paper 2 Section B: Mass Media

In this section of the Workbook, there are two exam-style questions on Mass Media. Once you have worked through the revision chapter on Mass Media, you should be ready to answer these questions. You could start by answering Question 1 and then check your answers before moving on to Question 2.

When you are answering each question, give yourself 30 minutes to complete your response. This is the amount of time you should spend on the Mass Media question if you choose this option in the Paper 2 exam. Answering these questions under timed conditions will help you to prepare for the exam by giving you practice in managing your time.

Mass Media Question 1

Answer **all** questions from this section.

Total for this question: 30 marks

Study **Items A** and **B** and then answer parts (a) to (g).

ITEM A

The digital divide refers to a division between those who have access to new media technology such as the internet and digital TV and those who do not have access to this technology. For example, people on high incomes are more likely than other people to have the equipment and means to access the internet. Digital divisions may also be based on education, geography and age.

ITEM B

One area of public debate concerns whether exposure to violence in the media can encourage copycat violence in everyday life, particularly among children. A lot of the earlier research on the relationship between media exposure and real-life violence was carried out in laboratories. Laboratory experiments are generally associated with the psychological approach. Sociologists tend to see labs as artificial settings and question how far experiments can tell us about the way people behave in everyday life.

(a) From **Item A**, identify **one** example of new media technology.

_____

_____ *(1 mark)*

(b) From **Item B**, with which approach are laboratory experiments usually associated?

_____

_____ *(1 mark)*

(c) Identify **two** ways in which the technology of the mass media has changed over the last 30 years.

_____

_____

_____

_____ *(2 marks)*

(d) Explain what sociologists mean by the traditional media.

_____

_____

_____

_____

_____

_____

_____ *(4 marks)*

(e) Describe **one** way in which the mass media may present stereotyped images of some ethnic groups **and** explain why this stereotyping can be seen as a problem.

_____

_____

_____

_____

_____

_____

Continue overleaf

_____

_____

_____

_____
                                                        (5 marks)

(f) Describe **one** way in which the mass media may contribute to the process of gender socialization **and** explain why the media's role in this process can be criticised.

_____

_____

_____

_____

_____

_____

_____

_____

_____

_____
                                                        (5 marks)

(g) **EITHER**

   (i) Discuss how far sociologists would agree that technological developments such as the internet help to spread power more widely among individuals and groups in modern Britain.

   OR

   (ii) Discuss how far sociologists would agree that exposure to violence in the media can encourage violence in everyday life.

_____

_____

_____

_____

_____

_____

(12 marks)

Mass Media Question 2

Answer **all** questions from this section.

Total for this question: 30 marks

Study **Items C** and **D** and then answer parts (a) to (g).

ITEM C

ITEM D

In general, readership of national daily newspapers in Britain has declined over the last 30 years. Data from the National Readership Survey shows, for example, that:

- 72% of respondents read a national daily newspaper in the 12 months to June 1978 compared to 44% in the 12 months to June 2008

- 28% of respondents read the *Daily Mirror* in the 12 months to June 1978 compared to 8% in the 12 months to June 2008

- 8% of respondents read the *Daily Telegraph* in the 12 months to June 1978 compared to 4% in the 12 months to June 2008.

(a) From **Item C**, identify **one** example of a mass media product.

_____

_____ *(1 mark)*

(b) From **Item D**, what percentage of respondents read the *Daily Mirror* in the 12 months to June 2008?

_____

_____ *(1 mark)*

(c) Identify **two** reasons why people might read newspapers.

_____

_____

_____

_____ *(2 marks)*

(d) Explain what sociologists mean by the digital divide.

_____

_____

_____

_____

_____

_____

_____

_____ *(4 marks)*

(e) Describe **one** way in which individuals or groups can create content on the internet **and** explain why they might want to produce content in this way.

_____

_____

_____

_____

_____

_____

Continue overleaf

_____

_____

_____

_____ *(5 marks)*

(f) Describe **one** way in which the mass media can create negative images of a social group **and** explain why this could be seen as a problem.

_____

_____

_____

_____

_____

_____

_____

_____

_____

_____ *(5 marks)*

(g) **EITHER**

(i) Discuss how far sociologists would agree that the mass media is the most powerful agency of political socialization in Britain today.

OR

(ii) Discuss how far sociologists would agree that the press owners in Britain control the content of newspapers.

_____

_____

_____

_____

_____

_____

(12 marks)

In this section of the Workbook, there are two exam-style questions on Power. Once you have worked through the revision chapter on Power, you should be ready to answer these questions. You could start by answering Question 1 and then check your answers before moving on to Question 2.

When you are answering each question, give yourself 30 minutes to complete your response. This is the amount of time you should spend on the Power question if you choose this option in the Paper 2 exam. Answering these questions under timed conditions will help you to prepare for the exam by giving you practice in managing your time.

Power Question 1

Answer **all** questions from this section.

Total for this question: 30 marks

Study **Items A** and **B** and then answer parts (a) to (g).

ITEM A

Percentage of respondents who watch current affairs or politics programmes on television: by age England 2006–07	
Age	*Percentage*
16–24	13
25–34	25
35–44	29
45–64	38
65 and over	40
All aged 16 and over	31

Source: adapted from Table 13.3, *Social Trends 39*, 2009, page 194. Office for National Statistics © Crown Copyright

ITEM B

Weber identified three types of authority: legal rational, traditional and charismatic authority.

- In the case of legal rational authority, people obey an individual or a group (such as senior managers at work) because of the position they hold within an organization.

- In the case of traditional authority, people accept an individual or a group's authority because it is customary to do so. For example, a King or Queen may exercise authority based on hundreds of years of tradition.

- In the case of charismatic authority, people obey an inspirational individual who has extraordinary personal qualities and who can get others to go along with his or her wishes.

(a) From **Item A**, what percentage of respondents aged 35–44 watch current affairs or politics programmes on television?

_____

_____ *(1 mark)*

(b) From **Item B**, identify **one** example of an individual who exercises legal rational authority.

_____

_____ *(1 mark)*

(c) Identify **two** reasons why there are far fewer female Members of Parliament (MPs) than male MPs.

_____

_____

_____

_____ *(2 marks)*

(d) Explain what sociologists mean by coercion.

_____

_____

_____

_____

_____

_____

_____

_____ *(4 marks)*

(e) Describe **one** way in which the police may exercise power over members of the public **and** explain the basis of their power.

_____

_____

_____

_____

_____

_____

_____

_____

_____

_____ *(5 marks)*

(f) Describe **one** way in which participation in the political process in Britain has declined over the last 50 years **and** explain why this could be seen as a problem.

_____

_____

_____

_____

_____

_____

_____

_____

_____

_____ *(5 marks)*

(g) **EITHER**

(i) Discuss how far sociologists would agree that the welfare state has been successful in significantly reducing poverty in Britain over the last 50 years.

OR

(ii) Discuss how far sociologists would agree that the state represents the interests of all individuals and social groups in British society today.

_____

_____

_____

_____

_____

_____

_____

_____

_____

_____

_____

_____

_____

_____

_____

_____

_____

_____

_____

_____ _(12 marks)_

Continue on lined paper if necessary

Answer **all** questions from this section.

Total for this question: 30 marks

Study **Items C** and **D** and then answer parts (a) to (g).

ITEM C

Some individuals are more likely than others to participate in social organizations such as political parties, trade unions or environmental groups. Participation varies according to factors such as income and employment status.

	More likely to participate in social organizations	*Less likely to participate in social organizations*
Income	People in higher-income households	People in lower-income households
Employment status	Employed people	Unemployed people
Educational qualifications	People with higher educational qualifications	People with no qualifications
Household composition	Households containing childless couples and non-related people	Households containing lone-parent families

Source: adapted from Table 3.3, *Social Trends 39*, 2009, page 30. Office for National Statistics © Crown Copyright

ITEM D

Source: Andrew Forsyth, RSPCA Photolibrary

(a) From **Item C**, are employed people more likely or less likely than unemployed people to participate in social organizations?

_____

_____ *(1 mark)*

(b) From **Item D**, identify **one** example of a pressure group.

_____

_____ *(1 mark)*

(c) Identify **two** ways in which British governments have tried to reduce unemployment levels during the last 20 years.

_____

_____

_____

_____ *(2 marks)*

(d) Explain what sociologists mean by a dependency culture.

_____

_____

_____

_____

_____

_____

_____

_____ *(4 marks)*

(e) Describe **one** way in which parents may exercise authority over their children **and** explain the basis of their authority.

_____

_____

_____

_____

_____

Continue overleaf

_____

_____

_____

_____

_____ *(5 marks)*

(f) Describe **one** factor that could increase the chances of pressure group activity being successful **and** explain how this factor could increase a pressure group's chances of success.

_____

_____

_____

_____

_____

_____

_____

_____

_____ *(5 marks)*

(g) **EITHER**

(i) Discuss how far sociologists would agree that all individuals and groups have opportunities to participate fully in the political process in Britain today.

OR

(ii) Discuss how far sociologists would agree that British governments have been successful in reducing discrimination based on age, gender and ethnicity over the last 30 years.

_____

_____

_____

_____

_____

(12 marks)

Paper 2 Section D: Social Inequality

In this section of the Workbook, there are two exam-style questions on Social Inequality. Once you have worked through the revision chapter on Social Inequality, you should be ready to answer these questions. You could start by answering Question 1 and then check your answers before moving on to Question 2.

When you are answering each question, give yourself 30 minutes to complete your response. This is the amount of time you should spend on the Social Inequality question if you choose this option in the Paper 2 exam. Answering these questions under timed conditions will help you to prepare for the exam by giving you practice in managing your time.

Social Inequality Question 1

Answer **all** questions from this section.

Total for this question: 30 marks

Study **Items A** and **B** and then answer parts (a) to (g).

ITEM A

Employment rates of working-age men and women United Kingdom

| Year | Percentage | |
	Men aged 16–64	Women aged 16–59
1971	91.7	56.3
1981	81.8	58.9
1991	79.5	66.1
2001	79.2	69.5
2008	78.8	70.4

Source: adapted from Figure 4.5, *Social Trends 39*, 2009, page 49. Office for National Statistics © Crown Copyright

ITEM B

Some people live on a low income on a long-term or persistent basis rather than on a short-term basis. Research shows that people living in some family types are more likely to have a low income over time. For example, 19 per cent of lone-parent families in Britain had incomes below average during 2002–5. By contrast, couples without dependent children are much less at risk of experiencing low incomes over time.

(a) From **Item A**, what is the **trend** in the proportion of women in employment between 1971 and 2008?

_____

_____ *(1 mark)*

(b) From **Item B**, identify one family type that is more likely than others to experience a low income on a long-term basis.

_____

_____ *(1 mark)*

(c) Identify **two** sources of income.

_____

_____

_____

_____ *(2 marks)*

(d) Explain what sociologists mean by life chances.

_____

_____

_____

_____

_____

_____

_____

_____ *(4 marks)*

(e) Describe **one** way in which the social position of women in Britain has changed over the last 50 years **and** explain the reasons for this change.

_____

_____

_____

_____

_____

_____

_____

_____

_____

_____

_____

_____ *(5 marks)*

(f) Describe **one** social group whose members are more likely than others to experience poverty **and** explain why this group is more at risk of experiencing poverty.

_____

_____

_____

_____

_____

_____

_____

_____

_____

_____

_____ *(5 marks)*

(g) **EITHER**

(i) Discuss how far sociologists would agree that modern Britain is a meritocratic society.

OR

(ii) Discuss how far sociologists would agree that inequality based on ethnicity is a more significant cause of social division than social class in modern Britain.

_____

_____

_____

_____

_____

_____

_____

_____

_____

_____

_____

_____

_____

_____

_____

_____

_____

_____

_____

_____

(12 marks)

Continue on lined paper if necessary

Answer **all** questions from this section.

Total for this question: 30 marks

Study **Items C** and **D** and then answer parts (a) to (g).

ITEM C

Employment rates of people aged 50 and over
United Kingdom

	Percentage			
Age	1997	2000	2004	2008
50–54	74.8	76.5	78.8	80.1
55–59	59.8	63.5	67.7	70.3
60–64	36.9	36.6	41.5	45.9
65 and over	5.0	5.2	6.0	7.4

Source: adapted from Figure 4.7, *Social Trends 39*, 2009, page 50. Office for National Statistics © Crown Copyright

---

ITEM D

The Duke of Westminster held on to third position in *The Sunday Times* Rich List 2009. He is worth £6500 million and the source of his wealth is property. Sir Philip and Lady Green were in sixth position in the Rich List 2009. They are worth £3830 million and the source of their wealth is retailing. Their assets include the Bhs department stores, Topshop, Topman and Miss Selfridge.

(a) From **Item C**, what is the **trend** in the proportion of people aged 55–59 in employment between 1997 and 2008?

_____

_____ *(1 mark)*

(b) From **Item D**, identify **one** source of wealth.

_____

_____ *(1 mark)*

(c) Identify **two** barriers to social mobility that some individuals might face.

_____

_____

_____

_____ *(2 marks)*

(d) Explain what sociologists mean by social exclusion.

_____

_____

_____

_____

_____

_____

_____

_____ *(4 marks)*

(e) Describe **one** way in which poverty can be defined **and** explain the problems with defining poverty in this way.

_____

_____

_____

_____

_____

_____

_____

_____

_____

_____ *(5 marks)*

(f) Describe **one** way in which social class can be measured **and** explain why it is measured in this way.

_____

_____

_____

_____

_____

_____

_____

_____

_____

_____ *(5 marks)*

(g) **EITHER**

(i) Discuss how far sociologists would agree that Britain is now a classless society.

OR

(ii) Discuss how far sociologists would agree that long-term unemployment is the most significant cause of poverty in Britain today.

_____

_____

_____

_____

_____

_____

_____

_____

_____

_____

_____

_____

(12 marks)

GCSE
Sociology
AQA

Glossary and Index

Absolute poverty: people experience absolute poverty when their income is insufficient to obtain the minimum needed to survive.

Achieved status: social positions that are earned on the basis of personal talents or individual merit.

Ageing population: in an ageing population, the proportion of the population over retirement age is gradually increasing.

Ageism: prejudice or discrimination based on age.

Agencies of social control: the groups and organizations in society that control or constrain people's behaviour and actions.

Agency of socialization: a social group or institution responsible for undertaking socialization. Examples include families, peer groups, schools, workplaces, religions and the mass media.

Agenda setting: the ability of the media to focus public attention on particular topics and, in doing so, to direct public discussion and debate onto these topics.

Antisocial behaviour: behaviour that causes harassment, distress or alarm to other people.

Ascribed status: social positions that are fixed at birth and unchanging over time including a hereditary title linked to family background (Princess or Lord, for example).

Authority: the exercise of power based on consent or agreement.

Beanpole family: a multigenerational family in which each generation has one or very few members.

Bourgeoisie: a term used by Karl Marx and others to refer to the capitalist or ruling class that owns the big businesses in capitalist society.

Capitalism: an economic system in which private owners invest money – or capital – in businesses in order to make a profit.

Charismatic authority: obedience based on an individual's charisma or extraordinary personal qualities.

Chivalry effect: the idea that female offenders are seen as deserving more lenient treatment within the criminal justice system and the impact of this on things like sentencing.

Citizens: members of a state who have full legal rights (e.g. to be treated equally before the law) and responsibilities (e.g. to obey the law).

Citizenship: either the political and legal status associated with membership of a particular state such as the UK or active involvement in public life and the political process.

Civil partnership: a relationship between two people of the same sex who register as civil partners and thereby have their relationship legally recognized.

Class dealignment: the weakening of the links between social class and voting behaviour.

Classless society: a society that does not have different social classes.

Coercion: obedience based on the threat or use of force.

Cohabitation: living with a partner outside marriage or civil partnership.

Conflict approach: a sociological approach which sees society as based on conflict, tensions and divisions between social groups, such as between different social classes.

Conglomerate: a huge corporation or company formed by the merging of different firms. Media conglomerates have stakes across a range of media such as newspapers, films and digital TV services. They operate on a global rather than a national scale.

Conjugal roles: the domestic roles of married or cohabiting partners.

Corporate crime: crimes committed by employees on behalf of the company or organization they work for. Examples include the manufacture and sale of unsafe products.

Crime: an illegal act (such as shoplifting or murder) which is punishable by law.

Cultural deprivation: this is said to happen when children's backgrounds do not provide them with the necessary cultural resources (e.g. encouragement from parents or visits to museums) to perform well at school.

Cultural diversity: culturally based differences between people in a society in terms of religion, ethnicity, social class and so on.

Culture: the whole way of life of a particular society or social group. Culture includes the values, norms, customs, beliefs, knowledge, skills and language of the society or group.

Cycle of deprivation: the idea that deprivation and poverty are passed on from parents to their children.

Democracy: government by the people.

Democratic relationships: relationships between, for example, married partners or parents and children, based on equality.

Demography: the systematic study of human populations, including their size, age and gender structures, birth and death rates and life expectancy.

Dependency culture: some people who rely on state benefits are seen as developing a way of life in which they become so dependent on benefits that they lose the motivation to work.

Deviance: behaviour which does not confirm to society's norms and values and, if detected, is likely to lead to negative sanctions. Deviance can be – but is not necessarily – illegal.

Deviancy amplification: the process whereby the social reaction to deviance from the mass media and public leads to an increase in (amplifies) the deviance, by provoking more of the same behaviour.

Digital divide: a division or gap between those who have access to new media technology and those who do not.

Discrimination: less favourable or unfair treatment based, for example, on an individual's gender, ethnicity or age.

Division of domestic labour: the division of tasks such as housework, childcare and DIY between men and women within the home.

Dual-earner household: a household in which two adults work in paid employment.

Dual-worker families: families in which both adult partners work in paid employment.

Ethical issues: these relate to morals and, in the context of sociological research, raise questions about how to conduct morally acceptable research which protects the rights of research participants and safeguards their well-being.

Ethnic group: a social group whose members share an identity based on their cultural traditions or cultural characteristics such as religion or language.

Ethnicity: cultural norms and values that distinguish one ethnic group from another.

Extended family: a group of relatives extending beyond the nuclear family. The classic extended family contains three generations who either live under the same roof or nearby. This type of extension is known as vertical extension. In modified extended families, members live apart geographically but maintain regular contact and provide support.

Family: a couple who are married, civil partners or cohabiting, with or without dependent children, or a lone parent with their child or children.

Family diversity: the variety of family types living in Britain today.

Feminism: this term describes the feminist movement in society. It is also used to describe an approach within sociology.

Feminist approach: a sociological approach which examines the ways gender operates in society against the interests of women.

Fertility: the average number of children born to women of childbearing age (usually 15–44) in a particular society.

Folk devil: a group that is defined as a threat to society's values.

Formal social control: control of people's behaviour based on written laws and rules. Formal social control is usually associated with the ways the state regulates and controls our behaviour. The agencies of formal social control include the police force, the courts and prisons.

Function: the role that a social structure such as the family or the education system fulfils on behalf of individuals or society.

Functionalist approach: a sociological approach which examines society's structures (such as the family, the education system and religion) in terms of the functions they perform for the continuation of society and for individuals.

Gay or lesbian family: a family in which a same-sex couple live together with their child or children.

Gender: social or cultural (rather than biological) differences between men and women that are associated with masculinity and femininity.

Gender roles: traditional social roles related to gender such as housewife and breadwinner (wage earner).

Gender socialization: the process through which individuals learn what is seen as appropriate masculine and feminine behaviour and acquire a gender identity.

Generalizations: general statements and conclusions that apply not only to the sample studied but also to the broader population.

Geographical mobility: moving house from one area to live in another area, region or country.

Government: in the UK, the government consists of those MPs who are ministers. They are selected by the Prime Minister, who is the leader of the political party that currently holds power.

Hidden curriculum: things learnt in school that are not formally taught such as valuing punctuality or obedience.

Hierarchy: a hierarchy is shaped like a layered pyramid and each layer has more power than the one below it. In schools, for example, the head teacher is typically at the top of the hierarchy and the pupils are at the bottom.

Household: this comprises either one person who lives alone or a group of people who live at the same address and who share at least one meal a day or facilities such as a living room.

Hypothesis: a supposition, hunch or informed guess, usually written as a statement that can be tested and then either supported by the evidence or proved wrong.

Identity: how we see ourselves and how other people see us. Sources of identity include age, gender, ethnicity and social class.

Income: the flow of resources which individuals and households receive over a specific period of time. Income may be received in cash (for example from earnings) or in kind (for instance a petrol allowance).

Infant mortality rate: the number of infant deaths (aged under one year) per 1000 live births per year.

Informal social control: control of people's behaviour based on social processes such as the approval and disapproval of others. Informal social control is enforced via social pressure. The agencies of informal social control include peer groups and families.

Informed consent: as part of ethical research practice, the researcher must ensure that all research participants understand what the study is about, why it is being done and what it will involve before they freely agree (or otherwise) to take part.

Insider group: a pressure group such as the CBI, the Automobile Association and the National Trust that has close links with government networks and is consulted by government departments, civil servants and ministers when policy proposals are being prepared.

Institutional racism: this occurs when an organization (such as a police force or hospital) fails to provide an appropriate service to people because of their ethnic origin, culture or colour. Institutional racism can be seen in organizational attitudes or behaviour that discriminates, even when individuals themselves act without intending this.

Inter-generational social mobility: movement up or down between the layers of a stratification system as measured between the generations of a family.

Interview effect: also known as 'interview bias', this occurs when the interview situation itself influences interviewees' responses. Interviewees may give answers that they think are socially acceptable or that show them in a positive light.

Interviewer effect: also known as 'interviewer bias', this occurs when the interviewer influences the interviewee's responses. It may be linked to the interviewer's dress, age, gender, ethnicity, appearance or accent.

Intra-generational social mobility: movement of an individual over the course of their life up or down between the layers of a stratification system, e.g. from one occupational classification to another.

Joint conjugal roles: this term describes domestic roles of married or cohabiting partners which are divided or shared in an equal way.

Kinship relationships: relationships between people based on ties of blood, marriage or adoption.

Labelling: the process of attaching a label (which is like a sticky tag) to individuals or groups.

Legal rational authority: a type of authority in which obedience is based on an individual or group's position in an organization.

Life chances: an individual's chances of achieving positive or negative outcomes (relating, for example, to health, education, housing) as they progress through life.

Life cycle of poverty: movement into and out of poverty at different stages during the course of a person's life.

Life expectancy: the average number of years a newborn baby may be expected to live.

Lone-parent family: a family consisting of one parent and a child or children who live together.

Long-range mobility: social mobility that involves significant movement e.g. from the bottom layer to the top.

Longitudinal studies: studies of the same group of people conducted over a period of time. After the initial survey or interview has taken place, follow-up surveys or interviews are carried out at intervals over a number of years.

Male-breadwinner household: a household which the adult male works in paid employment and earns the bulk of the household income.

Marketisation of education: the policy of bringing market forces (such as competition) into education.

Marxist approach: a sociological approach that draws on the ideas of Karl Marx and applies them to modern societies.

Mass media: forms of communication (media) that reach large (mass) audiences including newspapers, magazines, books, television, cinema and the internet.

Material deprivation: the lack of material resources such as money.

Means test: a test to establish need before financial help from public funds is given.

Meritocracy: a system in which an individual's social position is achieved on the basis of their abilities and talents rather than on the basis of their social origins and background.

Migration: the movement of people either nationally from one region of a country to another, or internationally from one country to another.

Minority ethnic group: an ethnic group that is in a minority in a particular society. Britain is home to many minority ethnic groups including those of Irish, Polish, Greek Cypriot, Indian and African Caribbean heritage.

Moral panic: a media-fuelled overreaction to social groups (such as 'hoodies'). This process involves the media exaggerating the extent and significance of a social problem. A particular group is cast as a folk devil and becomes defined as a threat to society's values.

Multimedia (or cross-media) conglomerate: a huge corporation or company that is formed when different firms merge and that has stakes across a range of different media such as newspapers, films and digital television services.

Negative sanctions: sanctions that punish those who do not conform to the group's expectations, for example by ignoring them.

...a based on new technology,
... and digital television.

...roach: an approach to studying
...mphasises the importance of the
...y and traditional family values.

News values: media professionals' values about what issues and personalities are considered newsworthy, topical or important.

Norm referencing: the ability of the media to present some behaviour, views and groups positively and others negatively, thereby shaping public opinion on these groups.

Norms: these define appropriate and expected behaviour in particular social contexts such as classrooms, cinemas, restaurants or aeroplanes.

Nuclear family: a family containing a father, mother and their child or children. It contains two generations and family members live together in the same household. The parents may be married or cohabiting.

Official curriculum: the formal learning that takes place in schools, e.g. during history and science lessons.

Official statistics: existing sources of quantitative data compiled by government agencies such as the Home Office.

Outsider group: a pressure group that is not consulted automatically by government.

Patriarchy: male power and dominance over women.

Peer group: a group of people who share a similar status and position in society, such as people of a similar age, outlook or occupation.

Peer pressure: the social pressure that a peer group puts on its members to encourage them to conform to the group's norms.

Peer review: before papers are accepted for presentation at conferences or before articles are published in journals, they are assessed (reviewed) by experienced sociologists (peers). This operates as a form of quality control.

Pluralist approach: an approach which argues that a range of views and opinions exists in society and this range is reflected in the varied media products available to consumers.

Political party: an organization (such as the Labour Party or the Liberal Democrats) that has policies on a range of issues (e.g. education and defence) and aims to have its candidates elected as MPs and to form a government.

Political socialization: the process via which we acquire our political values, beliefs and preferences.

Population: the particular group under study. The population may consist of people such as higher education students or institutions such as schools depending on the aims of the research.

Positive sanctions: sanctions that reward those who behave according to the group's expectations, for example through praise.

Poverty: there are two broad approaches to defining poverty: absolute and relative poverty. People experience absolute poverty when their income is insufficient to obtain the minimum needed to survive. People experience relative poverty when they cannot afford to meet the general standard of living of most other people in their society.

Poverty line: a government-approved line that divides people who are living below a set income level (living below the poverty line) from those who are living above it. In Britain, there is no official poverty line.

Poverty trap: people may be trapped in poverty when an increase in their income reduces the means-tested benefits to which they are entitled.

Power: the ability of an individual or group to get what they want despite any opposition they may face from other people. In social relationships between individuals (e.g. between spouses or parents and children) or groups, power usually refers to the dominance and control of one individual or group over others.

Prejudice: a pre-judgment in favour of, or against, a person, group or issue. Prejudice involves opinions and beliefs rather than action.

Pressure (or interest) group: a group of people who try to persuade the government to adopt a particular policy or to influence public opinion on an issue.

Primary research methods: research methods that collect primary data (data that are collected first-hand by doing research using techniques such as surveys or observation).

Primary socialization: the process of early childhood learning, usually within families, during which babies and infants acquire the basic behaviour patterns, language and skills needed in later life.

Proletariat: a term used by Karl Marx and others to refer to the working class, the oppressed group in capitalist society.

Promotional pressure group: a pressure group such as Amnesty International that seeks to promote a particular cause or campaign on a specific issue.

Protective pressure group: a pressure group, such as a trade union, that seeks to protect or defend its members' common interests.

Qualitative data: information presented in visual or verbal form, e.g. as words or quotations rather than numbers.

Quantitative data: information presented in numerical form, e.g. as graphs or tables of statistics.

Reconstituted family: a stepfamily or a blended family in which one or both partners have a child or children from a previous relationship living with them. Most stepfamilies comprise a stepfather, a biological mother and her child or children but they can combine biological and social parenting in more complex ways.

Relative deprivation: this occurs when individuals or groups feel that they are badly off in relation to the living standards of their peers.

Relative poverty: people experience relative poverty when they cannot afford to meet the general standard of living of most other people in their society.

Reliability: this refers to consistency. Research findings are reliable if the same or consistent results are obtained a second time using the same methods.

Replication: standardized methods such as questionnaires can be replicated or repeated by other researchers to check the reliability of the research findings. Getting the same or similar results a second time round confirms reliability.

Representative democracy: a type of democratic political system in which citizens elect representatives (such as MPs) who make political decisions on their behalf.

Representative: typical; a representative sample is one that reflects the characteristics of its population.

Role: the pattern of expected and acceptable behaviour of people who occupy a particular social position, e.g. the role of 'teacher' defines how we expect a teacher to behave during the working day.

Sample: a subgroup of the population selected for study.

Scapegoat: an individual or group (such as economic migrants) that is blamed for something that is not their fault.

School ethos: the climate or character of a school including its policies on behaviour, homework, uniform and discipline.

Secondary sources: sources of information that already exists and has previously been generated or collected by other people. Secondary sources include official statistics, the mass media, autobiographies and studies by other sociologists.

Secondary socialization: during secondary socialization, which begins during later childhood and continues throughout our adult lives, we learn society's norms and values. Agencies of secondary socialization (the social groups or institutions which contribute to this process) include peer groups, schools, workplaces, religions and the mass media.

Secularization: the process whereby the influence of religion in a society declines.

Segregated conjugal roles: this term describes domestic roles of married or cohabiting partners which are separated out or divided in an unequal way.

Selective education: a way of recruiting pupils to a school, based on a form of selection. For example, pupils may be selected on the basis of their performance in an entrance exam or their parents' ability to pay annual school fees.

Self-fulfilling prophecy: this occurs when a teacher makes a prediction (prophecy) about a pupil's likely performance or potential that comes to be true.

Self-report study: a survey that asks respondents whether they have committed particular offences during a specified time period such as the last year. Such studies provide information on offenders and offences that are not necessarily dealt with by the police or courts.

Sexism: prejudice or discrimination based on gender.

Sexuality: in broad terms, sexuality refers to the way an individual expresses themselves and behaves as a sexual being; it also refers to sexual orientation and preference (for example, being heterosexual, lesbian, gay or bisexual).

Short-range mobility: social mobility that involves limited movement e.g. from a semi-skilled to a skilled manual job.

Social class: a group of people sharing a similar economic position in terms of occupation, income and wealth.

Social cohesion: when a society is based on social cohesion, the different individuals and groups that make up society are united into a body of citizens rather than divided by conflicting interests.

Social construction: this term is often used in relation to age, gender and race and reflects the idea that, rather than being rooted in biology or nature, these are created by society or culture.

Social control: this refers to the control that a group or society exercises over people's behaviour and actions.

Social exclusion: being shut out or excluded from participation in society's social, economic, political and cultural life.

Social inequalities: the uneven distribution of resources (such as income and power) or opportunities and outcomes related to, for example, education and health.

Social issues: issues that affect communities, groups and people's lives. Contemporary social issues relating to families, for example, include the quality of parenting, relationships between adults and teenagers, care of the elderly and forced marriages. Issues related to the mass media include the question of whether exposure to the media (for example, watching violent films) encourages copycat violent behaviour. Social issues may be – but are not necessarily – social problems.

Social mobility: movement up or down between the layers or strata of a society.

Social order: this occurs when society is stable, ordered and runs smoothly without continual disruption.

Social policies: sets of plans and actions put into place by governments, local authorities or other organizations in order to address particular social issues or problems, in the fields of, e.g. welfare, criminal justice and education.

Social problems: problems facing society such as racism, discrimination, teenage crime, poverty, unemployment and domestic violence. Social problems are seen as damaging or harmful to society and therefore require tackling or solving through social policies.

Social processes: processes in society that involve interaction between individuals, groups and institutions. For example, socialization is a social process through which we learn the culture of a society or group. It involves interaction between individuals, groups (such as families) and institutions (such as schools).

Social stratification: the way society is structured or divided into hierarchical strata – or layers – with the most privileged at the top and the least favoured at the bottom. Social class is an example of a stratification system.

Social structures: the institutions that make up society such as the family, education and stratification systems.

Socialization: the process through which we learn the culture and appropriate behaviour (the norms and values) of the particular group or society we are born into. The socialization process also prepares us for the roles we will play in society.

Society: a group of people who share a culture or a way of life.

State: the various institutions (such as the civil service and the courts) that organize and regulate society by making, implementing and enforcing laws.

Status: status can refer to social positions linked, for example, to occupations and families such as child, parent, teacher or train driver. It can also refer to the amount of prestige or social standing that an individual in a particular social position is given by other members of the group or society.

Status frustration: Albert Cohen argued that working-class boys experience status frustration when they try – but fail – to meet middle-class expectations at school.

Stereotype: a fixed, standardized and distorted view of the characteristics of a particular group such as women. Stereotypes are often based on prejudice.

Streaming: pupils are grouped according to their general ability and then taught in this group for all their subjects.

Subculture: a social group which differs from the dominant or main culture in terms of its members' values, beliefs, customs, language, dress or diet and so on. Examples include travellers who have a nomadic way of life and youth subcultures such as 'Goths' or 'Emos'.

Symmetrical family: a family form in which spouses carry out different tasks but each makes a similar contribution within the home.

Traditional authority: a type of authority in which obedience is based on custom and tradition.

Traditional media: media based on older technology, e.g. newspapers and terrestrial television.

Underclass: this term has been used in different ways. It can refer to a group whose attitudes and values are different to those of mainstream society. It can also refer to people who experience long-term poverty and who are unable to obtain a living.

Unemployment: people experience this when they do not have paid employment but are actively seeking work.

Validity: this refers to truth or authenticity. Research findings are valid if they provide a true or authentic picture of what is being studied.

Values: beliefs or ideas about what is desirable or worth striving for. Values such as privacy and respect for life provide general guidelines for conduct.

Victim survey: a study which asks respondents about their experiences of crime, whether they have been victims of particular offences during a specified time period such as the last year and, if so, whether they reported the crimes to the police.

Wealth: ownership of assets such as property, land and works of art as well as money held in savings accounts and shares in companies.

Welfare dependency: the idea that some groups remain in poverty because the welfare state encourages them to depend on state provision.

Welfare state: a system in which the state takes responsibility for protecting the health and welfare of its citizens and meeting their social needs. The state does this by providing services (e.g. the NHS) and benefits (e.g. Income Support).

White-collar crime: this term refers broadly to crimes committed by people in relatively high status positions, such as accountants, doctors or solicitors, during their work. Examples include tax evasion and 'fiddling' expense accounts at work.

Index

Acknowledgements

The Publishers are grateful to the following for permission to reproduce copyright material.

p6 Item A. Department for Children, Schools and Families Adapted from Table 4.1.1. Youth Cohort Study & Longitudinal Study of Young People in England: the Activities and Experiences of 16-year-olds: England 2007. Statistical Bulletin.

p32 Item F. Adapted from Figure 2.13, *Social Trends 39*, 2009, page 20. Office for National Statistics.

p46 Item B. Adapted from the British Crime Survey, Home Office Research Development Statistics (2009).

p82 Focus on Gender report, Office of National Statistics, September 2008.

p119 Item A. Adapted from Table 3.8, *Social Trends 39*, 2009, page 34. Office for National Statistics.

p123 Item D. Adapted from Figure 9.5, *Social Trends 39*, 2009, page 131. Office for National Statistics.

p128 Item A. Adapted from Table 3.3, *Social Trends 39*, 2009, page 30. Office for National Statistics.

p132 Item C. Adapted from Table 3.7, *Social Trends 39*, 2009, page 33. Office for National Statistics.

p136 Item A. Adapted from Table 2.5, *Social Trends 39*, 2009, page 16. Office for National Statistics.

p140 Item D. Adapted from Figure 2.7, *Social Trends 39*, 2009, page 17. Office for National Statistics.

p144 Item A. Adapted from Table 9.1, *Social Trends 39*, 2009, page 128. Office for National Statistics.

p148 Item D. Adapted from Table 9.3, *Social Trends 39*, 2009, page 130. Office for National Statistics.

p160 Item A. Adapted from Table 13.3, *Social Trends 39*, 2009, page 194. Office for National Statistics.

p168 Item A. Adapted from Figure 4.5, *Social Trends 39*, 2009, page 49. Office for National Statistics.

p172 Item C. Adapted from Figure 4.7, *Social Trends 39*, 2009, page 50. Office for National Statistics.

Photographs

The Author and Publishers are grateful to the following for permission to reproduce photographs:

p70 Item F. iStockphoto/Dave Roberts.

p120 Item B. iStockphoto/Winston Davidian.

p136 Item B. iStockphoto/Alexander Shalamov.

p145 Item B. Wikipedia/Man Vyi.

p156 Item C. iStockphoto/René Mansi.

p164 Item D. RSPCA Photolibrary/Andrew Forsyth.

Every effort has been made to trace the copyright holders and to obtain their permission for the use of copyright material. The author and publishers will gladly receive any information enabling them to rectify any error or omission in subsequent editions.

GCSE
Sociology
AQA

Answers to exam
practice workbook

Answers to exam practice workbook

Different types of answer are provided in this section depending on the question:

- Part (a) and most part (b) questions require you to pick out information from the Items. There are usually only one or two possible answers to this type of question and these are provided so that you can check whether your own responses are correct.

- On other short-answer questions, there are usually several equally acceptable answers that would earn you full marks. The answers to these are presented as a checklist of the possible points that you could include in your responses.

- Extended-answer questions can also be addressed in several different ways. The answers to these are presented as a checklist of the points that you could include in your own introduction, main body and conclusion. This will help you to recognize the sort of information that you would need to include in your own extended answers in order to earn full marks.

Paper 1 Section A: Studying Society

Studying Society Question 1

Pages 120–123

(a) 62 per cent.

(b) (i) Any one of the following: social survey, questionnaire or structured interview.

(ii) Strengths of social surveys, questionnaires and structured interviews – answers could include any one of the following:

- Questions are standardized so answers can be compared and differences identified.
- Easy to replicate in order to check the reliability of findings.
- Generalizations are possible from a representative sample.
- Compared to some other methods, it is possible to collect a lot of information from many people.

Weaknesses of social surveys, questionnaires and structured interviews – answers could include any one of the following:

- Respondents have few opportunities to introduce their own issues so reducing validity.
- Respondents have few opportunities to develop their answers so reducing validity.
- In a structured interview, the interviewer's presence may influence the respondent's responses so reducing validity.

(c) (i) Possible differences include:

- Sociologists focus on groups while psychologists focus on individuals.

- Sociologists are concerned with the social/cultural influences on behaviour while psychologists are concerned with individual behaviour and differences between individuals in their behaviour.

(ii) Answers could cover ideas such as:

- the social pressure that a group (such as fellow students, work colleagues or friends) exerts on its members to encourage them to conform to group norms
- the pressure is exerted informally through rewards (e.g. being praised) and/or punishments (e.g. being ignored).

(d) Answers could suggest that:

- if research findings show that race discrimination is still common in Britain, then current laws (such as equality legislation) could be changed to take account of this finding or new policies (such as positive discrimination in employment or in selecting Parliamentary candidates) could be considered
- governments might use research findings on institutional racism to develop policies in order to raise awareness of this form of racism and to review practices within organizations such as hospitals, schools or universities.

(e) (i) Answers could refer to one of the following:

- Informed consent – making sure that the research participants (who are under the age of 18) understand fully what taking part will involve and do not feel under pressure to take part.

- Confidentiality – making sure that the research participants' responses are not disclosed (e.g. to their teachers) and that all information about them is kept secure.
- Research participants' well-being – making sure that the participants are not made to feel uncomfortable or upset by insensitive questioning.

(ii) Answers could suggest one of the following:

- Studies on this theme that other sociologists have carried out – the findings of the different studies could be compared and any similarities and differences identified.
- The school and college prospectuses – this would provide background or contextual information on the school and college, their curriculum and ethos and could help you to devise appropriate questions to ask.
- Statistics on the destinations of the school pupils including the number and proportion who transfer from the school to the college – this would provide useful background information on the research context and could suggest questions that you might ask.

(iii) Answers could suggest that:

- Structured interviews would enable the researcher to gather statistical data on male and female pupils' views and opinions of the transfer. The researcher could compare responses and identify connections between different factors, e.g. gender, ethnicity and views on the transfer.
- Structured interviews would be better than informal interviews because they are usually quicker and cheaper for the amount of data collected. The sample size is usually larger. The questions are standardized so pupils' responses can be compared and similarities and differences identified based on their gender, ethnicity and GCSE results.
- Unlike informal interviews, structured interviews can be replicated to check the reliability of the findings. If the findings are reliable and the sample is representative, then it is possible to generalize.

Alternatively, answers could suggest that:

- informal interviews could be used to investigate male and female pupils' experiences of the transfer – they would allow the interviewer to explore pupils' views, to probe their answers and to get a rich and detailed account of their perspectives and what it means to them to transfer from school to college

- informal interviews would be better than questionnaires. Questionnaires containing pre-set standardized questions are more suited to a study of attitudes and opinions rather than a study of pupils' experiences.

Studying Society Question 2

Pages 124–127

(a) The 16–24 age group.

(b) (i) Either simple random sampling or snowball sampling.

(ii) Answers could refer to:

Simple random sampling:

- One of the following advantages – all members of the sampling frame have an equal chance of being selected for inclusion in the sample; the sample is likely to mirror the population.
- One of the following disadvantages – by chance, some groups may be under-represented in the sample; by chance, the sample may not be representative of the population.

Snowball sampling:

- One of the following advantages – this technique can be used when there is no sampling frame; it may be the only way of getting a sample.
- One of the following disadvantages – the sample will not be representative of the population because it is not randomly selected and the people in the sample are likely to be similar to each other; it will not be possible to make generalizations.

(c) (i) Answers could suggest differences such as:

- journalists work to tight deadlines and so their research is less systematic and less thorough than that of sociologists
- sociologists are expected to be balanced in using evidence and interpreting data while journalists may present information in a one-sided way
- sociologists' research findings are subject to peer review while journalists' accounts are not peer reviewed.

(ii) Answers could refer to the following points:

- Ageism – people being treated differently and less favourably than others (e.g. when applying for jobs or promotion) on the basis of their age.
- In the labour market, age discrimination usually works against older workers. For example, some employers may think that older workers will not

adapt to new technology and, as a result, the employers appoint younger people.

(d) Answers could suggest:

- If sociological research findings identify some of the causes of antisocial behaviour or the factors associated with it, then this information could be used to devise evidence-based policies to reduce it.

- Findings may indicate that, in practice, current policies (e.g. the use of antisocial behaviour orders) are not working as intended or that antisocial behaviour is not always taken seriously by the police or local councils. Such findings may result in policy changes (e.g. reducing the number of ASBOs issued or changing the way the police or local councils deal with public complaints about antisocial behaviour).

(e) (i) Answers could refer to one of the following:

- The sensitivity of the subject matter – the topic of faith could be a sensitive issue for some research participants so all questions would need to be carefully worded to avoid causing offence.

- Informed consent – making sure that the research participants understand fully what taking part will entail and that they don't feel under pressure to take part.

- Anonymity – making sure that the research participants cannot be identified by name, description or in any other ways in publications based on the research.

- Confidentiality – ensuring that the research participants' responses (e.g. in interviews or questionnaires) are not disclosed.

(ii) Answers could suggest one of the following:

- Official statistics on the number of faith schools in the Local Authority (LA) and the number of pupils who attend faith schools – this would provide a cheap source of statistical data and it would provide useful information about the context in which you are carrying out your research.

- Studies by other sociologists on this theme – the findings could be compared and any similarities or differences identified.

- Media reports (e.g. documentaries on television or newspaper articles about faith schools) – these could provide useful background information on this issue.

(iii) Answers could suggest:

- A questionnaire (or structured interview) could be used to collect statistical information about parents' attitudes to faith schools. If closed questions are used, they could be answered quite quickly. The questions would be standardized so it is possible to compare the responses of parents from different ethnic groups and identify any similarities and differences in their attitudes.

- Questionnaires (or structured interviews) would be quicker and cheaper than informal interviews for the amount of data collected. Informal interviews are not useful for measuring social attitudes. Also, informal interviews are not standardized so they are hard to replicate to check the reliability of findings.

Paper 1 Section B: Education

Education Question 1

Pages 128–131

(a) Any one of the following: comprehensive school, selective school, modern (or secondary modern) school, city technology college or an academy.

(b) 42 per cent.

(c) Answers could suggest two of the following:

- Special schools are more likely to have specialist teachers with relevant qualifications/experience of teaching children with SENs.

- Special schools are more likely to have the necessary specialist equipment.

- In special schools, the buildings can be designed to meet pupils' needs while in mainstream schools, parts of the schools may not be easily accessible.

- Classes are often smaller in special schools.

(d) Answers could cover ideas such as:

- the things that pupils learn at school outside the official curriculum such as respecting teachers and getting to lessons on time

- while formal learning takes place through the official curriculum (e.g. learning French in lessons), informal learning takes place through the hidden curriculum (e.g. learning to obey rules).

(e) Answers could include one of the following:
- The publication of school league tables and information on exam results each year – to help raise standards in schools.
- The publication of Ofsted school inspection reports – to help raise standards in schools.
- Increasing parents' choice about which school to send their child to – to encourage local schools to compete as a way of helping to raise standards.

(f) Answers could suggest:
- Having a school culture with a focus on academic success – this could encourage pupils to work hard, compete with each other and value academic achievement and exam success.
- Having a culture in which progression to university is taken for granted – this could encourage pupils to work hard in order to meet university entrance requirements.

(g) (i) An effective introduction could:
- briefly explain the terms 'gender' and 'educational achievements'.

The main body might:
- begin by arguing that gender is the most significant influence (e.g. discussing the underachievement of boys compared to girls, 'laddish' cultures and anti-learning attitudes)
- move on to examine other significant influences such as ethnicity and social class (e.g. pointing out that not all boys underachieve and that middle-class boys tend to perform better in general than working-class girls and boys).

The conclusion might argue:
- that most sociologists would agree that gender is the most significant influence rather than one important influence or
- that most sociologists would agree that an alternative factor (e.g. ethnicity or social class) is the most significant influence or
- argue that the different influences (gender, ethnicity and class) overlap and are difficult to disentangle.

(ii) An effective introduction could:
- briefly explain the terms 'function' and 'social cohesion'.

The main body might:
- begin by referring to the functionalist approach and arguing that social cohesion is the most important function
- move on to examine other important functions such as socialization and meeting the needs of

the economy and link these to the functionalist approach
- examine how alternative approaches such as the Marxist approach would view the functions of the education system in capitalist society (e.g. serving the interests of the ruling class or reproducing the class system).

The conclusion might:
- argue that sociologists from the functionalist approach might agree that social cohesion is the most important function
- argue that other sociologists would disagree with the functionalist approach
- conclude on how far sociologists agree that social cohesion is the most important function rather than one important function.

Education Question 2

Pages 132–135

(a) Nursery and primary schools.

(b) 6.5 per cent.

(c) Answers could suggest one of the following advantages:
- The test results provide parents with information on their child's performance.
- The performance of pupils/schools can be compared.
- Testing helps to raise educational standards.

Answers could suggest one of the following disadvantages:
- Testing takes up too much time.
- Pupils may find the tests stressful.
- Some parents keep their children off school on test days.

(d) Answers could give definitions that refer to:
- Differences in educational attainments (e.g. in GCSE or A-level results) between groups according to social factors such as class, gender or ethnicity.

(e) Answers could include:
- The introduction of the Education Maintenance Allowance (EMA) to encourage pupils from low-income families to remain in education after they complete Year 11.
- Raising the participation age to 17 (from 2013) and to 18 (from 2015) so that young people remain in education or training for longer.

Governments want to increase the staying-on rates in order to:
- improve young people's life chances and opportunities

- address the issue of young people who are not in employment, education or training (NEET) and who are at risk of long-term social exclusion.

(f) Possible answers include one of the following:
- Secondary socialization – by teaching the norms and values of British culture.
- Encouraging 'Britishness' and social cohesion – through citizenship education, pupils identify with British culture. This helps to reinforce the social bonds that unite different groups.
- Serving the needs of the economy – by teaching the knowledge and skills that future workers will need in a competitive global economy.
- Social mobility – by providing equal opportunities in education so that gifted children from disadvantaged backgrounds can achieve good results and move up the social strata.

(g) (i) An effective introduction could:
- briefly explain the terms 'ethnic background' and 'educational achievements'.

The main body might:
- begin by arguing that ethnic background is the most significant influence
- develop this argument by examining home-based factors (e.g. economic circumstances may have a negative effect on some pupils' achievements while cultural background and parental values may have a positive effect) and school-based factors (e.g. teacher expectations and labelling of some minority ethnic pupils; the self-fulfilling prophecy; the curriculum)
- move on to examine other important social influences such as class and gender

- examine government policies (e.g. anti-discrimination laws) as a positive influence on pupils' achievements.

The conclusion might:
- argue that many sociologists would agree that ethnic background is the most significant influence rather than one important influence or
- argue that most sociologists would agree that an alternative factor (e.g. gender or social class) is the most significant influence or
- argue that the different influences (ethnicity, gender and social class) overlap and are difficult to disentangle.

(ii) An effective introduction could:
- briefly explain the terms 'school-based factors' and 'educational achievements'.

The main body might:
- begin by arguing that school-based factors (e.g. teacher expectations and labelling, school ethos, pupil cultures, school resources) are the most important influence
- move on to examine other important influences such as home factors (e.g. parental values and economic circumstances) and government policies (e.g. EMAs or league tables).

The conclusion might:
- argue that most sociologists would agree that school-based factors are the most important influence rather than one important influence or
- argue that most sociologists would agree that other factors (e.g. home background) are the most important influence or
- argue that many sociologists would see home-based and school-based factors as equally significant.

Paper 1 Section C: Families

Families Question 1

Pages 136–139

(a) Asian or Asian British.

(b) A nuclear family.

(c) Answers could suggest two from the following:
- Changing social attitudes to lone-parent families.
- More acceptable for unmarried women to raise a child alone.
- The general increase in divorce.

(d) Answers could cover ideas such as:
- a group whose members share an identity based on their cultural traditions or characteristics such as religion or language.

(e) Answers could include one of the following:
- More equal relationships between parents and children – linked to: changing attitudes to childrearing; less emphasis on discipline; the recognition that children have rights; smaller families.

- More equal gender relationships between adult partners – linked to: the impact of feminism; changing attitudes to gender; the changing role of women; more women in paid employment; the changing role of fathers.

(f) Answers could include one of the following:
- Women are generally having fewer children/smaller family size – this is linked to changing attitudes to family size, changing attitudes to the role of women, increased educational and employment opportunities for women and the availability of effective contraception.
- Women are generally delaying having children/having them at an older age – this is linked to later marriage, changing attitudes to women's roles, increased career opportunities for women and the availability of effective contraception.

(g) (i) An effective introduction could:
- briefly explain the terms 'nuclear family' and 'typical'.

The main body might: *a three generation family containing married or cohabiting parents + their children*
- begin by arguing that the nuclear family is the typical family form (e.g. it is seen as the norm, most people live in a nuclear family at some point in their lives, it is seen by the functionalist approach as the family type most suited to performing essential functions, it is seen by the New Right approach as most suited to meeting the needs of children)
- move on to discuss arguments against the view that the nuclear family is typical (e.g. family diversity, alternatives to the nuclear family such as lone-parent families and extended families).

The conclusion might:
- argue that some sociologists would agree that the nuclear family is typical or
- argue that most sociologists would disagree with the view that the nuclear family is typical.

(ii) An effective introduction could:
- briefly explain the terms 'families' and 'agency of socialization'.

The main body might:
- begin by arguing that families are a more important agency of socialization than schools. For example, families fulfil the key function of primary socialization
- move on to examine the role that schools perform as an agency of secondary socialization
- consider the argument that it depends on the age of the child (e.g. families are likely to be a

more important agency of socialization than schools for pre-school children).

The conclusion might:
- argue that most sociologists would agree that families are a more important agency of socialization than schools or
- argue that many/most sociologists would disagree with the view that families are a more important agency of socialization.

Families Question 2

Pages 140–143

(a) Any one of the following: lone parent family, a couple with children/nuclear family or a couple without children.

(b) 75 and over.

(c) Answers could suggest two of the following:
- becoming part of a blended/reconstituted family
- some children may lose contact with their father
- freedom from conflict/domestic violence
- continued conflict (e.g. over parenting and property) after divorce
- loss of income/risk of poverty
- loss of emotional support particularly for divorced men.

(d) Answers are likely to cover ideas such as:
- the variety of family types that exist in Britain today (e.g. nuclear, extended and lone-parent families)
- the diversity of family types linked to ethnicity and to whether couples are cohabiting, married or civil partners.

(e) Answers could suggest that:
- People are living longer – this is linked to improvements in: medical technology; treatment provided by the National Health Service; living standards and nutrition.

(f) Answers could suggest that gender relationships have become more equal/less patriarchal. Possible reasons for this include:
- The impact of feminism.
- Changing gender roles, e.g. the changing role of women in society/the changing role of fathers.
- Changing social attitudes to gender and gender roles.

(g) (i) An effective introduction could:
- briefly explain the term 'extended family'.

The main body might:

- begin by arguing that people's relationships with members of their wider/extended family have become less important. Possible arguments are that geographical mobility has weakened family ties; women in paid employment, in particular, have less time to invest in relationships with members of the wider family; friends are now the new family
- move on to examine the view that people's relationships with members of their wider/extended family have not become less important. Possible arguments are that people remain in regular contact by phone; family members provide help and support, e.g. with childcare; family members provide support (e.g. financial help) at a distance.

The conclusion might:

- argue that most sociologists would agree that people's relationships with members of their wider/extended family have become less important or
- argue that most sociologists would agree that these relationships may have changed but they have not become less important or
- argue that it is difficult to generalize in a culturally diverse society.

(ii) An effective introduction could:

- briefly explain the terms 'family' and 'function' and then link this to the functionalist approach in sociology.

The main body might:

- begin by arguing that families are necessary because they perform important functions such as primary socialization, emotional support, the economic function and reproduction. Brief reference to the functionalist and New Right approaches could be made
- move on to examine how far families actually fulfil these functions effectively
- examine alternative views about the role of families in modern society such as the feminist or Marxist approaches.

The conclusion might:

- argue that most sociologists would agree that families are necessary because they perform important functions for individuals and for society or
- argue that many sociologists/alternative approaches would disagree with the view that families are necessary because they perform important functions.

Paper 2 Section A: Crime and Deviance

Crime and Deviance Question 1

Pages 144–147

(a) 5 per cent.

(b) Court/crown court.

(c) Answers could suggest any two of the following:

- Physically, e.g. injury during an assault.
- Financially, e.g. having to replace stolen items that were not insured.
- Psychologically, e.g. feeling stressed after a burglary or fearful of crime.
- Socially, e.g. affecting the victim's relationships with family or friends.

(d) Answers could cover ideas such as:

- antisocial behaviour that does not conform to society's norms and is disapproved of, e.g. playing very loud music at night in a residential area
- behaviour that, if detected, is likely to lead to negative reactions.

(e) Answers could include one of the following:

- Informal rules may operate through social pressure, e.g. peer pressure to dress in a particular way.
- They may operate through social approval or rewards (positive sanctions) such as being accepted by the group and social disapproval or punishments (negative sanctions) such as being ignored by peers.

Group members might conform to these rules for the following reasons:

- To gain acceptance and approval.
- To avoid ridicule or negative sanctions.
- Because they identify with the group and its members.

(f) Possible examples include: knife crime, gun crime or youth crime.

These might be seen as a problem because:

- they have negative consequences, e.g. they affect victims, their families and communities
- they generate fear of crime

- the mass media have exaggerated their significance and created a moral panic.

(g) (i) An effective introduction could:

- briefly explain the terms 'deprivation' and 'crime'.

The main body might:

- begin by arguing that deprivation is the main cause of most crime in Britain and develop this argument by examining explanations based on relative deprivation
- move on to examine other important sociological explanations of the causes of crime such as inadequate socialization, subcultures, status frustration, labelling theory and Marxist approaches.

The conclusion might:

- argue that most sociologists would agree that deprivation is the main cause of most crime rather than one important cause or
- argue that most sociologists would agree that an alternative explanation identifies the main cause or
- argue that most sociologists would recognize that different crimes (e.g. theft of a mobile phone and white-collar crime) are likely to have different causes.

(ii) An effective introduction could:

- briefly explain the terms 'official statistics' and 'crime'.

The main body might:

- begin by arguing that the official statistics of police-recorded crime provide a complete picture of the extent of crime in Britain
- compare the picture provided by police-recorded crime statistics with that provided by statistics from victim surveys and from self-report studies
- move on to examine arguments that question how police-recorded crime statistics are compiled (e.g. the statistics exclude undiscovered, unreported and unrecorded crimes)
- discuss the view that police-recorded crime statistics are socially constructed.

The conclusion might:

- argue that many sociologists would not take police-recorded crime statistics at face value and/or
- argue that most sociologists would disagree with the view that these statistics provide a complete picture of the extent of all crime.

Crime and Deviance Question 2

Pages 148–151

(a) Any one of the following: teenage crime, domestic violence, poverty, racism or racially motivated crime.

(b) 1 500 000

(c) Answers could include any two of the following:

- Whereas formal rules are written down or codified, informal rules are unwritten or taken for granted.
- Whereas formal rules are enforced formally (e.g. by the police), informal rules are enforced informally (e.g. through peer pressure).
- Whereas formal sanctions (e.g. imprisonment) operate when formal rules are broken, informal sanctions (e.g. being ignored) operate when informal rules are broken.

(d) Answers could cover ideas such as:

- a fixed, standardized and distorted view of a social group such as women, travellers or asylum seekers
- stereotypes are often based on prejudice and may lead to discrimination.

(e) Any behaviour that causes harassment, distress or alarm to others can be classed as antisocial behaviour. Examples include:

- hanging round street corners in large groups and disturbing neighbours
- racist abuse
- verbal abuse
- playing loud music in a residential area after midnight
- rowdy behaviour such as swearing or fighting.

Answers could suggest that governments have tried to address antisocial behaviour through measures such as:

- antisocial behaviour orders (ASBOs)
- acceptable behaviour contracts (ABCs)
- child curfews
- dispersal of groups
- parenting orders.

(f) Examples of agencies of informal social control include:

- Peer groups, families, friends, work colleagues.

These agencies can influence behaviour by applying social pressure and through rewards and punishments. For example:

- Peer groups can influence people's behaviour by putting social pressure on members to conform to the group's norms and by using positive and negative sanctions.

- Families can influence the behaviour of family members by applying social pressure and by rewarding behaviour that complies with expectations and punishing inappropriate behaviour.

(g) (i) An effective introduction could:

- briefly explain the terms 'official statistics' and 'crime'.

The main body might:

- begin by outlining what the official statistics tell us about young people's involvement in crime, e.g. that young men are more likely than women and older men to be cautioned for, or found guilty of, serious crimes
- move on to examine explanations for young people's apparently greater involvement in crime, e.g. subcultural theory, peer pressure or lack of social control
- examine the argument that the statistics exaggerate young people's involvement in crime, e.g. by discussing labelling and policing methods
- discuss the view that police-recorded crime statistics are socially constructed and cannot be taken at face value.

The conclusion might:

- argue that some sociologists would agree that police-recorded crime statistics reflect young people's involvement in crime or
- argue that most sociologists would agree that the police-recorded crime statistics exaggerate

young people's involvement in crime to some extent.

(ii) An effective introduction could:

- briefly explain the terms 'official statistics', 'crime' and 'ethnic groups'.

The main body might:

- begin by outlining what the official statistics tell us about the involvement of members of different ethnic groups in crime, e.g. that white people are under-represented in prisons compared to their proportion in the population and black people are over-represented
- examine explanations for the apparently greater involvement of members of some minority ethnic groups in crime, e.g. unemployment, deprivation
- move on to examine the argument that the statistics exaggerate the involvement of members of some minority ethnic groups in crime by discussing, for instance, labelling, policing methods, institutional racism and bias within the criminal justice system
- discuss the view that police-recorded crime statistics are socially constructed.

The conclusion might:

- argue that most sociologists would not take official statistics at face value and/or
- argue that many sociologists would agree that the official crime statistics exaggerate or distort the involvement of members of some minority ethnic groups in crime.

Paper 2 Section B: Mass Media

Mass Media Question 1

Pages 152–155

(a) Either the internet or digital TV.

(b) The psychological approach.

(c) Answers could include two of the following:

- digitalization
- interactivity/ability to interact with the TV, e.g. by 'pressing the red button'
- the development of the internet
- the development of cable and satellite TV
- convergence.

(d) Answers could cover ideas such as:

- the means of mass communication (media) that are based on older technology
- examples include newspapers and terrestrial TV.

(e) Answers could suggest that the media may present stereotyped and distorted images of:

- people of Asian heritage by focusing narrowly on particular themes such as forced marriage rather than covering a range of news stories
- British Muslims by focusing narrowly on stories linked to extremism or terrorism.

Answers might suggest that this can be seen as a problem because:

- it may result in prejudice and discrimination

- it is linked to norm referencing
- it may contribute to the creation of moral panics.

(f) Answers could suggest that the media may contribute to the process of gender socialization by:

- presenting stereotypical rather than realistic images of gender (e.g. in lads' mags, TV advertisements or in tabloid reports of women's tennis)
- presenting a limited rather than a varied selection of gender roles.

Answers might suggest that this can be criticized because:

- over the long term, it may influence people's attitudes to gender (e.g. encouraging people to assume that females cannot fix cars or males do not work in childcare)
- when repeated over time, stereotyped images could reinforce sexism in society.

(g) (i) An effective introduction could:

- briefly explain the terms 'power' and 'technological developments'.

The main body might:

- begin by arguing that technological developments help to spread power, e.g. via the internet, anyone can become a producer of media content rather than just a consumer; the power of media owners is reduced; groups can use the internet to recruit members, communicate, debate and participate in the political process
- move on to examine views that question how far technological developments help to spread power, e.g. as a result of the digital divide, not everyone has access to the internet; most users use the internet for shopping or for entertainment rather than to participate in the political process.

The conclusion might:

- argue that some sociologists would agree that technological developments such as the internet spread power more widely by giving people more power to communicate, debate and participate or
- argue that most sociologists would agree that, in practice, power is still concentrated rather than distributed widely in Britain and/or that media owners still have more power than other individuals or groups to influence public opinion.

(ii) An effective introduction could:

- briefly explain the term 'media'.

The main body might:

- begin by arguing that exposure to violence in the media can encourage copycat violence in everyday life (e.g. by drawing on the hypodermic syringe approach)
- move on to examine views that question how far the media can encourage violence (e.g. by criticizing much of the early research which was carried out in laboratories; by pointing out that evidence from research does not suggest a strong link between viewing and violence; by discussing the decoding approach which argues that viewers actively interpret media messages).

The conclusion might:

- argue that some sociologists would agree that exposure to media violence can encourage violence in real life or
- argue that most sociologists would agree that there is insufficient evidence from research to suggest that the media encourage violence.

Mass Media Question 2

Pages 156–159

(a) Newspapers.

(b) 8 per cent.

(c) Answers could include two of the following:

- as a source of information, e.g. about current affairs/celebrity news/sport/finance
- to pass time/for entertainment, e.g. doing the crossword or reading horoscopes
- to find out about the latest film or album reviews and theatre listings.

(d) Answers could include ideas such as:

- a gap between people who have access to new media technology such as the internet and digital TV and those who do not have access to these
- the digital divide may be linked to wealth and income, education, age and geography.

(e) Answers could suggest that individuals or groups could create content by:

- setting up a website, blogging, twittering, contributing to a social network site or internet forum or uploading music.

Answers could suggest that they might want to produce content in this way:

- to publicise a pressure group or a cause

- as a marketing tool
- to communicate with others
- to buy and sell
- to organize events or demonstrations
- to engage in political debates.

(f) Answers might suggest that the mass media could create negative images of some social groups (such as teenage mothers or asylum seekers) through norm referencing or through biased and one-sided reporting.

Answers might suggest that this can be seen as a problem because it could:

- result in prejudice and discrimination
- contribute to a moral panic about the group and its activities.

(g) (i) An effective introduction could:

- briefly explain the terms 'mass media' and 'agency of political socialization'.

The main body might:

- begin by discussing the role of the media as an agency of political socialization, e.g. as a key source of information about politics and current affairs; in influencing people's voting behaviour during election campaigns
- move on to examine other agencies of political socialization such as the education system, families, peer groups and workplaces.

The conclusion might:

- argue that many sociologists would agree that the mass media is the most powerful agency rather than one important agency or

- argue that most sociologists would disagree with the view that the media is the most powerful agency.

(ii) An effective introduction could:

- briefly explain that this debate concerns the relationship between press ownership and control.

The main body might:

- begin by outlining the pattern of press ownership in Britain (e.g. by discussing concentration of ownership)
- argue that press owners control content (e.g. by examining the conflict view on this debate)
- move on to examine arguments that press owners do not control content (e.g. by drawing on the pluralist approach)
- examine other influences on content, e.g. laws of libel, advertisers and media professionals such as editors.

The conclusion might:

- argue that many sociologists would agree that press owners have the power to control content or
- argue that most sociologists would disagree with the view that press owners have much power to control content or
- argue that many sociologists would agree that there are several influences on content including ownership.

Paper 2 Section C: Power

Power Question 1

Pages 160–163

(a) 29 per cent.

(b) A senior manager.

(c) Answers could suggest two of the following:

- sexism/discrimination
- the male culture or ethos of Parliament
- many women combine paid work with domestic labour and caring responsibilities so it is more difficult to find time to pursue a career in politics.

(d) Answers could include ideas such as:

- the exercise of power based on the threat or

use of force rather than on authority; people being forced to obey others against their will
- examples of coercion include the use of torture and kidnapping.

(e) Answers could suggest that the police have the power to:

- stop and search
- arrest and detain
- obtain a warrant to conduct a search of a property such as a house.

Answers could suggest that police officers exercise power on behalf of the state. Their authority is based on written rules laid down by the state and their interaction with members of the public is based on codes of practice.

(f) Answers could refer to the decline in:
- voter turnout in elections
- political party membership.

Answers might suggest that this could be considered a problem because the active participation of citizens is seen as:
- a feature of a thriving democracy
- a way of controlling the government and politicians between general elections.

(g) (i) An effective introduction could:
- briefly explain the terms 'welfare state' and 'poverty'.

The main body might:
- begin by arguing that the welfare state has been successful in reducing poverty, e.g. through the national minimum wage and a system of welfare benefits including means-tested benefits paid to those in financial need
- move on to examine alternative arguments such as the view that child poverty persists in the 21st century; welfare benefits can trap people in poverty; benefits are too low; the welfare state has created a dependency culture.

The conclusion might:
- argue that many sociologists would agree that the welfare state has been successful in removing absolute poverty and in reducing relative poverty or
- argue that most sociologists would disagree with the view that the welfare state has been successful in significantly reducing poverty.

(ii) An effective introduction could:
- briefly explain the term 'state'.

The main body might:
- begin by arguing that the state represents the interests of all individuals and social groups, e.g. by discussing the pluralist approach; the role of pressure groups
- move on to examine the view that the state represents the interests of some groups (e.g. middle class white men, the bourgeoisie/ruling class, big business) more than others (e.g. the socially excluded, NEETs, some minority ethnic groups). Alternative approaches such as conflict, Marxist or feminist views could be examined.

The conclusion might:
- argue that some sociologists would agree that the state represents the interests of all individuals and groups or

- argue that many sociologists would agree that the state represents the interests of the powerful and privileged groups in society.

Power Question 2

Pages 164–167

(a) More likely to participate.

(b) The RSPCA.

(c) Answers could suggest two of the following:
- job creation/work experience schemes
- improving claimants' skills through education and training
- improving claimants' motivation through counselling services
- specific programmes such as New Deal
- giving claimants a financial incentive to work, e.g. through tax credits.

(d) Answers could refer to the following:
- Some people who receive state benefits are seen as developing a way of life (or a culture) in which they become so dependent/reliant on welfare state provisions that they lose the motivation to work in paid employment.

(e) Answers could suggest that:
- parents may exercise authority over their children by laying down rules and expectations about behaviour and by disciplining them
- their authority is based on their adult status but its scope is regulated by legislation, e.g. on the use of physical punishment.

(f) Answers could refer to one of the following factors:
- Having insider status – this gives the pressure group close links with government networks and means it will be consulted by government departments or ministers when new policies are being prepared.
- Having human resources such as a large staff and lots of volunteers – this could increase the pressure group's chances of success by enabling it to organize petitions and publicity stunts or raise funds.
- A large membership – membership fees could provide financial resources to help the group to generate publicity for its cause.
- Celebrity backing of the group and its cause – this could generate media interest and publicity.

- Widespread public support for the cause – this can strengthen the pressure group's case for introducing new policies or legal changes.

(g) (i) An effective introduction could:
- briefly explain the phrase 'participate fully in the political process' and outline one or two of the different opportunities to participate.

The main body might:
- begin by arguing that individuals can participate in traditional forms of politics by voting in elections, joining political parties or standing for office. Individuals and groups can also participate through pressure group activity, trade union membership or consumer boycotts
- move on to examine the argument that, in practice, not everyone takes up the opportunities to participate. Participation varies according to factors such as age, income, employment status and educational background. Some groups are under-represented among MPs
- discuss the possible reasons for non-participation such as disillusionment, apathy and satisfaction with the government.

The conclusion might:
- argue that some sociologists would agree that all individuals and groups have opportunities to participate or

- argue that most sociologists would agree that, in practice, participation levels vary according to factors such as age and income.

(ii) An effective introduction could:
- briefly explain the term 'discrimination' and outline the different bases of discrimination (age, gender and ethnicity).

The main body might:
- begin by arguing that governments have successfully tackled much discrimination, e.g. through equality legislation covering education, employment and the labour market; by tackling institutional racism; and by funding bodies such as the Equality and Human Rights Commission
- move on to examine the argument that discrimination based on age, gender and ethnicity still exists within employment, criminal justice and in the media.

The conclusion might:
- argue that some sociologists would agree that governments have successfully reduced these forms of discrimination or
- argue that most sociologists would agree that, in practice, governments have not succeeded in significantly reducing these forms of discrimination.

Paper 2 Section D: Social Inequality

Social Inequality Question 1

Pages 168–171

(a) An increase/growth/rise.

(b) Lone-parent families.

(c) Answers could refer to:
- wages and salaries
- pensions
- benefits
- income from self-employment
- income from investments.

(d) Answers could include ideas such as:
- an individual's chances of achieving positive or negative outcomes (e.g. in relation to health, education, housing and employment) as they progress through life
- life chances are linked to social factors such as social class, gender and ethnicity.

(e) Possible ways include:
- Significant improvements in the educational achievements of females.
- A higher proportion of women are in paid employment.
- More women are now entering professions such as medicine.
- More scope for women to combine motherhood and a career.

Possible reasons include:
- The impact of anti-discrimination legislation.
- The impact of equal opportunities policies in education/in the workplace.
- The impact of feminism/changing attitudes to gender.

(f) Answers may refer to the following:
- Some older people (particularly older women living alone) may be at risk of poverty when

their only source of income is their state pension.

- Children in lone-parent families are at risk of poverty – these families are more likely to have low incomes.
- Women may be at risk of poverty because they are more likely than men to head lone-parent families; women in paid work earn less than men on average; they are more likely than men to work part-time.
- Members of some minority ethnic groups may be more at risk of poverty because of racism in the labour market.

(g) (i) An effective introduction could:

- briefly explain the term 'meritocratic society'.

The main body might:

- begin by arguing that Britain is a meritocracy, e.g. there is equality of opportunity in education to facilitate social mobility; equality legislation outlaws discrimination; status and class position are achieved rather than ascribed; Britain is now a classless society
- move on to examine the argument that Britain is not a meritocratic society, e.g. research on social mobility indicates that working-class children have much less chance of getting managerial or professional jobs than children from professional backgrounds; equality of educational opportunity does not exist when not everyone has access to private education; inequalities based on gender, ethnicity and age mean that Britain is not a meritocracy
- refer briefly to the functionalist, Marxist and feminist approaches.

The conclusion might:

- argue that some sociologists would agree that Britain is largely a meritocracy/that society is becoming increasingly meritocratic or
- argue that most sociologists would disagree with the view that Britain is a meritocratic society.

(ii) An effective introduction could:

- briefly explain the terms 'inequality', 'ethnicity' and 'social class'.

The main body might:

- begin by arguing that inequality based on social class is no longer significant, e.g. by suggesting that Britain is becoming a classless society; class identity is declining; traditional working class communities based on mining or shipbuilding have declined; higher education is

now a mass experience rather than a middle-class experience; the links between class and voting are declining

- move on to argue that ethnicity is a more important division, e.g. the underachievement of some minority ethnic groups in education; discrimination in employment; the under-representation of people from minority ethnic groups in positions of power
- discuss the argument that class inequalities are as important as ethnic inequalities, e.g. research findings indicate that long-range social mobility is limited; class divisions in education persist; class differences in life chances related to health and life expectancy persist.

The conclusion might:

- argue that some sociologists would agree that inequality based on ethnicity is a more significant cause of social division than class or
- argue that some sociologists would disagree with the view that inequality based on ethnicity is a more significant cause or
- argue that most sociologists focus on the relationship between ethnicity and social class.

Social Inequality Question 2

Pages 172–175

(a) An increase/growth/rise.

(b) Either property or retailing.

(c) Answers could refer to two of the following:

- discrimination based on gender/ethnicity
- lack of skills
- lack of qualifications.

(d) Answers could include ideas such as:

- Being shut out or excluded from participation in the social, economic, political and cultural life of society.
- Groups likely to experience social exclusion include young people who are not in education, employment or training (NEETs) and older people without skills and qualifications.

(e) Answers could suggest:

- Absolute poverty – when people's income is insufficient to obtain the minimum they need to survive. The problem with this definition is that, in practice, it is very difficult to decide what the minimum needed to survive is (e.g. bread and water alone or fresh vegetables as well).

- Relative poverty – when people are poor compared with others in their society and they cannot afford to have the standard of living that most other people enjoy. The criticism of this definition is that it means we will always find poverty in a society unless incomes are distributed more or less equally.

(f) Answers could suggest that:
- Social class can be measured through occupation – this is because occupation is linked to life chances (e.g. income and health) and to status.
- In research on education, being entitled to free school meals is often taken to indicate social class background when information on parents' occupations is not available. This is because entitlement to free school meals is linked to low household income and deprivation.

(g) (i) An effective introduction could:
- briefly explain the term 'classless society'.

The main body might:
- begin by arguing that Britain is now a classless society, e.g. social class is no longer an important division; class identity is declining; traditional working class communities based on mining or shipbuilding have declined; higher education is now a mass experience rather than a middle-class experience; the links between class and voting are declining; other divisions (e.g. based on gender, age and ethnicity) are more important
- move on to examine the argument that class divisions persist in Britain, e.g. class divisions exist alongside inequalities based on gender, ethnicity and age; research on social mobility indicates that working-class children have

much less chance of getting managerial or professional jobs than children from professional backgrounds; class divisions in education including higher education persist; class differences in life chances related to health and life expectancy persist; Britain is not a meritocracy
- refer briefly to the Marxist approach.

The conclusion might:
- argue that some sociologists would agree that class differences are becoming less significant/ Britain is now becoming a classless society or
- argue that most sociologists would disagree with the view that Britain is now a classless society.

(ii) An effective introduction could:
- briefly explain the terms 'long-term unemployment' and 'poverty'.

The main body might:
- begin by arguing that the main cause of poverty is long-term unemployment, e.g. during an economic recession, unemployment increases and poverty also increases; welfare benefits for unemployed people are inadequate
- move on to examine alternative explanations for the persistence of poverty such as the culture of poverty; the cycle of deprivation; welfare dependency; the Marxist approach.

The conclusion might:
- argue that some sociologists would agree that long-term unemployment is the most significant cause of poverty or
- argue that many sociologists would disagree with the view that long-term unemployment is the most significant cause of poverty.